D0161312

CAMBRIDGE AIR SURVEYS

GENERAL EDITORS

DAVID KNOWLES   J. K. S. St JOSEPH

H. GODWIN

I

MONASTIC SITES FROM THE AIR

MONASTIC SITES FROM THE AIR

BY

DAVID KNOWLES

PROFESSOR OF MEDIEVAL HISTORY IN THE
UNIVERSITY OF CAMBRIDGE

AND

J. K. S. St JOSEPH

CURATOR IN AERIAL PHOTOGRAPHY IN THE
UNIVERSITY OF CAMBRIDGE

WITH 138 PHOTOGRAPHS

CAMBRIDGE
AT THE UNIVERSITY PRESS
1952

PUBLISHED BY
THE SYNDICS OF THE CAMBRIDGE UNIVERSITY PRESS

London Office: Bentley House, N.W. I
American Branch: New York

Agents for Canada, India, and Pakistan: Macmillan

Printed in Great Britain at the University Press, Cambridge
(Brooke Crutchley, University Printer)

PREFACE

THIS book had its origin in some photographs of monastic sites, taken among many others of archaeological and historical interest by Dr St Joseph in 1947. These seemed to the present writer to show the plan and surroundings of a medieval monastery so clearly that he proposed a collaboration such as has in fact taken place in assembling the photographs and letterpress that follow. A list of representative sites was drawn up, and in the summers of 1948–51, and on other isolated occasions, most of these and a number of others added from time to time were photographed. When the descriptions of certain selected plates had been completed, the project was laid before the Syndics of the University Press and accepted by them for publication as the first of a series of books intended to illustrate the uses of air photography in various fields of archaeology, social history, geography, ecology and the like.

The aim in the present book has been to make the selection as large and as representative (both of regions and of orders) as possible, and by no means to restrict it to religious houses noted for the extent or beauty of their remains; but circumstances of one kind or another have necessarily limited the choice in some respects. Thus flying restrictions made it impossible to obtain views of sites, such as Westminster Abbey, the London Charterhouse and Barking Abbey, which lie within the area of London or some other great city; the accident of weather conditions sometimes excluded a particular locality which could not again be visited; and a few sites, such as Iona in the Hebrides, could not easily be fitted into a flying programme. Nevertheless, the number of sites represented by photographs either in this book or in the Cambridge University collection of air photographs is both large and comprehensive, and may claim, as a collection, to illustrate the plans and surroundings of the religious houses of Britain more adequately than any other hitherto assembled.

For this reason the book is primarily the work of Dr St Joseph, since all depended on his skill in directing the aircraft to an often unfamiliar site identifiable only by a name on the map, and in obtaining a clear and significant photograph in the few seconds of opportunity granted him. For the letterpress the present writer is responsible, but Dr St Joseph has read and amended the whole to its great advantage and has himself contributed the description of the sites at Milfield and Yeavering, and part of that of Grace Dieu, which he was able to visit after he had taken the photograph.

The photographs have all been taken from aircraft of the Royal Air Force, and the collection could not have been obtained so quickly and conveniently without the generous assistance extended at all times by those concerned with the flying operations. We are also indebted to the Air Ministry for permission to reproduce the

plates, which are Crown copyright, at a fee that was little more than nominal. Our thanks are, in addition, due to the following for their kindness in giving information of one sort or another which aided in the interpretation of certain views, or in lending unpublished plans of excavations: Mr F. T. Baker, Mr C. H. Hunter Blair, Mr H. S. Braun, the Rev. J. C. Dickinson, Lt.-Col. C. D. Drew, Major P. C. Fletcher, Mr Angus Graham, Dr W. G. Hoskins, the late Sir Alfred Clapham, Mr B. H. St J. O'Neil, the Very Rev. the Prior of St Hugh's Charterhouse, Parkminster, the Very Rev. the Prior of Buckfast Abbey (Dom J. Stephan, O.S.B.), and Dr H. Talbot.

DAVID KNOWLES

Cambridge
26 *October* 1951

CONTENTS

INTRODUCTION

I

THE collection of plates here presented is reproduced from air photographs of the sites of medieval religious houses taken for this book. A very few illustrations of other medieval sites and of modern religious houses have been included for purposes of comparison. It is hoped that a fairly ample collection of such views, including examples of almost every religious order in every part of the country—houses large and small, celebrated or almost unknown—may help to serve a number of purposes. It will, in the first place, illustrate the resources and potentialities of air photography as a technique applied to a particular field of archaeology. For the general reader or the tourist it may serve to give an idea of the wealth of such medieval sites existing in Great Britain, of the important architectural features that remain in so many places, and of the great natural beauty of so many of the sites. Those who have a more specialized interest, whether antiquarian, architectural or purely historical, may be glad to find a large and representative selection of material grouped within the covers of a single moderately sized book.

Air photographs, when taken by a competent hand under favourable conditions, lay bare the ground plan of a great monastery almost as completely as the most elaborate measured drawing; at the same time, by showing such of the elevation of the fabric as remains, together with the natural surroundings of the site, they give a more vivid visual impression, and a richer material for interpretation, than either a plan or a photograph from the ground can hope to do. The views given in these pages of Roche, Byland, Kirkham and Castle Acre (to name but a few) will be sufficient proof of this. Moreover, the marshalling of a large number of sites may help to give even those who are familiar with monastic history a new precision in their grasp of the material framework of medieval religious life, and of the differences between the homes of the various orders.

In addition, air photographs often give information not conveyed by existing plans, either by showing features omitted for clarity's sake or, in the case of unplanned or unexcavated sites, by indicating features altogether unknown. Even where excavation has been attempted, an air photograph may show that the foundations of other buildings exist outside the field of work. An exceptionally interesting example of discovery of this kind can be seen in the non-monastic sites of the plates on p. 271, but the views of Sempringham and Robertsbridge (pp. 243–4, 135), and perhaps those of Tilty and Calder (pp. 131, 77) show traces of buildings not hitherto reckoned with, and many of the views show the course of canals, conduits, walls, drains and fishponds with a clarity that no map or surface photograph could hope to equal.

Besides showing the remains and the natural surroundings of a site, a numerous collection of plates gives a striking picture of the post-Dissolution history of the sites. Thus we see a pre-Reformation cathedral priory such as Ely (p. 5) converted without much change to house the officials and clergy of the new regime, who were in many cases the previous occupants of monastic offices. Abbeys in similar urban surroundings were adapted to a similar purpose, as at Chester and Gloucester (pp. 9, 13). Other urban sites were more often than not heavily plundered, as Bury St Edmunds, St Albans, and St Mary's, York (pp. 15, 7, 21) and such abbeys rarely became the nucleus of a modern mansion. Battle (p. 27) is scarcely an exception, as the town there was small and entirely monastic property.

As for rural sites, their destinies might seem at first sight to have been settled by the caprice of fortune, though in almost every case a knowledge of regional economic conditions or of individual history would give the key. Why, we might ask, have Bardney, Barlings and Sempringham (pp. 23, 171, 243) vanished almost to the last stone, while Fountains, Cleeve and Furness in large part remain (pp. 96, 143, 79)? No attempt can be made in this book to give an answer in every case; a few general observations must suffice. The best chances of survival lay with a house in a (then) comparatively remote situation (e.g. Fountains), or with one immediately occupied by a lay owner (e.g. Forde). There was, however, the difference that with houses of the first class the shell of the church was likely to survive, since plundering its fabric was difficult and dangerous, whereas in the second class the church was usually the first part to disappear, as a useless encumbrance to the new mansion, while the remainder might either be permanently preserved, as at Forde, or subsequently swept away by a new tide of architectural ambition, as at Welbeck. Sometimes the cause of total disappearance is obvious: thus St Benet's of Holme (p. 25) lay indeed in a remote spot, but water transport was conveniently at hand and stone was precious for house and road making; moreover, since the revenues of the abbey had been annexed to the see of Norwich there was no lay grantee to make a mansion or farm of the ruins. Prevailing economic conditions would probably explain the almost total disappearance of the numerous and important Lincolnshire and fenland houses, and would equally account for the general survival of ruins in counties, such as Shropshire and Kent, which were not notably more remote from habitation. Yet the personal equation of the new owner must often have had decisive weight. A modest Premonstratensian abbey and an insignificant Augustinian priory are reborn in Welbeck Abbey and Longleat House. Others become stately mansions (e.g. Forde, p. 145, St Osyth, p. 227), beautiful houses (e.g. Much Wenlock, p. 54), abodes of substantial squires (e.g. Notley, p. 223), yeomen and small farmers (e.g. Cleeve, p. 143, and Beauvale, p. 237), cottagers (e.g. Eggleston, p. 159) or cattle (e.g. Waverley, p. 63), while elsewhere, on the sites of great churches and populous cloisters,

> Lies the hawk's cast, the mole has made his run,
> The slow-worm creeps, and the thin weasel there
> Follows the mouse, and all is open field.

II

Besides the specialist's interest which the antiquary or religious historian finds in the study of monastic sites, there is the wider appeal to all students of the life of the Middle Ages. To the present writer, the preparation of the notes in this book has given a new sense of the genius for order and beauty of the twelfth and thirteenth centuries. While much in the public and private life of those times was disorderly, brutal and squalid, it was an epoch when order, symmetry and centralization at the highest levels attained a perfection and a beauty found only at the peak of a culture's development. The system of papal administration and judicature in the age of Innocent III, the theological and philosophical system of St Thomas Aquinas, the standardization of a clear and beautiful script and precise language in all the chanceries of Europe—these are typical examples of a phenomenon that is apparent in a number of departments of life. Not the least striking instance of the medieval genius for order is the uniformity of plan, realized with the widest flexibility in details and in artistic interpretation, which makes a Cistercian or Augustinian abbey of Elgin or Cardigan or Essex the recognizable sister of one in Galloway, Northumberland or Devon. Moreover, this uniformity is joined to an almost unfailing excellence of design and workmanship, and to the employment, even in remote sites among an upland population, of good and durable materials and of complicated works of plumbing and draining. The stylistic and constructional experiments of the past century and a half, and the not infrequent decline in workmanship and use of makeshift or composite materials to which two world wars have inured us, make the high standards of medieval craftsmanship and their lavish use of good freestone very refreshing to the spirit. It is this uniformity of plan and solid excellence of construction that give a strong intellectual interest, as well as an aesthetic delight, to the excavator of the monastic site and to one who follows him either on the ground or by means of a plan or a photograph. It is a species of mental stimulus which will be wanting to the excavator, some hundreds of years hence, of a hospital or school of the present age, or even of the less regular and less distinctive buildings of a modern religious house.

III

English antiquaries have for long given attention to monastic remains, and in addition to learned monographs, several excellent short accounts exist of the normal monastic plan and of the varieties of building erected by the different orders. Nevertheless, to make the present volume in a sense self-contained, it may be well to give once more a brief sketch of the subject.

The ancestry of the typical plan of the medieval monastery can be traced back to the early days of monachism in the East. When organized community life developed in the fourth century in Egypt, Palestine and Syria, a number of monastic buildings devoted to the various activities of daily life immediately made their appearance—the cells of the brethren, often replaced by a common dormitory and work-rooms; an oratory for common prayer; a refectory for community meals, and a large apartment for deliberative assemblies and spiritual conferences. It was natural that the whole group of buildings should be enclosed by a wall, and the architectural and social traditions of the portico and the arcade were so strong in Mediterranean countries that this, too, soon became a normal part of the monastery. The general type was fixed very early and has continued in the Orthodox Church till the present day, though the Greek monastic plan (here resembling Greek monastic organization in general) never reached the same degree of uniformity as did the Western plan in the twelfth and thirteenth centuries. There was, also, one very great difference of overall planning. Whereas in the West the typical monastic plan in its final development invariably included a cloister surrounded by conventual buildings and bounded along one side by the church, the typical Greek plan was that of a large oblong enclosure wholly or partially surrounded by buildings with an inward-looking portico around the interior space: the church and often the refectory and other main conventual buildings stood free in the centre.[1]

When monasticism came to the West its buildings took various forms in different regions—Ireland, Gaul and Italy—and they were at first on the whole small and irregular. The Rule of St Benedict (*c.* A.D. 540) exercised a considerable influence here as in other respects owing to the insistence of the legislator on the necessity of containing within the precinct wall of the monastery all essential services and offices —garden, mill, workshops and the rest. Of strictly monastic buildings, the *Rule* mentions or implies an oratory (small and without architectural divisions), a refectory, a common dormitory, a common assembly room (not yet used for the quasi-liturgical chapter-assembly), and quarters for the novices and guests, but there is no mention of a cloister or of any symmetrical arrangement. The cloister was not a feature of early Gallic or Irish monasticism; it probably first appeared in the basilican monasteries of Rome and other Italian cities in the sixth century. The suggestion has been made that it derived from the *atrium* of the Roman house, the interior court into which the living rooms opened, but it is more likely that its immediate ancestor was the atrium or porticoed court at the west end of the basilica such as can be still seen, e.g., at Sant'Ambrogio in Milan. This was transposed from the end to the side of the nave, and the conventual buildings were then grouped around it. This in Mediterranean lands is the ideal plan for a large establishment, and it rapidly became so stereotyped that it passed with little modification beyond the Alps and even into northern countries where its amenities were less obvious. The only modification it underwent was that whereas in Italy, where the desideratum was shade, the cloister was normally north of the church, in northern lands, where sunshine and shelter from the north and east winds were appreciated, a southern position was normal, thus making the best use of the protective walls of nave and transept. But as we shall see, this rule was far from absolute; in fact it is a tendency rather than a rule.

[1] See *Dictionnaire d'Archéologie chrétienne*, ed. Cabrol et Leclercq, art. 'Cloître'.

When once the cloister alongside the nave had become the norm, the other buildings grouped themselves in certain fixed positions. Thus the dormitory came naturally in the eastern walk, whence the brethren could pass easily from it to their quire for the night offices. The southern walk was the convenient place for the refectory, so that the fumes and bustle of the kitchen might be furthest from the church and from the walk of the cloister lying alongside the church, which, as shadiest or sunniest, was the normal place for work and study. The western range was thus left for storage and the cellarer's offices; it was easy of access to the outer world as the great court and gateway usually lay near the west front of the church, through which lay people or pilgrims would have access to the nave or shrine of the minster. It is interesting to see that as early as 853 (and probably much earlier) the monastic plan had become stereotyped in its main features. The contemporary plan[1] of the Carolingian abbey of St Gall in Switzerland shows the cloister south of the church, the dormitory along the eastern range, the frater and kitchen to the south, and cellarage to the west, with the main exit from the cloister to the outer world near the west end of the church, and with infirmary and guest-rooms nearer the periphery of the mass of buildings. The only important differences between the plan of St Gall and the later monastic norm are that the dormitory of the Swiss abbey was on the ground floor and that there was as yet no chapter-house; meetings apparently took place in the north walk of the cloister.

St Gall is an example of a type of monastery, common enough on the Continent, especially in the Rhineland and south Germany, which is not found in England on the same elaborate scale. St Gall and others like it were not so much monasteries as, so to say, religious county-towns. The great complex of buildings included not only the monastery proper but the administrative offices of its vast estates, hospitals for monks and lay people, schools for boys and young clerks, guest-houses for monks and pilgrims, almonries for the poor—to say nothing of the workshops and stores needed to keep the whole fabric and its population well found and in good condition. Nothing in Britain was on this scale in Saxon times. Even celebrated abbeys like those of St Hild at Whitby or St Aethelfryth at Ely were less complex and, architecturally speaking, were on a far smaller scale. Still later, after the revival of the tenth century, the buildings, in common with all Anglo-Saxon architecture, remained small, cramped and confined. For the purpose of this book all pre-Conquest monastic architecture can be neglected, for Saxon monastic church or domestic building was rarely left standing by the newcomers, nor is there any evidence that the Normans took the slightest notice of the Saxon plan in determining their layout, save that the area of the chancel of the Saxon church usually lay within that of the apsidal presbytery of the new Norman minster. In other words few extant English monastic buildings are, like Deerhurst, older than the Conquest; and all those in this book derive ultimately from models in Normandy, Burgundy or elsewhere on the Continent.

[1] Reproduced in *Encyclopedia Britannica* (11 ed., 1910), art. 'Abbey'.

IV

Benedictines

By 1066 the monastic layout had become standardized in north-western Europe, partly in the houses of the great congregation of Cluny, but more completely in the new monasteries of Normandy which, though following Cluniac traditions, never formed part of the family of Cluny. Here in Normandy what almost amounted to a new species developed, owing to the Norman genius for large-scale planning and construction: the distinctive feature of this type was a more spacious arrangement which was soon regarded as a material *sine qua non* of every monastery worth the name. The only two major changes since the days of St Gall were, as has been suggested, the appearance of the chapter-house as an architectural feature in the eastern range and, perhaps in some way connected with it, the lifting of the dorter to first-floor level, thereby giving room for the chapter-house beneath, and at the same time leaving the ground floor of the eastern range free of any important spatial demands and devoted to a number of minor and often varied purposes, some of which are obscure to the modern investigator.

The main features of the eleventh-century plan were:

(i) The great abbey church, consisting of aisled apsidal presbytery of varying length; transepts with eastern apsidal chapels; and a long aisled nave used for the frequent liturgical processions which were a notable element in monastic observance, based upon Cluniac customs.

(ii) The great cloister, of which the north walk was backed by the south aisle of the nave;[1] this walk had processional doorways to the church at the eastern and western ends. The eastern walk began at the north-west angle of the south transept; along it on the ground floor came normally, in the following order, (*a*) a passage to the graveyard near the east end of the church, (*b*) the chapter-house, (*c*) a passage to the offices east of the range; this was used also as a parlour, (*d*) a long undercroft running south, divided in various ways and for varying uses; the northern part was often the treasury and muniment room, the southern part was the warming-house.

Near the south-east corner of the cloister there was usually a staircase—the 'day-stairs'—giving access to the dorter. Over the whole eastern range, and determining its length, ran the dorter, at the southern end of which, usually at right angles, lay the rere-dorter, or latrines. The north end of the dorter usually abutted on the transept, through the south wall of which there was direct access to the church by the 'night stairs', though at some houses, for one architectural reason or another, this stair debouched into the cloister between the chapter-house and the church. As a general practice, the alleys of the cloister, which had either open arcading or large windows on their inner side, were roofed with a pentise resting against the walls of

[1] The reader will note that Gloucester abbey (p. xv) is one of the fairly numerous Benedictine houses where the cloister lies *north* of the church; the dorter also is abnormal.

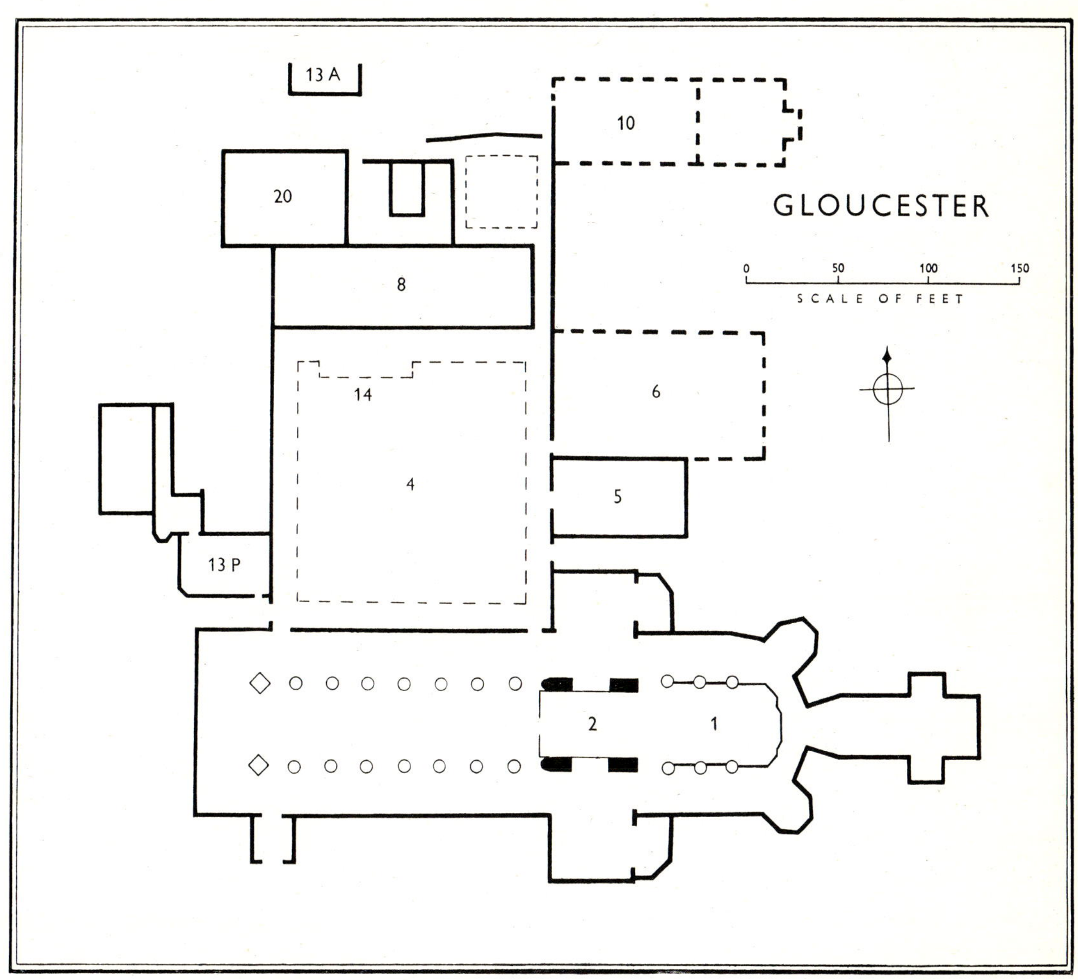

Note: the italicized titles are of features not found in this plan.

1. Presbytery
2. Quire
3. *Lay brothers' quire*
4. Cloister garth
5. Chapter-house
6. Dorter (on first floor)
7. *Warming-house*
8. Frater (on subvault)
9. *Rere-dorter*
10. Infirmary
11. *Cellars*
12. *Guest-house*
13A. Abbot's Lodging
13P. Prior's Lodging
14. Washing-place
15. *Lay-brothers' Dorter*
16. *Lay-brothers' Frater*
17. *Lay-brothers' Infirmary*
18. *Lay-brothers' Rere-dorter*
19. *Stream or Drain*
20. Kitchen

b 2

the church and other main buildings, i.e. they were not within the main walls of the claustral blocks. Later however in small houses, particularly those of the friars, the cloisters were passages within the main walls of the range. The area enclosed by the alleys, usually approximately a square, was under grass, and originally used as a burying-ground, though this was later discontinued in favour of a graveyard to the north-east of the church. Along the south walk lay the frater, originally a simple hall at cloister level, with an entrance from the cloister and another at its west end leading to the kitchen, which was at its south-west angle. Later, the frater was sometimes built or rebuilt on an undercroft, used sometimes partially as a warming-house, partially as cellarage; in this later form it was often of the type rendered familiar by its near relation, the college hall at Oxford and Cambridge. The frater thus developed had a partition or wall at its west end, beyond which came the lobby or 'screens', approached from the cloister by a staircase of some dignity, and from the kitchen by a western door. The kitchen lay outside the cloister range at the south-west angle. Along the western range lay, on the ground floor, cellarage and the cellarer's office or 'chequer', and on the first floor the (originally simple) reception rooms of the abbot or prior, with accommodation for notable guests. Near this, at the north-west angle of the cloister in the western range, was usually the only direct exit from the cloister to the *curia* and the outer world.

Outside this claustral nucleus lay two other groups of buildings:

(iii) To the south-east of the eastern range—that is, in the most secluded part of the precinct—lay the infirmary block. As this housed not only the sick but all who for any reason of age or disability or temporary inactivity (such as was caused by the periodic blood-letting) were unable to follow the common round of duties, it had to be large; it was in fact a monastery *in parvo* with hall (dorter), frater, chapel, accommodation for the infirmarian, and herb garden. Later, it was augmented or adjoined by cells for students and copyists.

(iv) To the west of the western range—that is, where the monastery made contact with the world—lay the *curia* or great court, entered from outside by a gatehouse, and bordered by offices of all sorts—mill, bakehouse, brewhouse, almonry, guest-house and stabling. Later, when the abbot's or prior's establishment increased in complexity, it was in this direction that it extended with its chapel, hall and small court. Often, indeed, outside the western range there was an inner court, with a gate, beyond which lay the great outer court. These quasi-secular appendages differed greatly from period to period, and from house to house, and their layout was necessarily conditioned by the exigences of the site. They therefore occupied no fixed area or position, but in urban, and particularly in cathedral, monasteries their main outlines have been preserved to the present day as may be seen at Ely (p. 5), Durham (p. 3), Worcester (p. 11) and Chester (p. 9).

The arrangement of buildings set out above will be found in its main outlines in all the houses of black monks—that is, the traditional Benedictines, as they were called in a later age. It must, however, be remembered:

(1) That Norman builders scarcely ever had a virgin site on which to plan. Most of the Old English monasteries lay within the built-up area of towns, large or small, which cramped the site with roads on one or more sides, and often with a large public graveyard on one side of the church as at Gloucester and Bury St Edmunds (pp. 13, 15). Moreover, as has been said, the church was a fixed point; it could be rebuilt, but it was rarely transferred; and this often intensified the difficulties.

(2) That natural conditions, which had not affected the small Old English buildings, often presented problems to the Norman planners, with their love of space and new technique of water supply and drainage for a large community. Thus Durham and Worcester, where the west end of the enlarged church stood on the edge of a steep declivity with a river below, could only be planned at a sacrifice of traditional arrangements. In consequence, it will be found that the old black monk abbeys and cathedral priories exhibit more idiosyncrasies of planning than any other class of monastic building. The cloister is often north of the church (e.g. Canterbury, Bury St Edmunds, Gloucester and Chester) and even east of the transept (e.g. Rochester where it is south-east); the great court is often south or south-west of the conventual buildings (e.g. Durham and Worcester), and even the dorter is transferred to the western range (e.g. the later dorter of Durham) with, at Worcester, the additional eccentricity of a perpendicular position.

V

To the main features of this plan several orders added characteristic differences:

Cluniac Houses

The monasteries of the family of Cluny, which began to be established in England shortly after the Conquest, show no variations from the normal black monk plan, though in the minor architectural features of the church and in decoration in general many peculiarities appear. The only English Cluniac house of the first rank, St Pancras of Lewes, which must have been one of the most magnificent and complex monastic buildings in England, has been peculiarly unfortunate since its surrender in 1539. The great church was efficiently razed to the ground by a demolition squad a few weeks after the monks had left, and the site, after the customary vicissitudes at the hands of the grantee and pillaging townspeople, was ploughed up in 1845 by the main line of railway to Brighton, which passes over the site of the high altar. Thetford and Castle Acre (pp. 57, 59) are good examples of Cluniac sites of secondary importance.

Austin Canons

The houses of this order followed in general the monastic plan. A minor difference was that the frater almost always stood on an undercroft, part of which was a warming-house. The Augustinian houses differed greatly among themselves in size, from large abbeys such as Dunstable, Bristol and Cirencester to priories of five or six canons set deep in the fields or woods of Cambridgeshire or Sherwood Forest. These last are often small and irregular buildings, whereas the large abbeys are indistinguishable from black monk houses of the first or second rank.

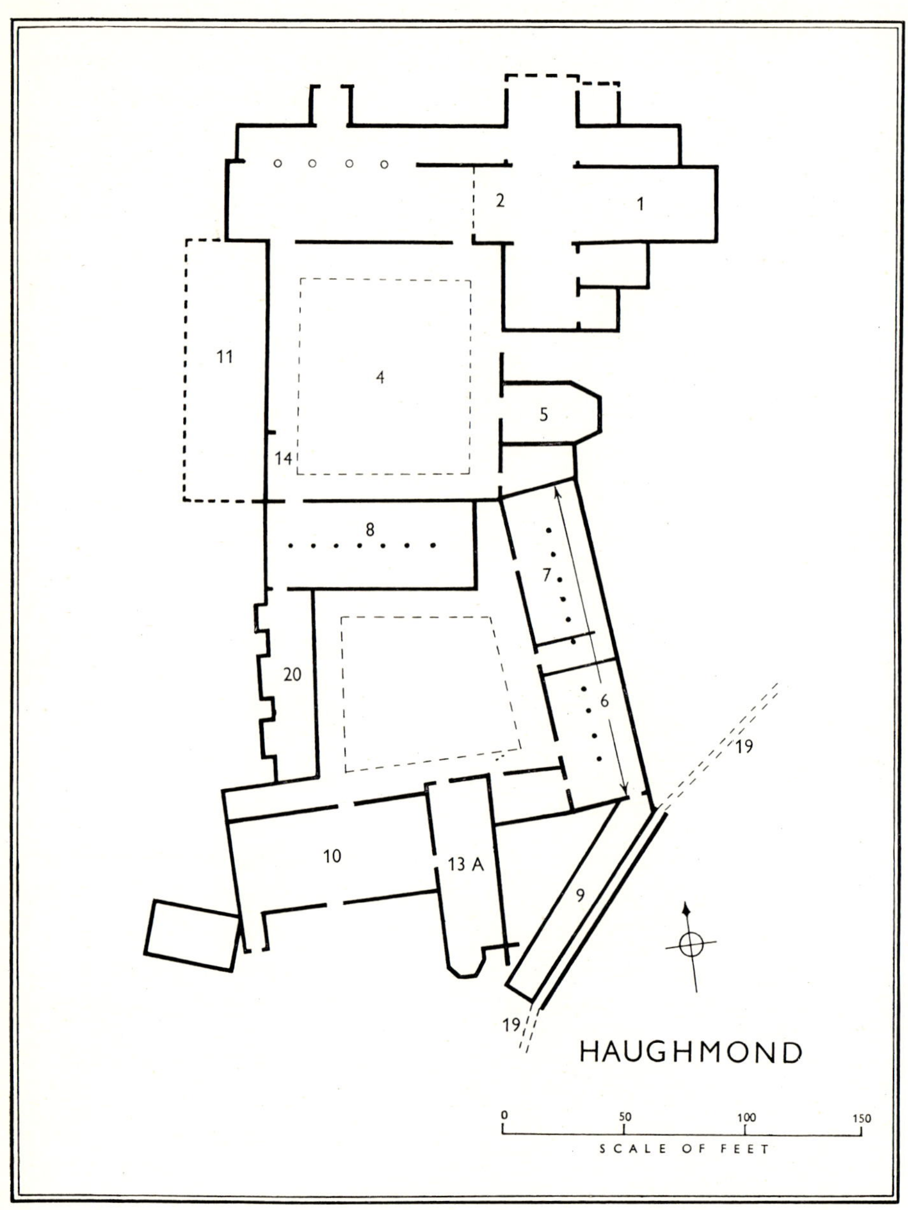

1.	Presbytery	8.	Frater (on subvault)	14.	Washing-place
2.	Quire	9.	Rere-dorter	15.	*Lay-brothers' Dorter*
3.	*Lay brothers' quire*	10.	Infirmary	16.	*Lay-brothers' Frater*
4.	Cloister garth	11.	Cellars	17.	*Lay-brothers' Infirmary*
5.	Chapter-house	12.	*Guest-house*	18.	*Lay-brothers' Rere-dorter*
6.	Dorter (on first floor)	13A.	Abbot's Lodging	19.	Stream or Drain
7.	Warming-house	13P.	*Prior's Lodging*	20.	Kitchen

VI

Cistercians

The Cistercians, whose first settlement in England was in 1128, claimed to follow exactly the Rule of St Benedict, and had no intention of innovating upon the traditional monastic plan, though they certainly aimed at reducing it to its simplest terms. Their way of life, however, did in effect bring about a number of changes which gave to the Cistercian abbeys a very distinctive architectural character:

(i) The exact uniformity which was demanded of all Cistercians brought it about that a single plan, derived originally from one or two of the original Burgundian houses of the order such as Cîteaux, Clairvaux and Fontenay, became standard for all the early foundations and was reproduced in its main features even in later houses. In consequence, the white monk abbeys, though varying in size and beauty of architecture and quality of material used, follow a single plan and form a single family more completely than those of any other religious order. A blind Cistercian of the first generation, if removed to a strange house, might have found little difficulty in moving about the conventual buildings.

(ii) The white monks were invariably newcomers; all their houses (save for one or two very late foundations) were on rural sites, and as a rule they chose—and were given—remote and desolate territory to exploit. Hence they were able to plan their monastery without having to consider their neighbours. Indeed, they considered their neighbours so little that on occasion they were willing to create the solitude which they had failed to find by removing cottages and even villages from the vicinity of their abbeys.

(iii) Their lay-brothers (*conversi*), equal and often superior in numbers to the quire monks, were from the start a new factor which influenced planning. The western range of the cloister was devoted to them, and the principal domestic buildings were duplicated: the dorter of the *conversi* ran along the western range on first-floor level, with their rere-dorter at its south-western angle; their frater was placed in the southern part of the dorter undercroft, near the kitchen which served also the frater of the monks; and their infirmary lay usually west of the southern end of the range. The western portion of the nave of the church became their quire, and to give them access to this without impairing the seclusion of the cloister a narrow passage or 'lane', parallel to the west walk of the cloister, was constructed within the ground floor of the range alongside of the cellarage.

(iv) The numbers of quire monks and *conversi* together, in the early days of the order, often made up a total far exceeding that of even the largest English black monk house. The largest of these latter, Christ Church, Canterbury, had as its maximum in the twelfth century a monastic population fluctuating between 100 and 150; Fountains and Rievaulx, at the middle of the same century, counted a total of 500 or 600. As a result, the two dorters (of monks and brothers) expanded to the south, and the ranges extended far beyond the quadrangle of the cloister; the frater parallel to the south walk was found to be too small, and it was rebuilt at right angles to the range where it could expand indefinitely.

(v) As the abbey stood in the open, and often wild, country, a precinct wall was a necessity and could contain as great an area as might be desired. At Fountains and Furness, for example, it had a very long perimeter, and large area. The wall at Fountains enclosed 90 acres; that of Jervaulx 100. It was entered by a main gateway, which usually had alongside it a chapel (the *capella ad portas*) for those externs who were not allowed in the abbey church. Sometimes, as at Furness and Beaulieu, there were two courts, an outer and an inner, both protected by gateways.

(vi) The abbey church was reserved for the use of the monks, and only in exceptional and late cases (such as Hailes) did it become a resort of pilgrims. It did not therefore need to undergo a wholesale rebuilding and extension so frequently as did the churches of black monks and canons, though it was common for the presbytery and often also for the transepts to receive additions. The church was usually long, so as to contain the two quires, and narrow. The monks' quire normally extended into the first or second bay of the nave, and was terminated by a screen; after an interval of a bay, used as the retro-quire, or quire of the sick, there was another screen, marking the eastern end of the lay brothers' quire. Since elaborate processions were among the Cluniac superfluities cut off by the Cistercians—the only regular one left being the Sunday procession with holy water around the cloister—the aisles were not needed for circulation, and often, in fact, were not constructed. When they existed, they were used to give accommodation for altars for private Masses, with screens in each bay. The Cistercian church, therefore, narrow, unadorned, whitewashed and cut up longitudinally and transversely by screens and walls, must have presented an austere, confined, and even a mean appearance. It is probable that the restrained grace and admirable proportions of Rievaulx, Tintern and Fountains in their open, ruined state would have been far less apparent when the fabric was enclosed and in use.

After these general observations we may consider the normal Cistercian plan. The east walk of the cloister began, as did those of the black monks and canons, at the angle where the south transept met the nave. Along it lay, in order from north to south: (1) a narrow room, divided by a partition, of which the eastern portion was used as a sacristy, the western as a book-room, while over it, in later centuries, was often the treasury; (2) the chapter-house, often entered through a vestibule; (3) a parlour; (4) a passage to the infirmary; and finally (5) the undercroft of the southern extension of the dorter, originally used partly as a warming-room and partly as a noviciate. Later, the noviciate was moved to a special building south-east of the range, and the warming-room to a new site next to the reconstructed frater, while the abandoned undercroft was used as a work-room for the monks. Over the whole range on the first floor ran the dorter, with the rere-dorter ordinarily at right angles at its end. The dorter of Waverley, which was on the ground floor, is an exception, possibly unique in England. East of the range lay the infirmary and the abbot's lodging which, at least in the first century or so of Cistercian planning, lay furthest from the outside world near the dorter, so as to observe the Rule, and not, as with the black monks, at the angle most accessible to visitors. The abbot's lodging in later centuries often included a set of rooms for visiting abbots.

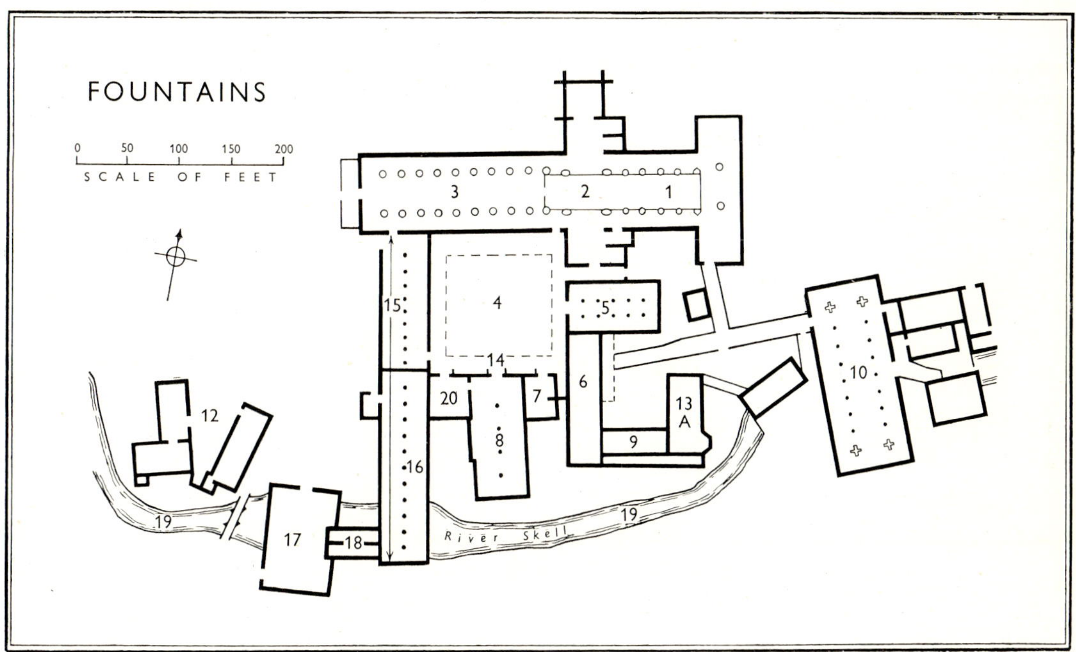

1. Presbytery
2. Quire
3. Lay brothers' quire
4. Cloister garth
5. Chapter-house
6. Dorter (on first floor)
7. Warming-house
8. Frater (on subvault)
9. Rere-dorter
10. Infirmary
11. *Cellars*
12. Guest-house
13A. Abbot's Lodging
13P. *Prior's Lodging*
14. Washing-place
15. Lay-brothers' Dorter
16. Lay-brothers' Frater
17. Lay-brothers' Infirmary
18. Lay-brothers' Rere-dorter
19. Stream or Drain
20. Kitchen

Along the southern range in the first planning lay the frater, but, as has been mentioned, this was usually rebuilt at right angles to the range and at the centre of the walk; the greater space thus left between the frater and the east and west ranges was filled by a new warming-house and a new kitchen. Thus the Cistercian kitchen, unlike that of the black monks, formed part of the southern range. The composition of the western range has already been sufficiently described. The guest-house was usually a separate building standing free, at a distance to the west.

This nucleus is traceable in all Cistercian houses, but great abbeys such as Fountains and Rievaulx naturally threw out tentacles and galleries in all directions, while often, as at the two abbeys just mentioned, natural obstacles, with which the modest original buildings had not come into contact, taxed the ingenuity of the later architects. At many sites, all the care and scholarship of the excavators has failed to give a perfectly satisfactory account of the functions of all the buildings that have been unearthed.

A word may be devoted to the water supply and drainage of the abbeys. Here again the white monks were at an advantage. Choosing their sites on virgin ground, they could lay their plans and their drains untrammelled, and many of their abbeys show systems of great complexity and efficiency. For a large abbey housing several hundred souls a swiftly running stream was a prime desideratum. This of itself explains the choice of a site in a valley which might appear to have drawbacks in other respects. The ideal site was one to the north of a stream flowing from west to east (cf. Fountains, where this condition obtains naturally, and the Premonstratensian Dryburgh, where it is achieved artificially), and the not infrequent cases where Cistercian cloisters lie to the north of the church (e.g. the Savignac Buildwas) are usually due to the awkward lie of the river, for it was the normal practice to set the church on the highest point of the site. The stream (as at Fountains) or the conduit (as at Beaulieu) was passed under the infirmaries, rere-dorters and kitchens, with branches to the abbot's lodging and guest-house. When the stream was near its head, a lead for domestic use was sometimes drawn off above the abbey; more normally, a supply of absolutely pure water was taken directly from a spring, and brought by a conduit or a lead pipe often from a distance of a mile or more. Thus Waverley, though its walls were washed by the Wey, drew its drinking water from a hillside spring, and Stanley (Wilts), though surrounded by watercourses, had a pipe-line of considerable length. Indeed, in the twelfth and thirteenth centuries the water-supply, sanitary arrangements and care of the sick must have reached a level of excellence in the abbeys which was unsurpassed in the land, and hitherto unattained in north-western Europe since the decline of the Roman Empire.

VII

Premonstratensians

The white canons of Prémontré, though in many ways modelled on the Cistercians and settling in similar remote places, bear little resemblance to the white monks in their planning. They are, in fact, to speak for Great Britain alone, the least uniform of all the orders as they are also, generally speaking, the least ambitious as planners. Though *conversi* were originally a part of their economy, provision is rarely made for them in the claustral buildings or the church, and those resident at the abbey must have been few in number. In consequence, the western range of the cloister, which was needed neither for the purposes required by the black monks, nor for the accommodation demanded by the *conversi*, became an insignificant feature, sometimes a narrow cellar, sometimes, as at Dryburgh, a screen wall only. In the same way the Premonstratensian churches are often narrow, somewhat gaunt structures; the naves have no aisles, or a northern aisle only. Occasionally at the east end, after rebuilding, some sort of magnificence is attained, as at St Radegund's and Bayham. For the rest, the normal claustral plan is followed, with the frater parallel to the southern walk.

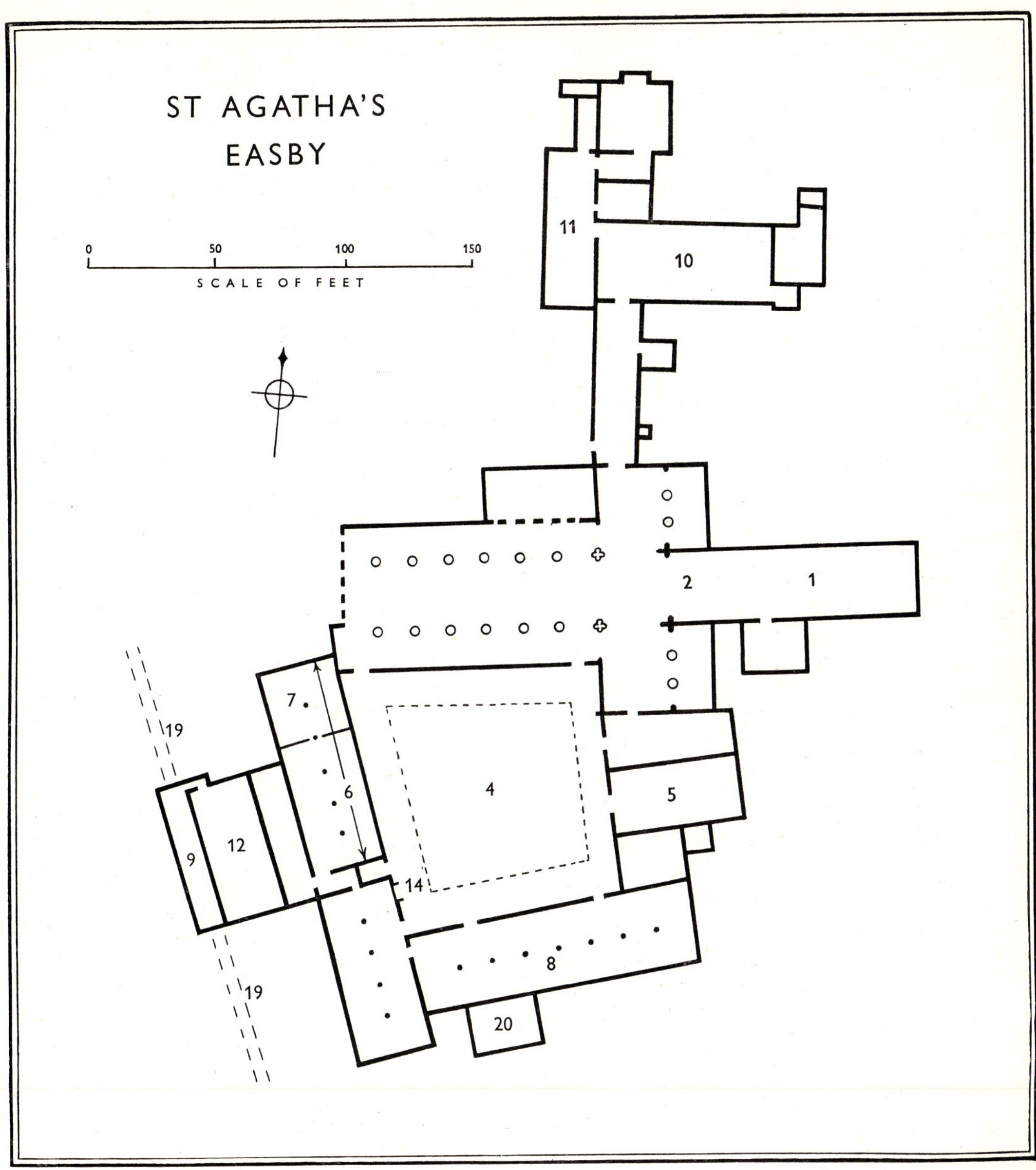

1. Presbytery
2. Quire
3. *Lay brothers' quire*
4. Cloister garth
5. Chapter-house
6. Dorter (on first floor)
7. Warming-house
8. Frater (on subvault)
9. Rere-dorter
10. Infirmary
11. Cellars
12. Guest-house
13A. *Abbot's Lodging*
13P. *Prior's Lodging*
14. Washing-place
15. *Lay-brothers' Dorter*
16. *Lay-brothers' Frater*
17. *Lay-brothers' Infirmary*
18. *Lay-brothers' Rere-dorter*
19. Stream or Drain
20. Kitchen

Carthusians

The Carthusian plan is so unlike that of any other English monastic order that it can best be studied from the individual examples given below.

The Nuns

Generally speaking, a nunnery resembled in plan very closely the monks' or canons' house of its order. There were, as has often been remarked, relatively few nunneries in medieval England, and of these more than half were small houses deep in the country. Their buildings, never large, have in most instances either perished or have been absorbed into farms or small country houses. The only large Benedictine nunneries were the ancient houses of Wessex and the London area, and of these several of the largest (e.g. Shaftesbury in Wiltshire and Barking in Essex) have either disappeared to the last stone or have been buried under urban encroachments. At Romsey, where the beautiful church remains intact, little else survives. The only other group of large nunneries is that of the Gilbertines in south-east Yorkshire and Lincolnshire. This again is a region where few remains of any monastic houses survive, and though two large Gilbertine houses, Watton and Sempringham (pp. 247, 243) have been excavated, the sites have been covered in again and no photographic impression can be given of the buildings. For different reasons, no photograph can fully show the plan of Lacock, where much remains, but is concealed from the camera by an overlay of subsequent additions. The section devoted to nunneries is therefore somewhat meagre.

The Friars

When the first Friars, Preachers (Dominicans) and Minors (Franciscans) arrived in England in the third decade of the thirteenth century, their needs were of the simplest. They invariably settled in, or on the outskirts of, towns, in mean huts or tenements, without even a chapel in early days, and when they received a more permanent home this was usually a nest of small houses knocked into a single habitation, with a few rough additions, the original chapel and cloister being usually of wood or wattle daubed with clay. As they became more numerous and their life became less austere, all the orders of friars tended to adopt a simplified form of the monastic complex, with church (made up of large nave for preaching and narrow quire), cloister, chapter-house, dorter, frater and the rest. There were, however, one or two features peculiar to their buildings:

(1) The cloister, which was used less than that of the monks for daily life and work, was often reduced to a corridor within the range.

(2) The north wall of the cloister often stood free of the south wall of the church, with a narrow space between.

(3) The quire was separated from the nave not by transepts, but by a narrow passage passing beneath a slender lantern-tower.

(4) The main entrance to the friary was often north of the church, the cloister being approached by means of the passage, known as the 'walking place', through the church.

As almost all the friaries were in towns or cities, in cramped and valuable sites, they were invariably broken up and absorbed at the Dissolution, though the large churches sometimes remained, as at Chichester, Norwich and in the City of London. Though in many cases considerable traces have been discovered and described, they can in no case be effectively recognized from the air. Consequently, the sites that figure below are in a sense hardly characteristic; they are those rare houses which were built on virgin sites in rural areas, and therefore approximated very nearly to the normal monastic plan. Walsingham, a late foundation in the meadows (p. 253), and Hulne, an early foundation of the Carmelites in remote Northumberland (p. 257), have little in them to distinguish them from houses of Austin canons. It has unfortunately not been possible to include a single Dominican site. Their only house in the country built on the monastic scale was the royal foundation of King's Langley (Bucks) used as a noviciate for the province, and this has been almost wholly destroyed or absorbed.

VIII

Hitherto we have been considering the normal monastery of the twelfth and early thirteenth centuries, and the monastic plan has been spoken of as something static and changeless. In essentials, this was indeed the case in England in medieval times. It was not until the sixteenth century that the development of domestic architecture and the spread of Renaissance sentiment in Europe brought about considerable modifications in such countries as remained Catholic. Nevertheless, no house remained without change. The collapse of one part, the need to enlarge another, the ambition to build on a greater scale, the necessity of meeting new needs, led all through the Middle Ages to repeated additions. Many indeed of the Norman churches were planned on such a magnificent scale that complete rebuilding has never been necessary. The naves of Ely, Winchester and St Albans, and the presbytery of Norwich have not been substantially altered or increased. In almost every great church, however, the east end has received either alterations or additions; the Lady Chapel, in particular, as an architectural feature of importance, is a new appearance of the thirteenth and fourteenth centuries. So with the conventual buildings; almost all, including the cloister itself, were altered and amplified and recased in the new mode. Among the many developments some were more widespread than others.

(1) Everywhere, first among the black monks and canons, but later with the Cistercians and Premonstratensians, the general rise in the standard of comfort led to the gradual domestication of the original bare and cheerless halls of the common life. In the dorter, wainscoted cubicles took the place of dividing curtains or low partitions; in the cloister, glazed and wainscoted carrells replaced the open benches. The chapter-house was often rebuilt with vaulting; in the infirmary, abbot's and

prior's lodging, and guest-house the great common rooms were replaced by panelled chambers with fireplaces and garderobes; the great refectory, rendered still more cheerless when numbers shrank, was relinquished on ordinary days or for many meals in favour of a smaller and warmer room where meat could be eaten. In consequence, some of the most magnificent of the late monastic structures, as at Forde and St Osyth, are architecturally almost indistinguishable from the contemporary secular mansions of the scale of Compton Wynyates and Layer Marney.

(2) With the Cistercians in particular a great change took place with the all but complete disappearance of *conversi*, *c.* 1350. Though some houses (e.g. Whalley, p. 103) appear to have built a western range even in the fifteenth century, and other houses made no structural alterations that can be seen in the ruins, the more common practice was to adapt old buildings to new conditions. The dorter and frater of the lay-brothers, and their infirmary also, were remodelled as accommodation for the abbot, cellarer and guests, while on the ground floor the 'lane' was thrown into the cellarage. In at least one case (Sawley, p. 101) the nave of the church, no longer needed as a quire for the *conversi*, was allowed to fall into ruin and then walled off from the remaining part of the fabric.

(3) Finally, two very different features that grew in elaboration may be mentioned. The one is the gatehouse, especially that of the rural establishments. This had originally been no more than a gate in a wall or at a bridge, but when the risings and wars, and later still the development of domestic architecture, made a great gateway a necessity or a desirable luxury, an architectural form of great magnificence and variety was evolved which influenced, and was itself influenced by, a parallel development at the mansions of secular magnates. The gatehouses of Butley, Thornton and St Osyth, to name but three, are examples of magnificent building too rarely visited by those familiar with other forms of medieval architecture.

The other feature is the system of moats and fishponds. It was only when studying the photographs here collected, and those of other sites not included, that the present writer became aware of the complexity of the channels surrounding many houses, especially those in the river valleys and fens of the eastern part of the country. The purpose and course of many of these channels will probably always remain problematic, but there would seem to be room for a study of medieval fish breeding, based partly on the many elaborate series of fish stews which have left their impression in the meadows surrounding the great Cistercian and other abbeys. Kirkstead, Barlings and Thornton are not the only ones to supply extensive evidence.

IX

As the primary purpose of this book is to exhibit the sites and planning of the various orders, the plates are grouped according to the divisions of the religious families, and within that division they are arranged roughly by geographical distribution from north to south-west.

The letterpress has been designed simply to explain the plates, with the primary aim of indicating to one who has the photograph before him what the site is, how the principal buildings lie, and what are their points of interest or singularity. The method of description may at first sight appear complicated to those unfamiliar with the monastic plan, but it is hoped that this impression will not be permanent, and that readers without any specialized knowledge of monastic antiquities, and those who may have the book with them when visiting the site, will get their bearings without difficulty. With this end in view, historical and architectural notes and dates have usually been reduced to a minimum; those who wish for further information will turn to the more elaborate guide or monograph or article dealing with the place. The present writer has visited many, though by no means all, of the sites illustrated and he has in every case attempted to base his notes on the most modern and reliable account of the remains. Detailed bibliographical notes would be altogether out of place here, but reference has been given in each case, wherever possible, to at least one published account which contains a good plan. When an official guide of the Ministry of Works exists reference has been made to this, as both competent and easy of access,[1] but antiquaries will be aware that such guides themselves often rely on previous articles in learned journals.

It has been impossible to make even this cursory exploration of antiquarian literature without recognizing very vividly the debt owed by all lovers of monastic antiquities to the pioneer work of a few distinguished scholar-antiquaries who have, within the past sixty or seventy years, converted the excavation of medieval sites from a haphazard, dilettante and often ineffectual pursuit into an exact and scientific process capable of yielding fruitful and permanent results. Foremost among these pioneers was, of course, the late Sir W. St J. Hope, who by a series of patient excavations, conducted autumn by autumn over more than thirty years, set up a tradition of sound technique and elucidated in great detail the normal plan of the various orders. Second only to Hope, as the notes below will show, was his friend and fellow-worker in later years, the late Sir Harold Brakspear. These two men were, in the best sense of the word, amateurs; their lead has been followed and their technique still further developed by those who in one way or another, as advisers or administrators, have been officially responsible for the conservation of the monuments they have explored. They have thus been able to command greater resources and touch wider fields, as representing H.M. Commissioners (later the Office, and later still the Ministry) of Works, while at the same time they have as antiquaries and scholars been in the counsels of the antiquarian societies or served on the Royal Commissions set up to report on the ancient and historical monuments of Britain. Among these the names of Sir Charles Peers and the late Sir Alfred Clapham must find a place in any account of the preservation of monastic ruins. It is owing to their learning and discernment that many of the sites that figure in this book present so clear a plan to the reader. There were those who, thirty years ago, were still apprehensive, when hearing that a ruin had

[1] These pamphlets, when in print, can be obtained on the site itself, or through any bookseller.

come under national guardianship, that something of the beauty and the charm of the place would for ever be gone. There are still probably those who find in an utterly lonely site, even if it be overgrown and unexcavated, something that is lacking in a fenced and tidied ruin, however reverently it may be cared for; but granted that the more celebrated ruins are to be visited by thousands, and to be preserved for future generations, the task could scarcely have been better done than it has been by those responsible in the past few decades. If a suggestion may be made, it is that in future excavations the debris of the site and its surroundings should be examined with care and the finds, however humble, of the minor ornamentation and of the domestic life of the monks should be preserved. The technique of the archaeologist, added to the knowledge of the antiquarian and the skill of the architect, might thus make the preservation of a ruin still more historically valuable.

MONASTIC SITES FROM THE AIR

1

DURHAM

BENEDICTINE

THE CATHEDRAL MONASTERY OF DURHAM lay to the south of the great church, sharing with it the superb situation on a lofty peninsula all but encircled by the Wear. Protected on three sides by the river and on the fourth by the castle, the cathedral and its satellite buildings have a stern beauty which accords well both with their site and with their function in the later Middle Ages as a bastion of religion and government in the path of Scottish encroachment. Durham became a cathedral when the body of St Cuthbert came finally to rest there shortly before 1000, but monks were not introduced till *c.* 1083. Thenceforward the cathedral priory rapidly became, and remained till the Dissolution, one of the wealthiest, most populous, most cultivated and most observant of the monasteries of England. Originally a small group of houses under the shadow of the castle, Durham has in modern times developed into a straggling city, the lower levels of which are often obscured by 'industrial haze'. Nothing, however, can impair the majesty of the cathedral, 'perhaps the most impressive single building in the country', the distant view of which from the railway is for many the most memorable feature of a journey to or from the North.

The priory buildings are exceptionally well preserved. A great part of the medieval library and the muniments is intact *in situ*, while the original records contain what is almost a complete list of the monks as well as a detailed description of the house and its life on the eve of the Dissolution; it is therefore probably true to say that English monasticism of a certain type can be studied more fully at Durham than anywhere else in the land.

The cloister is in the normal position south of the church, which lies almost exactly east and west. In the eastern range the apsidal roof of the chapter-house, rebuilt *c.* 1400, can be seen; to the south beyond it is the roof of the original dormitory, part of which, together with the prior's house to the south-east, forms the modern deanery. Along the south walk lay the frater, rebuilt as the Chapter Library in the seventeenth century; this great hall, as the *Rites of Durham* tells us, was in the last phase used by the whole community only on great feasts. At its south-west corner is the octagonal kitchen (1370), a less graceful building than the abbot's kitchen at Glastonbury. Along the western range, over a subvault, lay the new dormitory, built *c.* 1400; the lower row of small windows lighted the wainscoted cubicles. At right angles to the range, running west, the rere-dorter is visible. The whole layout of the western range may be compared with that of Worcester. The extent of the

relatively small precinct can be seen, bounded by the cathedral to the north, by a street to the east, and by a row of houses and the wooded cliff to the south and west. The great court, though still clear of buildings, has been planted with scattered trees. The great gateway can be seen to the east, with the almonry to its north-west. Granaries lay along the south wall and the guest-house to the west, now broken up into canons' houses.

Plan and short description in *Durham: Cathedral Books*, 2 (1948), by W. A. Pantin. See also *The Rites of Durham* (Surtees Society, cvii, 1903).

2

ELY

BENEDICTINE

THE ABBEY OF ELY was originally founded as a nunnery on an island in the fens by Aethelfryth (Etheldreda), daughter of Anna, king of the East Angles, shortly after the middle of the seventh century. Destroyed by the Danes, it was refounded as an abbey of monks *c.* 963–9. It was a very wealthy house, second only to Glastonbury in Domesday, and in 1109 it was converted into a bishop's monastery. Even so, it retained vast estates, and continued to be one of the most active of the black monk monasteries. No account will here be expected of the great constructions of the fourteenth century which, in addition to its magnificent Norman nave, give the cathedral a unique place among its fellows.

The abbey had originally enclosed a large, almost triangular area bounded to the north by the open space west of the church known as The Green; by High Street and Fore Hill north of the church; by Broad Lane (off the plate) to the east; and by Back Hill and Silver Street (the winding road in the west foreground) to the south and west. The straight road, known as The Gallery, seen in the plate running from north to south from The Green to its junction with Silver Street, is not primitive. Its function developed when, at the partition of property between the new see and the monastery, the part of the original area lying west of the cathedral and the conventual buildings was assigned to the bishop. Within the monastic precinct itself there was likewise a clear division, still visible, between the area occupied by buildings and small yards, and that taken up by large gardens, orchards and vineyards.

Owing partly to the artificial division made at the creation of the see, the priory had no great court west of the church and cloister. Instead, a relatively small walled court was created between The Gallery and the road, known for part of its course as Oyster Lane, which runs through the precinct towards the Cathedral in the centre of the plate. To the south of this court parallel to The Gallery was the gatehouse; the southern limit was formed by the great barn, still standing with its long, low roof, and now used as a part of the cathedral school. Between this court and the cathedral lay an unusually irregular mass of buildings, many of which have survived almost intact. Generally speaking, the large conventual buildings have disappeared; the smaller, capable of adaptation into houses for the cathedral clergy, have survived.

North of the outer court, beyond a walled garden containing a large, dark-foliaged tree, is a group made up of the prior's house and guest-halls. The southernmost member of the group, a small building with a steep roof, is the exquisite chapel built by Prior Crauden in 1324–5. From the north-east corner of this the prior's hall runs northward to meet other apartments. The high building running from east to west beyond (i.e. north of) the prior's house is the great guest-hall, with the lesser

Queen's Hall returning from it parallel to the road. Between this group and the cathedral the open garth of the cloister can be seen, but the great frater which lay along the south walk has disappeared, as has also the western range containing cellarage. In the eastern range the chapter-house has gone, and the south end of the south transept stands quite clear of buildings. The dorter and its undercroft, which ran south from the chapter-house, lay almost entirely beyond (i.e. south of) the cloister, and the southern end of the range would have been near the foot of the single dark tree now standing at the fork of the road. In contrast to the eastern range, the great group of the infirmary with its halls, chapel and cellarer's lodging is still standing to the south-east of the cathedral, and the parts can be readily identified in the plate from a plan.

Ely was unique among great monasteries in having some of its precinct and offices separated from the rest by the church. The sacristy and almonry lie along the south side of the modern High Street; they are visible immediately over the roof of the quire of the cathedral.

Elaborate plans and description by T. D. Atkinson in *The Architectural History of the Benedictine Monastery of St Etheldreda at Ely* (1933).

3

ST ALBANS

BENEDICTINE

THE BENEDICTINE ABBEY OF ST ALBANS stood on the reputed site of the martyrdom of the proto-martyr of England, a third of a mile outside the east angle of the Roman town of Verulamium. Founded, according to its own venerable tradition, by King Offa in 793, and refounded or reformed by St Oswald in 968, it enjoyed thenceforward, and especially after the Conquest, a long career of splendour. In wealth and influence it ranked among the very greatest houses, and its rich artistic and intellectual life, vitalized by its situation on the Great North Road near London, entitled it to claim with some justice the title of premier abbey of England. It was the home, in the thirteenth century, of a group of artists and chroniclers of whom Matthew Paris is the most celebrated, and it was ruled in the fourteenth century by a succession of great abbots of whom Thomas de la Mare (abbot, 1349–96) was the last and greatest.

The church, with many of its appurtenances, survived the Dissolution, to suffer severely at the hands of a nineteenth-century restorer. Until he attacked it, the vast shell of the Norman minster remained almost intact, much of it constructed in the rose-red Roman bricks from Verulamium, but the original triple apse was, between 1257 and 1310, replaced and extended by the ambulatory and Lady Chapel. Of the conventual buildings scarcely a trace remains, save for the great gateway to the outer court, seen to the west of the church, now forming part of a well-known school. The cloister lay in the usual position south of the nave, and the main domestic buildings were in the normal order. The precinct covered practically the whole area seen in the photograph south-west and south-east of the church.

As the church of St Albans has, since 1877, held cathedral rank, it has been the subject of numerous monographs with plans. One of the best and fullest descriptions of abbey and site is that of C. R. Peers in *Victoria County History of Hertfordshire*, II (1908), 483–570; see also the same writer in the *Hertfordshire Inventory* of the Royal Commission on Historical Monuments (1910), pp. 177–88.

4

CHESTER

BENEDICTINE

CHESTER, a pre-Norman church of canons, was refounded by Hugh Lupus in 1093 from Bec as the black monk abbey of St Werbergh. Its career was on the whole fairly prosperous, but not distinguished. Shortly after the Dissolution, in 1541, it was converted into the cathedral of a new and vast diocese, which at its inception included parts of Yorkshire and Westmorland as well as Lancashire. The buildings were constructed almost entirely of the warm red local sandstone, which is extremely friable, and it has in consequence endured much renovation. The choir stalls are among the finest surviving in England.

The abbey church and conventual buildings owe much of their plan to their situation in a town crowded within the walls of a Roman legionary fortress. Of the original Norman church only the north transept and part of the nave remain; the original east end was greatly enlarged in the thirteenth century, and in the fourteenth the south transept, which had been used as the parish church of St Oswald, was rebuilt with east and west aisles. The cloisters, which lie to the north of the church, are complete, dating in their present state from the fifteenth century. The rectangular chapter-house adjoins the north transept, but the dorter, which extended over the whole eastern range at first-floor level, has disappeared. The frater, long used as a schoolroom by the King's School, occupies the whole of the north walk. Of the western range only the cellarage of the ground floor remains; the narrow rectangular building next to the church is the early abbot's chamber, which later became the chapel of the abbot's lodging (now destroyed) on the first floor of the range. The great court (now Abbey Square) to the north-west of the cloister is entered by the medieval gateway visible among the houses to the west of the frater. The road running across the top right-hand corner of the plate (Foregate Street—Eastgate Street) is on the line of one of the main streets of the Roman fortress, of which the wall, extensively rebuilt in the Middle Ages, bounded the precinct to the east, and can be seen beyond the open space east of the frater.

Description and plan in numerous handbooks dealing with the cathedral; short account and plan in *Archaeological Journal*, XCIV (1938), 308–10.

9

5

WORCESTER

BENEDICTINE

THE BENEDICTINE MONASTERY OF ST MARY'S at Worcester had, in common with several of its sister cathedral priories, a long history before the Conquest. It had been refounded or reorganized by St Oswald in the tenth century, and at the time of the Norman Conquest there was a small community serving the cathedral church where St Wulfstan, their sometime prior, was bishop—the only Anglo-Saxon bishop to retain his see throughout the reign of the Conqueror. Much research on the part of historians and antiquaries has been devoted to the topographical history of the priory and cathedral before 1066; here we are concerned only with the buildings erected after the Conquest. A view has been given from a somewhat unfamiliar angle showing the cathedral from the south-west, in order to give a clear sight of the remaining conventual buildings.

The ancient precinct lay on an elevated site on the east bank of the Severn, and a new cathedral and monastic complex began to go up shortly after the Conquest. As often, the layout was conditioned by practical considerations. No source of running water was available on the site, which lay to the south of the church, but below it, to the west, flowed the river. On this, the western side of the cloister, the dorter was therefore planned. Besides its abnormal position (cf. Durham, where a similar problem received a similar solution) it had a further unique abnormality in that it lay not along, but at right angles to, the western range, and was extended westward by a further block, of which the floor levels were stepped down towards the river. This block contained the rere-dorter on the second (or top) floor, and the infirmary on the first and ground floors. The great drain, which usually ran beneath the rere-dorter at ground level, here fell at a steep angle within the building to the Severn, and its position shows that it can have been flushed only by rain water from a cistern on the roof. All the upper part of the wing has disappeared, but ruins of the infirmary stand between the grassy banks that slope towards the river. The frater can be clearly seen along the south walk; it stands above cloister level, and is now used by the Cathedral School. The polygonal chapter-house, the earliest of its kind (*c.* 1170), Norman in origin but re-roofed at the beginning of the fifteenth century, is in the usual position near the church. Beyond it to the east is a ruined arcade that was part of the guest-hall. The great gateway, known as the Edgar Tower, giving access to the city from the outer court, stands at the eastern end of the large quadrangle. Beyond the cathedral lie the streets of the old city, and beyond these again the

haphazard spread of nineteenth-century industrial buildings, through which winds the Worcester and Birmingham Canal. The bridge of the western road over the Severn lies off the plate to the left near the left-hand bottom corner: also off the plate lies the eastern boundary of the county cricket ground, whence the cathedral shows to great advantage.

Description, and plan of the dorter range, by Harold Brakspear in *Archaeologia*, LXVII (1916), 189–204.

6

GLOUCESTER

BENEDICTINE

THE BENEDICTINE ABBEY OF ST PETER at Gloucester began as a small foundation of Cnut's in 1022 which replaced a community of 'canons'. After some vicissitudes the monastery, when at a very low ebb of its fortunes, was rescued by the first Norman abbot Serlo who, appointed by the Conqueror in 1072, recovered and increased its possessions, raised its community to one hundred before his death, and may well be called the real founder of the medieval abbey. Henceforth, though never among the very greatest abbeys in landed wealth or intellectual distinction, Gloucester remained always in the forefront, partly owing to a distinguished series of abbots which included Gilbert Foliot, the rival of Becket, and John de Gamages, the great rebuilder; partly to its situation in a city which for long was the scene of an annual Great Council and was at least once (1278) the meeting place of parliament; partly to its possession of the body and shrine of the murdered Edward II, which proved a gold-mine to the monks; and in part, finally, to the excellent use made of this new source of wealth to rebuild church and monastery in a new and (as many would say) very beautiful style of architecture which ultimately became the reigning mode.

The conversion of the church into a cathedral shortly after the Dissolution helped, as at the old cathedral monasteries, to preserve intact not only the minster itself but a number of buildings great and small, though relatively less than at Durham or Ely. The architecture of the church, which, with the exception of the fifteenth-century tower and Lady Chapel, is largely a brilliant masking and reconditioning of the Norman fabric, has been treated and illustrated in so many excellent handbooks and guides that no comment is necessary here, and the photograph is included principally as an exhibition of what is perhaps the most noble purely monastic church to survive in its entirety.

The precinct is included within the plate save for a small triangle on the left (western) side. The precinct wall which runs from west to east along the line of houses in the foreground, was broken by St Edward's gate leading to the south-west porch of the nave, and by the cemetery gate opposite the south transept. Turning north at right angles, it ran to the south-east corner of the Lady Chapel and thence, from the north-east corner, to the road (Pitt Street) which it skirted, until, almost directly above the west end in the plate, it turned south at right angles along St Mary's Street.

The cloister, as at Bury St Edmund's and elsewhere, lay north of the church

owing to the presence of the town cemetery to the south; the arcading of the north walk can be seen above the roof of the nave. The beautiful lavatory, which projects into the garth, can be seen in its four westernmost bays. The roof of the chapter-house is hidden by the high roof of the presbytery, and the dorter, which lay in an unusual position at right angles to the eastern range, has disappeared. Above the roof of the presbytery, at some distance, the arcading of the infirmary hall is visible. The two blocks of building seen immediately above the north-west corner of the nave made up the original abbot's lodging; subsequently they became the prior's house, and are now the deanery. The later abbot's lodging lay on the site of the modern building to the left of the cathedral tower.

Detailed description and plans by W. H. St John Hope in *Archaeological Journal*, LIV (1897), 77–119.

7

BURY ST EDMUNDS

BENEDICTINE

THE BLACK MONK ABBEY OF ST EDMUNDSBURY, in the centre of West Suffolk on the River Lark, was founded in 1020 at the shrine of the murdered king of East Anglia, and soon became one of the half-dozen greatest houses, distinguished alike by its wealth, its local and regional influence, and its literary and artistic possessions. Already magnificent in its buildings and treasures, it was towards the end of the twelfth century the home of Abbot Samson and his biographer Jocelin of Brakelond, in whose pages the daily life of the cloister is mirrored with a fidelity found in no other medieval chronicle. Throughout the Middle Ages East Anglia contained a large part of the population and wealth of England, and Bury was often visited by kings and magnates; in 1267, 1296 and again in 1447 it was the meeting place of a parliament.

Few great abbeys have disappeared more completely, and the casual visitor can make little of the site. The best guide to the points of the compass in the plate is given by the church of St James, with its conspicuous roofs, which runs due east from its west front on the main street. The photograph includes almost the whole area of the precinct, east and north of the broad road. The west front of the abbey church lay some 200 ft. east of this road, and the tall Norman tower of St James, which is visible to the right of the plate just beyond the church, and which gave access to the cemetery, was almost exactly opposite its central doorway. The position of the west end of the minster is consequently almost coincident with the western front of the present large house. The abbey church, some 500 ft. long, would therefore, if still in existence, dominate the view; it remained Norman in its main outlines to the end, the later additions taking the form of chapels flanking the presbytery.

The cloister which, though large, extended only half-way along the wall of the great nave, lay to the north of the church, the ground to the south being occupied by the town cemetery and its churches. The cloister garth coincided roughly with the present lawn, which, in the plate, is shaded by a large dark tree in its south-eastern angle. The frater, of which low walls remain, lay along the north walk with the chapter-house in the east walk and the infirmary beyond it still further to the east. The great outer court covered a large part of the area now taken up by the modern public gardens; it had two main entries: the great western gateway, built in 1347, standing in the main street some distance north of St James's church, and a northern gateway, of which the remains are barely visible in the plate at the end of the northern arm of the cruciform path. The abbot's lodging, unusually elaborate, extended in a long line of buildings which bounded the great court to the east; fragments of masonry can be seen among the trees between the oval open space in the gardens and the three-branched path.

The cemetery, a large area to the south-west of the original shrine, contained at least seven small churches in Saxon times. Two of these, the sites of which were absorbed by the new Norman church, were rebuilt by the monks at the edge of the precinct, accessible from the road. The northernmost of the two, St James's, now the cathedral of the diocese of Bury St Edmund's, has already been indicated; it adjoins St James's tower, but has no architectural connection with it. Its east end reached to within 50 ft. of the west front of the abbey. The other, St Mary's, is just off the right-hand top corner of the plate.

No adequate monograph exists on the abbey site as a whole; there is a description (excellent for its date) with plans in the *Journal of the British Archaeological Association*, XXI (1865), 32 ff., 104 ff. It is to be hoped that this remarkable lacuna in antiquarian literature may be filled before long.

8

DUNFERMLINE

BENEDICTINE

THE BENEDICTINE ABBEY OF DUNFERMLINE in the south-west of Fife, some three miles from the northern coast of the Firth of Forth, and fifteen miles by road and ferry from Edinburgh, was founded on a modest scale by monks from Christ Church, Canterbury, some time before 1120. They were given as their church the small building erected by Queen Margaret *c.* 1070, the foundations of which, under the nave of the present kirk, were discovered in excavations from 1916 onwards. The scale of the monastery was greatly enlarged when King David I, in 1128, secured Geoffrey, prior of Canterbury, as the first abbot, and a great church was erected between that date and 1150. Of this church the nave alone remains. The crossing and eastern limb were rebuilt in the thirteenth century, and received various modifications, but this part of the church fell into disrepair after the Reformation and collapsed piecemeal in the late seventeenth and early eighteenth centuries. The remnants were cleared away in 1819 to make way for another rebuilding. The present parish kirk consists of a twelfth-century nave with a nineteenth-century crossing and east end. It is very nearly the same length as its predecessor, the medieval chapel-shrine of St Margaret, foundations of which lie exposed immediately east of the small eastern apse, in the shadow of the dark tree.

The abbey soon became one of the greatest in Scotland, rivalled only by Arbroath. Edward I of England stayed here in 1290 and again in 1303, and it became a favourite burial place for the Scottish royal line, including Alexander III and Robert Bruce.

The cloister garth, now partly graveyard, partly garden, lay to the south of the nave. The eastern range has wholly disappeared save for the south end of the dorter and, parallel to this, the south end of the rere-dorter, which can be seen in the plate, with the line of the drain outside it to the east. To the north-west of this stands the magnificent fourteenth-century frater. The ground here falls steeply to the south and west, and the frater proper, which lies somewhat above the level of the cloister, is on the second floor of the building as seen from the road to the south. It was served by kitchens placed in an unusual and inconvenient site beyond the present roadway and communicating with the frater by passages and stairs through the gateway or 'Pens'. The kitchens lay at the south-eastern end of the block beyond the gateway; the rest of the range, originally a guest-house, was rebuilt as a royal palace in the sixteenth century. It was the birthplace in 1600 of Charles I. The only other portion of the medieval monastery remaining is the abbot's house, embodied in a building beyond the burial ground to the north-east of the kirk.

Description and plans in the *Fife, Kinross and Clackmannan Inventory* of the Royal Commission on Historical Monuments (1933) pp. 106–21.

9

WHITBY

BENEDICTINE

FEW GREAT CHURCHES of medieval England can have stood more magnificently than Whitby Abbey, which rises from the turf on the open summit of a cliff, far seen and far seeing, its pinnacles and windows assaulted by the gale and resounding to the surf. The history of the site is of course far older than that of the stones now visible, and begins with the foundation of the Saxon community of men and women founded in 657 by Hild, shortly to be the resort of Caedmon and Wilfrid. Sacked by the Danes, it was not refounded till after the Conquest, when some of the band of monks from Evesham and Winchcombe, who had refounded Jarrow and Wearmouth and Durham, laid the foundations of a new life here also. Yet despite its past glory and its architectural splendour Whitby was never a very distinguished house in the later medieval centuries.

The church was left intact at the Dissolution, no doubt as a landmark familiar to mariners, and was almost complete as late as 1711, but during the last two centuries the fabric has sadly disintegrated, the nave having partly collapsed in the eighteenth century and the central tower early in the nineteenth. When at last there were hopes that the process of dissolution had been arrested, the ruins received several direct hits when a German cruiser squadron approached the Yorkshire coast in 1914. Since then the ruins have been cleared of debris, but no attempt has been made to excavate the conventual buildings to the south of the church. The latter, some 300 ft. in overall length, had an unusually long aisled presbytery; the transepts also had eastern aisles. The east end dates from 1220; the transepts and eastern bays of the nave from 1260, and the western part of the nave from the fourteenth century.

Recent excavations on the north side of the abbey church have revealed considerable traces of the Saxon monastery; its church or churches were no doubt overlaid by the later edifice. In the extreme left-hand lower margin of the plate the graveyard surrounding the medieval parish church can be seen. The two dark areas to the east of the abbey are shallow meres; beyond them a fair is in progress.

For description, plan and photographs see A. W. Clapham in *Victoria County History of Yorkshire: North Riding*, II, 508 ff. This was in print, though not published, in 1914. For the Saxon monastery, see Sir C. R. Peers and C. A. Ralegh Radford, *Archaeologia*, LXXXIX (1943), 27–88.

10

ST MARY'S, YORK

BENEDICTINE

THE ABBEY OF ST MARY at York was the wealthiest of the few black monk houses in the northern province. Though a monastery of some sort may have been in existence before the Conquest, the history of the house begins with the settlement at York of a band of monks who had met with difficulties in re-establishing monastic life at Whitby; its expansion dates from gifts by William II in 1088. In 1132 the life had become so relatively luxurious that a group of thirteen monks, many of unusual distinction, seceded to found the Cistercian abbey of Fountains, and no less than seven of the group became Cistercian abbots. The abbey weathered this storm, and at the end of the thirteenth century (1270–80) a great building abbot, Simon of Warwick, rebuilt the church on a grand scale; later still, in 1318, the great precinct wall was built and crenellated. At the Dissolution, the abbot's house was converted into a palace for the Lord President of the North, and in 1827 the area of the eastern range was handed over to the York Philosophical Society.

The abbey lies some 200 yds. west of the Minster; the site is bounded on the south-east by the city wall (visible in the plate, with the well-known multangular tower in the foreground), on the south-west by the River Ouse (just off the plate) and on the other two sides by its own precinct wall, which can be seen to the north. The view is taken from the south-east, the main axis of the church lying almost east-north-east. The lay-out of the whole has been ascertained by excavation, but the church alone reveals its plan in the plate. As rebuilt by Abbot Simon it was large and magnificent, 350 ft. in length, aisled throughout, and with a particularly long and spacious presbytery. The claustral buildings were in normal positions to the south, but save for the vestibule to the chapter-house which is incorporated in the museum on its site, nothing now remains above ground. The frater stood on a subvault along the south walk. The great gateway is visible at the west end of the church of St Olave, the original gift to the monks from Whitby; a small medieval building, west of the abbey church and known as the *hospitium* lies just outside the plate to the left.

Detailed plans and short description in *Archaeological Journal*, XCI (1935), 383–5.

11

BARDNEY

BENEDICTINE

THE ABBEY OF BARDNEY lay in the fens by the Witham, eight and a half miles due east of Lincoln. Originally a Saxon foundation, whither King Ethelred of Mercia retired in 704, it was ravaged by the Danes two centuries later and became derelict. The house was refounded in 1087 by Gilbert of Ghent as a cell of the black monk abbey of Charroux in Poitou, and in 1115 was established as an independent abbey by Gilbert's son William. A great church and extensive buildings were gradually erected, and Bardney had a good income, but it never became an abbey of the first rank, and in its latter days, known to us from copious visitation documents, an air of mediocrity seems discernible. It escaped dissolution in 1535, but was implicated in the Lincolnshire revolt of 1536 and six of the monks were executed, the remainder surrendering the abbey two years later. Part of the buildings were converted into a dwelling, but early in the eighteenth century all had gone to ruin and fifty years ago nothing was visible save a few low mounds. Scientific excavation was undertaken by H. Brakspear in 1909, and the plan of almost the whole abbey was elucidated and carefully measured and photographed. Since then nature has once more resumed her sway, and save for a few fragments of masonry the whole is once more under grass.

The large precinct, across which the view is taken from the east, was surrounded by a wide and deep ditch, of which the eastern and southern channels and traces of the western are visible in the plate. The main entrance lay west of the church, where the road turns at right angles, and remains of the great gateway still stand; they are concealed in the plate by a dark tree. Between this and the church ran a wall, to the south of which lay the inner court, while to the north stretched the great court, bounded by a large barn. In the south-eastern corner of the precinct was a large fishpond, of which the outline can be seen.

The great church, as the mounds of the piers show, was aisled throughout, save for the short extension of the presbytery which replaced the original apse. Next to the south transept came a small treasury, then the chapter-house of which the walls stand to the height of a few feet. South of this lay the undercroft of the dorter and beyond this again, and partially overlapping it, the rere-dorter; the lines of the great drain are distinguishable. The frater lay along the south walk of the cloister on the ground level. The western range was occupied by the cellarer's stores and checker, and by the abbot's house, built round a small court. At the southern end of the range lay the kitchens. Still further south, and detached from the range, the outlines of the guest-house can be distinguished, south-west of the southernmost tree. The infirmary lay to the east of the eastern range, where the mounds are visible under the turf.

There is an elaborate description, with large plan and an interesting appendix on the remarkable series of tombstones, by H. Brakspear in *Archaeological Journal*, LXXIX (1922), 1–92.

12

ST BENET'S OF HOLME

BENEDICTINE

The Black Monk Abbey of St Benet's lay on the left bank of the River Bure, seven and a half miles in a direct line from the coast, and some ten miles in a direct line north-east of Norwich. It was founded in 1020 by the Danish King Cnut, and within a few years helped to form the original community of Bury St Edmunds. Lying as it did among the marshes at the periphery of the country's activity, it never grew after the Norman Conquest, and maintained throughout the Middle Ages an undistinguished existence. At the end, however, it enjoyed the negative distinction of being the only abbey never to be suppressed. The last abbot, William Repp, was appointed to the see of Norwich with commendatory rights over the abbey; its revenues were annexed to the see, and successive bishops of Norwich have continued to enjoy the lands and revenues in virtue of their position as abbots of Holme.

The dyke enclosing the precinct can be clearly seen in the plate, which is taken from the west, but the church and conventual buildings have completely disappeared, the only fabric to retain any shape being the great gatehouse. This, incorporated into a windmill, itself now derelict, can be seen in the left foreground. It forms the subject of a well-known sketch by Cotman.

The outline of the abbey church can be seen in the centre of the precinct. It was of unusual design; the nave and transepts were aisleless, but the presbytery had aisles, and possibly an eastern extension. There was a circular central tower and another tower at the west end (cf. Wymondham and Ramsey); a corner of this can be seen. The rest of the site has been systematically robbed, the stone having gone to walls and roads, and even the soil and bones of the cemetery have been used for top-dressing. Some lines of buildings can be seen to the south-east (perhaps infirmary and abbot's house) and to south-west (possibly rere-dorter and guest-hall). The outlines of fish-stews are discernible to the east of the gateway.

Though remote from roads and rural communications, its situation on a navigable river in the midst of waterways must have made St Benet's accessible enough to visitors and traders. To-day, as can be seen from the photograph, the stream in summertime is alive with small craft.

There is no adequate description or plan of St Benet's of Holme. For some notes see *Journal of the British Archaeological Association*, XXXVI (1880), 15–26.

13

BATTLE

BENEDICTINE

THE ABBEY OF ST MARTIN DE BELLO, soon known as Battle Abbey, was founded by William the Conqueror in 1067 on the site of the battle of Hastings, as a thank-offering for his great victory and to provide prayers for the souls of the fallen. It was colonized by black monks from Marmoutier in Touraine. Tradition had it that the Conqueror ordered that the high altar should stand on the exact spot where King Harold fell, and that when the monks settled upon a lower site which was more sheltered and had a better supply of water the king insisted on his original design. Certainly, excavations carried out in 1929 established that the original high altar stood on the highest spot of the whole site, which would have been the natural station for King Harold to choose, and that the level of the other buildings was adjusted to this.

In the photograph, which is taken from the south, the great gateway, erected in 1328, is seen in the centre; to the right is the building put up by Sir Anthony Browne on the site of the almonry soon after the Dissolution. From this spot the wall of the precinct behind the trees follows the line of the main road, which was deflected from its original course as this traversed the proposed site of the church. Beyond the trees to the extreme right can be seen the parish church. The abbey church lay at right angles to the modern mansion beyond the grass quadrangle; it extended under the present garden and trees, where was the high altar of the first Norman church. A fragment of the south wall of the church can be seen.

The walks of the cloister are approximately indicated by the paths surrounding the lawn; to the east, next the church, lay the chapter-house, and the eastern range was continued by the great dorter, of which the walls and gable end are visible. The rere-dorter, of which low ruins remain, lay at right angles to the eastern range at its southern end. The infirmary ran out to the east from the centre of the dormitory range, under the present trees. The refectory, parallel to the walk, formed the south side of the cloister and the western range was occupied by the abbot's house. This, rebuilt in the thirteenth century, was unusually elaborate, and forms the nucleus of the existing dwelling-house, which in recent years has accommodated a well-known girls' school. South of the site of the refectory lie the foundations of the kitchen and cellar; south of these again, and running westwards, was the guest-house range, on the undercroft of which Sir Anthony Browne erected a large wing, intended to be the residence of the Princess Elizabeth, of whom he was for a short time guardian.

This, too, has disappeared, save for the two octagonal turrets which form a conspicuous feature in any view from the south.

The town of Battle is the classic example in England of a medieval borough which owes its material and civic existence entirely to a black monk abbey. Beginning as a settlement of masons and carters engaged in the construction it became a small town composed of workpeople, craftsmen, purveyors and dependants of all kinds. The triangular market place, long controlled by the monks, can be seen immediately beyond the gatehouse, and away from it stretches the High Street.

There is a full description of Battle abbey and town, with a plan, in the *Victoria County History of Sussex*, IX (1937), 102–5. For the abbot's house, see the elaborate paper, *The Abbot's House at Battle*, by Sir Harold Brakspear, in *Archaeologia*, LXXXIII (1933), 139–66.

14

GLASTONBURY

BENEDICTINE

OF ALL THE MONASTIC SITES of England Glastonbury, standing on the slope of its far-seen Tor at the edge of the Somerset meres, makes in some ways the greatest appeal to the imagination. Reaching back as a Christian settlement in actual fact to the early Dark Ages and in legend to apostolic times and even to the childhood of Christ, the church, when given its final monastic character by St Dunstan in 943, soon became the wealthiest in England, and retained this position, with some fluctuations of fortune, until the Suppression. Its buildings were commensurate in size and magnificence with its wealth. Both church and domestic offices received addition after addition until the very end, and the immense minster, with its western and eastern accretions, finally attained an overall length of some 550 ft. Its history ended with the execution—some would say, martyrdom—of the last abbot on the hill overlooking his abbey and the wide lands of his domain.

The remains of this splendour make—or at least until a few years since made—a somewhat melancholy spectacle, and often produced in visitors a depression of spirit not felt among other ruins. In part this was no doubt due to a sense of the transience of mortal things, nowhere more keenly felt than here, and in part to the too frequent intrusion into the little town and abbey precinct of a certain vulgarity which is not so apparent at other sites of the kind; most of all, perhaps, it was due to the appearance of desolation, rather than ordered care or pure solitude, that seemed to possess the place. This last reproach has now been fully removed by the labours of a group of eminent archaeologists, and, as the photograph shows, the site has now been excavated and much of it marked in the turf, though even now it lacks the faultless *décor* and map-like precision of some other ruins.

No brief paragraph can give even the barest outline of the church's history, over many details of which learned opinion is still divided. Even when all legends, Arimathean, Arthurian and the rest, have been shorn away it remains certain that a church of immemorial antiquity—the wattle *vetus ecclesia*—existed and was given a protective covering and roof by St Paulinus in 633. This survived till the great fire of 1184, when it was immediately replaced by the coincident chapel of St Mary, a work of delicate late Romanesque which still stands and is seen in the view. To the 'old church' a number of successive eastward additions were made by King Ine, St Dunstan and others. These occupied the area later covered by the narthex or galilee of which the wall can be seen, as well as by the westernmost bays of the Norman church. To the west of the *vetus ecclesia* and visible in the second photograph lie the foundations of the chapel of St John the Baptist erected by St Dunstan shortly after he re-founded the monastic community. The pre-Conquest monastic buildings

must therefore have occupied the space, immediately beyond a tree in the photograph, where a path leads east.

The first Romanesque church probably ran eastwards from a little short of the east end of the Saxon church. It was wholly ruined by a disastrous fire in 1184, and rebuilt on a larger scale. Part of the transept of this second church, remodelled to carry a larger tower, and the broken arch of the crossing, are the most striking features of the ruins. The east end, as so often, was rebuilt and extended in the fourteenth century (the site of the high altar can be seen marked in the turf) and, finally, only forty years before the Suppression, the so-called Edgar chapel was added by Abbot Bere east of the presbytery.

The Norman cloister was in the normal position with one corner of the garth in the angle between the south transept and the nave; it was relatively small and cramped owing to the presence, immediately to the west, of the *sacrum coemeterium* round which Dunstan's monastery had been built. The chapter-house has not been excavated, but its site can be seen; then comes the long subvault of the dorter, stretching far to the south of the cloister. The figure recessed in the turf to the south of this is the plan, unique in shape for a building of this kind, of the rere-dorter, which lay in the normal position.

Returning to consider the cloister, the excavated site of the long frater is distinguishable; to the west of this came the square kitchen and further still to the south-west the abbot's lodging. The foundations of these have been excavated but not marked in the turf. Further west the abbot's kitchen, which has survived intact, can be seen, its familiar shape disguised in a vertical view, but clearly seen in the first plate. The western range has wholly disappeared.

There is a plan of the church and other buildings then excavated opposite p. 1 of the Somerset Archaeological Society's *Proceedings*, LXXVI (1930), 26–33, and year-to-year reports of the excavations, by Sir C. Peers, Sir A. W. Clapham, and Abbot Horne, will be found in numerous volumes of the same journal, and (in shorter form) in the corresponding volumes of the *Antiquaries' Journal*. The work is still in progress, and important traces of the Saxon monastery were found in the summer of 1951.

15

MUCHELNEY

BENEDICTINE

THE ABBEY OF MUCHELNEY, as its name suggests, stood on an island one and a half miles south of Langport in Somerset, near the southern limit of the marshes traversed by the River Parrett and known by the generic name of Sedgemoor. Until recent times Muchelney was inaccessible by land during several of the winter months, and though a modern road on a causeway now connects it with Langport the waters occasionally reassert their sway, and at the moment of writing (February 1950) the village has been entirely isolated for almost a fortnight by flood water.

The abbey, founded by King Athelstan in 939, remained a small and poor house in Saxon times, and was one of the few to escape immediate reorganization at the hands of the Normans. It had, however, to fight for long against the domination of its powerful neighbour, Glastonbury; it was successful and had a not unprosperous career in the later medieval period.

The domestic buildings have suffered almost total destruction, and until a few years ago the site was covered by an orchard; nothing remained visible save part of the abbot's house, still inhabited as a farm-house. Within the last few years, however, the Ministry of Works has obtained control of the site and has begun excavations which were still in progress when the photograph was taken (summer, 1949). The plan of the large abbey church some 200 ft. in length, can be clearly seen. The excavation of the interior has not yet been completed, but four stages of growth can be clearly discerned: the original small apsidal Saxon church entirely enclosed by the later building; the original Norman apse; the second and larger Norman apse; and, finally, the square Gothic east end (? or Lady Chapel).

The lines of the cloister, which lay to the south of the nave, have been indicated, but hitherto the eastern range has not been excavated. To the south and west a large and beautiful group of buildings remains, the work of the years immediately preceding the suppression (cf. St Osyth and Forde). The high-roofed building along the south walk, recently used as a cider cellar, embodies the original wall separating the cloister from the frater. The latter lay in what is now a grass-grown court (the line of the southern wall is marked in the turf), but the ante-room still exists to the west, in the ground floor of what was the abbot's lodging and which still stands to full height, built largely of the beautiful and durable Ham stone.

North of the abbey is the parish church, with a fine tower of the Somerset type, and north of that again, across the road, the medieval cottage that was the priest's house.

Partial plan and photographs in H. A. Tipping, *English Homes*, II (1921), 261–70. A *Guide* of the Ministry of Works may have appeared by the time the present pages are published.

16

MILTON

BENEDICTINE

MILTON ABBAS lies in a deep and now peaceful valley below the Downs of north-east Dorset, thirteen miles north-east of Dorchester and six miles south-west of Blandford. The abbey, one of the old Wessex Benedictine houses, founded in 964, lay out of the stream of national life and remained small and modest of means. The existing church, seen from a little south of east, replaced a Norman fabric, which was struck by lightning and burnt down in 1309; it was almost a century in building, and shows a gradual change of style. It is probable, though not certain, that the nave was never rebuilt, but an eastern Lady Chapel has been destroyed.

The monastic buildings lay to the north, the south side not being then available; they were converted into a mansion by Sir John Tregonwell, one of Cromwell's agents and the original grantee, and remained largely intact for two centuries. Secluded as the valley now is, it contained, throughout the medieval and later centuries, a small market-town clustering with grammar school, almshouses, shops and inns where now is lawn south-east of the church. The whole aspect of the site was changed by a new owner, Joseph Damer, who became Baron Milton and earl of Dorchester in the late eighteenth century. Having swept away the Tregonwell mansion, save for the abbot's hall which was embodied in the south wing, he erected a Georgian mansion and called in Wyatt to deal with the church. Then, irked by the proximity of the town, he bought in the leases, demolished the houses and transplanted such of the inhabitants as clung to the soil to a 'model' village built expressly for the purpose in a valley half a mile to the south-east. The only trace that now remains of Milton is a fragment of the market cross, hidden in the plate by trees.

Standing thus bereft upon an expanse of lawn and veiled by noble trees, the church has a visionary beauty comparable to that possessed by Fountains. After the Georgian changes it became the private property of the landowner, and in 1933 there was a prospect of its returning into monastic hands; in the event, it was purchased by the Ecclesiastical Commissioners. St Catherine's chapel, seen on the hill in the foreground, was an indulgenced place of pilgrimage in the Middle Ages. There is no modern description or plan of the monastic buildings, which have never been excavated.

35

17

BUCKFAST

BENEDICTINE

The Abbey of St Mary at Buckfast in south Devon is included to show a Benedictine abbey in being, which has an additional interest as occupying the site, and in some measure reproducing the architectural design, of a medieval Cistercian abbey. It lies in the valley of the Dart, midway between the source and mouth of the river, near the little town of Ashburton, nineteen miles from Exeter and nineteen miles from Plymouth.

The present abbey is the third of its name. The first, an Anglo-Saxon monastery of black monks founded in the tenth century or before, was decaying at the Conquest and disappears from history *c.* 1100. Savignac monks were introduced to the site in 1134 by Stephen, count of Mortain and later king, who had already founded Furness in the north. They received the lands which had belonged to the previous abbey and soon afterwards became Cistercian in the merger of 1147. This house was never of the first rank, and after an uneventful life was surrendered in 1539. The buildings disintegrated or were plundered and in 1806 a small mansion was constructed, in part out of the masonry on the site. A painting by Turner shows the house and its surroundings, somewhat romanticized, as they were in 1828.

The history of the present monastery begins in 1882, when the house and site came into the possession of exiled monks of the French abbey of Pierre-qui-Vire (Morvan). The colony sent to Buckfast was small in numbers, but the medieval associations of the place attracted benefactors, in particular the ninth Lord Clifford of Chudleigh, and monastic buildings were begun. In 1902 the house became an abbey with full rights, and the work of uncovering the medieval foundations was undertaken, but proceeded slowly for lack of funds. The decisive impetus was given by the second abbot, Dom Anscar Vonier (1906–38), who at the time of his election was only thirty years old. He resolved to proceed immediately with the construction of a great church of the same dimensions as the medieval fabric, relying upon domestic labour and future benefactions. The work was begun to the designs of the late F. A. Walters and the fabric was erected by half a dozen monks, mainly lay-brothers; the church was opened for public worship in 1922 and consecrated ten years later.

The buildings as seen in the plate follow the main lines of the medieval Cistercian plan, adapted to modern conditions of life and the somewhat different needs of a community which, though not unlike the Cistercians in much of its employment, is Benedictine in its organization and liturgical life. The ground plan of the church resembles that of many Cistercian churches; it has an aisled nave and transepts with eastern chapels; but it departs somewhat from the normal Cistercian plan by its

aisled presbytery and eastern transept of six chapels (cf. Fountains). Interiorly, it is adapted to the liturgical requirements of a Benedictine community and to congregational use; there are therefore none of the screens and walls that divided the area of the Cistercian nave. The style is Romanesque transitional, save in the upper storey of the tower (a recent addition) which is a not wholly satisfying blend of Gothic and Romanesque. Taken as a whole the result is pleasing, especially when seen in the mass and from a distance; on the ornaments and decoration of the interior opinions are more divided.

In the conventual buildings the ground plan of the eastern and southern walks of the cloister reproduces the main features of the Cistercian plan, though the internal divisions are different and the chapter-house, which includes the area devoted to the book cupboard and parlour in the medieval houses, is in actual use as a large sacristy. The refectory is on what is said to be the Cistercian site parallel to the south walk. The west range is composite. At its north end is the 1806 mansion, used as abbot's apartment and guest-house; south of this is the present chapter-room, and at right angles to the southern end, the large library with lay-brothers' quarters in a medieval building beyond. On the upper floors no attempt has been made to reproduce medieval conditions, and the modern usage of individual rooms or cells for the monks has been followed; accommodation for fathers, lay-brothers and novices extends over all three ranges.

The precinct extends southwards to a lane bordered partly by a wall and partly by the long modern building visible in the plate, which houses the various industries carried on by the monks such as bee-keeping, book-binding, etc. Besides extensive gardens the monks run a large farm of 260 acres. The Dart, which bounds the precinct to the east, is no longer used for domestic purposes as in Cistercian days, but has been canalized and provides power for the large mill visible in the distance, which does not form part of the abbey's property.

Description and plan in latest (1948) edition of the *Historical Guide to Buckfast Abbey*, by Dom John Stephan.

18

MALMESBURY

BENEDICTINE

THE ABBEY OF MALMESBURY in Wiltshire lay on the northern extremity of the area of high ground covered by the town. The existing parish church represents only the western half of the medieval minster which attained a length of 240 ft., with a large central tower crowned by a lofty spire. Little remains of the monastery, and only a part of the cloister, which lay to the north of the church, has been excavated.

The chapter-house stood normally, but the fall of the ground made it necessary for the dorter to run east and west on the same axis as the frater, which stood on an undercroft along the north walk. The rere-dorter remains in the basement of the Abbey House visible to the north-east of the church. West of the cloister was the guest-house, fragments of which are now embodied in the Bell Hotel. The main gateway lay north of the present market cross; north-east of this the site of the great court, where once Leland saw the 'vast Houses of Office' filled with the looms of the local clothier William Stumpe, is now covered by buildings. The abbot's house stood beyond the square tower to the south of the church; the infirmary lay where now is lawn in front of the Abbey House.

Description with plans by H. Brakspear in *Archaeologia*, LXIV (1912), 399–436.

19

LINDISFARNE

BENEDICTINE

LINDISFARNE or Holy Island, which lies off the coast of Northumberland ten miles south-east of Berwick, though less visited than many monastic sites, may claim with justice to be one of the most venerable. Founded as a monastery of the Irish type, and as the seat of a bishopric, by St Aidan in 634 and hallowed anew by the presence of St Cuthbert in 685–7, it was the centre from which Northumbrian religion and culture radiated. Of the seventh-century church nothing remains, though one of its ornaments may have been the Lindisfarne Gospels now in the British Museum. The ruins visible to-day are those of the cell or priory dependent upon Durham and founded *c.* 1082. This is now under the guardianship of the Ministry of Works.

The priory church is seen in the photograph standing to the east of the parish church and almost upon the same axis; its west end and the west wall of the cloister form the south-eastern limit of the graveyard, in which the tombstones, caught by the western sunshine, cluster like sheep. The small precinct, which was strengthened, if not actually fortified, to repel marauders who might arrive from the sea, consists of a cloister court and larger outer court; the latter had a gateway at the north-west angle and was bounded on the south by a steep ridge which falls abruptly to the shore. The church, of massive Romanesque architecture (1095–1145), which time and the sea-winds have made rugged, consisted of nave, transepts and presbytery with apse. The last, towards the end of the twelfth century, was replaced by a larger presbytery with a square end. The church is otherwise unchanged from its original shape.

The priory was never a large one and the original buildings, probably small and irregular, have disappeared. Those that remain are nearly all of the fourteenth century and were built at intervals. As Professor A. Hamilton Thompson observes, they are of a plan which in its final form shows monastic building gradually becoming domestic, with the added complication of semi-fortification. They should be compared with a similar development in a wholly peaceful setting at another of Durham's priories, Finchale (p. 43).

To the south of the transept was the chapter-house, with the dorter above. The southern range contains the original frater, with warming-house to the east and kitchens to the west, but as a result of re-building and additions the whole range became a unit—a domestic building with living-rooms to the east and offices to the west. The living-rooms were the prior's lodging, and there is some evidence that the prior's house became the quarters of all the small community as numbers decreased. It is symptomatic of the change that the original infirmary, probably on part of the site of the prior's lodging, disappeared with the domestication of the other buildings. In the western range, as usual, was the cellarage and storage. The door into the outer

court from the lobby of the frater at its south-west corner was strengthened in the fourteenth century by a barbican, of which the foundations are visible. The foundations at the south-eastern corner of the outer court are probably those of the guest-house. Those extending from the north-western angle of the court are the remains of a gatehouse and barbican.

Plan and description in the *Guide* of the Ministry of Works, by A. Hamilton Thompson.

20

FINCHALE

BENEDICTINE

THE RUINS OF FINCHALE PRIORY, a dependency of the neighbouring cathedral monstery of Durham, are beautifully situated on the west bank of the River Wear, some four miles downstream and four and a half by road north of the city. The site was originally the cell of the celebrated hermit and ex-merchant and shipowner St Godric. In his latter years he received visits and ministrations from the Durham monks and after his death in 1170 the place came into their hands. For a time only two or three monks lived there, but it was ultimately founded as a small conventual priory *c.* 1195, and the body of St Godric attracted pilgrims and funds. This phase of the house's life did not, however, last very long, and about the middle of the fourteenth century its existence as a self-contained monastery ended, and it was used by the cathedral priory as a rest-house and *villegiatura* for the monks, all in turn spending a week or two there. Henceforward, and till the Dissolution, the monastic population of Finchale was smaller and floating, and the prior was often a distinguished elderly monk of the mother house; in the latter half of the fourteenth century the post was held at intervals over twenty years by the eminent theologian Ughtred of Boldon. The buildings are of interest as reflecting the various stages of organization and as giving a good example of a monastery in miniature which was partly, but never wholly, transformed into a quasi-domestic building.

The nucleus of the priory was the original stone chapel of St John the Baptist erected by the monks for St Godric; remains of this, enclosed within the later quire, are still in existence below the present floor level, and a cross marks the spot where the tomb of St Godric was found. The foundations visible east of the church are those of a building of quasi-domestic type which housed the few monks in residence between the death of Godric and the erection of the priory. The remaining ruins are those of the priory.

The church and cloister date from 1250–1300, the rest is later work. The nave and quire of the church originally had aisles; these were destroyed in 1364–5, probably, as Sir Charles Peers suggests, to avoid repairs when numbers had fallen. The south aisle of the nave was later used as the north walk of the cloister; the line of the original interior wall of the north walk can be clearly seen. The chapter-house adjoined the south transept; then come some passages and rooms which formed the subvault of the dorter; the wall of the rere-dorter can be seen running east from the end of the dorter. The walls of the frater are standing parallel to the cloister, but there is no kitchen in the usual position at the west end of the frater, its place being taken by one in what is now the open space to the north of the rere-dorter. Nor are there any remains of a western range, but a building at the north-west angle of the

cloister where it joins the church may have been either the cellarer's lodging or a guest-house.

The large building running out eastwards from the dorter was the prior's house of later times. It is an example of the normal domestic arrangements of the period, with a hall, prior's chamber and small chapel. There is some indication that the monks on vacation used part of the prior's lodging, and a special day-room was allotted to them there. The range beyond the prior's house and at right angles to it contained the bakehouse and brewhouse.

Description and plan by Sir C. Peers in the *Guide* of the Ministry of Works; this is an abbreviation of a more elaborate account by the same author in *Archaeologia Aeliana*, 4th ser. IV (1927), 193–220; there is also a plan in *Archaeological Journal*, LXV (1908), 331.

21

BINHAM

BENEDICTINE

THE PRIORY OF BINHAM, near the Norfolk coast, lay some five miles south-east of Wells-next-the-Sea and three miles north-east of Walsingham. It was a cell of St Albans, founded shortly before 1093, and is noteworthy as an example of a small dependent priory planned as a complete monastery *in parvo* (cf. Finchale). The presbytery, crossing, and easternmost bay of the church were the property of the monks, and so destroyed after the Dissolution; the nave continued to be used by the parishioners, though both aisles have disappeared save for their western walls, which still form part of the fine west façade.

The church, though relatively small, was designed from the beginning with transepts and an apsidal east end, flanked by apsidal chapels. The line of the apse is visible in the presbytery and northern chapel; later, the east end was rebuilt and extended, as can be seen; the site of the new high altar is visible east of the line of the apse. The conventual buildings follow the normal black monk plan, with spacious chapter-house, parlour, passage and warming-room; the dorter extended over the whole eastern range, and projected beyond the cloister to the south. The frater lay along the south wall, and was presumably built on an undercroft; the kitchen stood at its south-west corner. The western range was of some importance, with cellarage on the ground floor and presumably the prior's lodging above. The range, as at Castle Acre, extended west of the west end of the church, with a projecting wing containing accommodation for guests.

Plan and short description in *Archaeological Journal*, LXXX (1923), 335. A guide will soon be published by the Ministry of Works, which has charge of the site.

22

EWENNY

BENEDICTINE

THE BLACK MONK PRIORY OF EWENNY lies on the left bank of the river of that name one and a half miles south of Bridgend between Cardiff and Swansea in Glamorganshire. It lies in a region thick with Norman and Edwardian castles, and is a remarkable example of a semi-fortified monastery surrounded by a defensive wall. Founded early in the twelfth century, it was one of a numerous group of small communities settled by Norman barons in or near their castles. They were, or soon became, cells of larger abbeys, and in most cases soon changed their abode to a site outside the castle precinct (cf. Castle Acre below, p. 58). Ewenny, however, which became a cell of Gloucester in 1141, was from the first a fortress in its own right, and so remained.

The church, which is seen from the north-west, was immediately after erection divided into two parts by a screen in the western arch of the crossing: a parish church in the nave and a monastic church in the presbytery and crossing. Over the crossing itself is a massive, fortress-like tower. The small cloister lay to the south of the nave; the eastern range has disappeared since the beginning of the nineteenth century, and the frater is embodied in the rear of the modern dwelling-house. The western range was taken up by the prior's lodging, which has partially survived.

The precinct wall, either standing or in ruins, can be traced for a great part of its length. The north gate can be clearly seen in the plate; the south gate is in the part of the wall immediately opposite. Two other towers exist in a ruined condition; the north tower is partly visible in the precinct wall just beyond the triangular road-junction; the south-eastern tower can be seen among trees at the corner of the lawn towards the top of the plate. The river from which the priory takes its name (='bright water') can be seen north of the wall along the line of trees and bushes.

Description with rough plan, by St Clair Baddely in *Archaeologia Cambrensis*, 6th ser. XIII (1913), 1–50.

23

ST MICHAEL'S MOUNT

BENEDICTINE

ST MICHAEL'S MOUNT is an islet in Mount's Bay, two and a half miles across the water from Penzance and connected with the mainland at Marazion at low water by a causeway a third of a mile long. The dedication to St Michael—'the great vision of the guarded mount'—dates from pre-Conquest times, and a Celtic religious community had probably been already succeeded before 1066 by monks from the Norman abbey of the same name. In any case, an alien priory was established there by *c.* 1087, and the island was owned by the abbey of Mont St Michel till the reign of Henry V, when it was confiscated with its companions and ultimately passed to Syon Abbey who installed an archpriest with two companions. After the Dissolution the priory was converted into a mansion, and has for long been the residence of the St Aubyn family (Lord St Levan). The frater and Lady Chapel have been incorporated into the house; the church remains, somewhat altered, with its wide view from the tower out over the Atlantic, 'toward Namancos and Bayona's hold'.

Historical account, without plan, in *St Michael's Mount* (Oxford, 1932) by Canon T. Taylor.

24

WILMINGTON

BENEDICTINE

THIS VIEW of the 'alien' priory of Wilmington, on the north side of the South Downs almost midway between Lewes and Eastbourne, is included as an example of a class of monastic establishment, common enough in medieval England, which has left few complete memorials of its existence—the 'alien' priory which never contained a community living the full monastic life.

The manor of Wilmington was given to the Norman abbey of Grestain by Robert of Mortain, half-brother of the Conqueror, before the date of Domesday; Grestain acquired a number of other possessions, rents and rights in England, some of them in Sussex, and Wilmington, lying near the English Channel, became in time the administrative headquarters and collection centre for the Norman abbey. No attempt was made, however, to build a regular monastery or to develop conventual life, and the structure, even in medieval times, probably resembled a manor-hall far more than a religious house. Confiscated more than once during the Hundred Years War the place was finally granted to the Dean and Chapter of Chichester by Henry V in 1413.

In the photograph, taken from a little west of south, the church, still in use, is seen towards the top centre of the plate among trees; the walled enclosure in the foreground is not part of the site. The church has a shingled broach spire over a belfry loft, and consists of chancel and nave, northern chapel or transept, and short modern south aisle, which may have replaced a larger medieval south chapel. There is no physical connection at present between the church and the old priory buildings, but it has been suggested that a pentise or gallery may once have joined the north-east wing to the southern chapel. This north-east wing, now roofless and in ruins, is built over a vaulted undercroft, and its southern portion was probably part of the 'old hall' (thirteenth century) referred to in documents concerning the priory. The block to the south is largely medieval and contains the 'new hall' of the priors on the first floor (fourteenth century) with what was the chapel adjoining to the east. No trace remains, either architectural or documentary, of a cloister and its offices, and it is improbable that one ever existed.

There is a full architectural description and plan, by W. H. Godfrey, in *Sussex Archaeological Collections*, LXIX (1928), 1–28. Historical notes, by W. Budger, will be found *ibid.* 29–52.

25

ALBERBURY

GRANDMONTINE

THE GRANDMONTINE PRIORY OF ALBERBURY in Shropshire stood on the right (south) bank of the Severn eight miles west of Shrewsbury. The order of Grandmont, founded near Limoges in France early in the twelfth century by St Stephen of Muret, was in origin extremely austere, and chose to settle in sites of a desolate and inhospitable character.

The Grandmontine priories of England reproduce a plan normal to the French houses, and at Alberbury the only unusual feature was a rectangular east end to the

church in place of an apse; this may have been due to the original design of the founder to introduce Austin canons. Considerable remains exist of this church in a farmhouse known as White Abbey, and the plan of the whole has been recovered by excavation in 1925. The existing house, here seen from the north-west, is made up of a section of the quire and nave of the church and of the parallel chapel of St Stephen, both now covered by gabled roofs. The prominent cross-wing, running north and south, is not in the main medieval, though it embodies part of the church. The small (45 ft.) cloister lay south of the church, with the conventual buildings in their customary positions round it.

For an account with plan see 'The Order of Grandmont and its Houses in England', by R. Graham and A. W. Clapham in *Archaeologia*, LXXV (1926), 159–210.

26

MUCH WENLOCK

CLUNIAC

THE CLUNIAC PRIORY OF MUCH WENLOCK lies at one side of the little town of that name twelve miles south-east of Shrewsbury on the road to Bridgnorth. A nunnery here was founded for St Milburge *c.* 680; it was destroyed by the Danes *c.* 874, but what are believed to be the foundations of its church have been discovered under the crossing of the Cluniac minster. A second foundation for men was made by Earl Leofric, earl of Mercia and founder of Coventry, and by his widow, Lady Godiva, *c.* 1050; he built a church of which the apsidal foundations have been discovered east of the crossing. Finally, *c.* 1080, Earl Roger de Montgomery incorporated the property of Leofric's church in his foundation for Cluniac monks from La Charité-sur-Loire. Begun in a small way, this grew and ultimately had half a dozen small priories of its own. It remained an alien priory till 1395, when it purchased denizenship, and came to rank as one of the greater monasteries, thus escaping dissolution until January, 1540.

The church was a noble building, 350 ft. in overall length, and the portions of the transept that remain show it to have been of a remarkably beautiful design of the early thirteenth century. Both quire and nave were aisled, and the transepts had an eastern aisle with chapels. A Lady Chapel was later added to the east of the presbytery, and a small hexagonal sacristy in the angle of the south transept. No trace of a primitive Norman church has been discovered, and it is probably that the first monks, few in number, used Leofric's church till the great rebuilding.

The nave has perished, save for a remarkable and perhaps unique chamber, visible in the photograph, which occupies the upper half of the three westernmost bays of the south aisle. Its purpose must be conjectural, but Dr Rose Graham has made the happy suggestion that it was a chapel of St Michael, such as is not infrequently found in upper storeys of French churches. The priory is known to have shown particular devotion to the archangel. Another peculiarity, also visible in the plate, is the long room on first-floor level lying between the south transept and the cloister. That such a site should have been available was probably a consequence of a maladjustment of cloister and transept in rebuilding; the room itself was almost certainly used as a library. The chapter-house, somewhat abnormally, adjoins the south transept—another result of rebuilding which made a separate library and sacristy necessary—and above it lay the dorter, which was continued along the

---

NOTE. The plate of the Grandmontine, Alberbury, which should come after the Cluniac houses, became available only when the rest of the book had been set up in type. Its position opposite was therefore dictated by exigencies of printing.

vanished eastern range. No trace of the rere-dorter remains, nor has the line of the great drain been recovered. The dorter ended at, and its line was continued by, the now detached building with steeply pitched roof; this has been identified as the prior's hall and guest-chamber.

The frater lay in the usual position alongside the south walk but, as the photograph shows, its line for some reason was not exactly parallel to the church, but inclined slightly to the south-east. In the south-west corner of the garth can be seen the remains of the circular lavatory, originally surmounted by a stone canopy on pillars. The western range has entirely disappeared.

To the south and east of the cloister lay the infirmary and prior's lodging, which form to-day the most beautiful and interesting features of the priory. They occupy two sides of a large court of which the dorter bounded the west and a gallery, and perhaps the rere-dorter, the south. The northern range embodies the infirmary hall and private rooms; at the north-east angle (not visible in the photograph) on the ground floor is the infirmary chapel, with its altar still *in situ*. The eastern range, with its long rows of windows lighting a corridor and gallery, and its lofty, stone-tiled roof, is an extremely fine specimen of fifteenth-century domestic architecture which, both externally and internally, has retained its principal features. Part of it is three storeys in height, and it contained the infirmarian's apartment to the north and the prior's lodging to the south. These two ranges were converted into a dwelling-house at the Dissolution, and their warm, rich tints and opulent architecture, set off by the smooth lawns and formal parterres, give a unique character to Wenlock.

The approach to the priory was from the road to the west, and a medieval gateway tower can be seen near the lower margin of the photograph.

Dr Cranage described his excavations and survey, with a plan, in *Archaeologia*, 72 (1922), 105–32; Dr Rose Graham added a few architectural points, and reprinted the plan, in her historical article in *Journal of the British Archaeological Association*, 3rd series, IV (1939), 117–40.

27

THETFORD

CLUNIAC

THE CLUNIAC PRIORY OF THETFORD, on the southern boundary of Norfolk eleven miles north of Bury St Edmunds, was founded in 1103–4 by Roger Bigod, a veteran of the Conqueror's host. Its original community came from Lewes, but it was soon recognized as directly dependent upon Cluny. The first foundation was in the town, but the priory was soon transferred to its present position where work was indeed begun as early as 1107, though the church was not occupied till 1114. The site has recently been excavated in a truly exemplary fashion by the Ministry of Works; as the photograph shows, a beautiful setting is given by the trees that surround the ruins.

The church, which was never rebuilt on the grand scale, can be clearly distinguished in the view, which is taken from an angle slightly north of west. Like all large Romanesque churches, it ended in three apses, but early in the thirteenth century the square-ended Lady Chapel was added on the north side of the presbytery to give worthy housing to an image reputed to be miraculous, and at the end of the same century the presbytery, slightly extended, was given a square eastern end, level with the Lady Chapel. In the centre of the presbytery can be seen the concrete slab covering the tomb of the second Howard duke of Norfolk (*ob.* 1524), and at the extreme east end is the reconstructed high altar.

The rest of the plan follows normal lines. Adjoining the end of the south transept is the sacristy, then the chapter-house and then, beyond passages, the subvault of the dorter with the rere-dorter at right angles at its end. East of the dorter was the infirmary cloister, and traces of the infirmary itself extend under the trees. The large frater ran parallel to the south walk of the cloister, with the kitchens at its west end in the range that completed the square and contained the cellarage. The only exit to the outside world from the cloister was the narrow passage at its north-west corner, where a row of trees now begins.

There is a plan in the *Guide* of the Ministry of Works, by F. J. E. Raby and P. K. Baillie Reynolds.

28

CASTLE ACRE

CLUNIAC

THE CLUNIAC PRIORY OF CASTLE ACRE lies in the valley of the Nar, some four miles north of Swaffham in Norfolk. It was founded *c.* 1090 by William second earl of Warenne. The earl's father had introduced Cluniac monks to England at Lewes, and the first community of Castle Acre was drawn thence. The original scheme was that the monks should be part of the population of the new castle. This was a common practice of great barons in the early days after the Conquest, especially on the Welsh border, but at Acre, as elsewhere, it soon proved unworkable and a site was given to the monks nearby to the west, where building was begun at once. The ruins, seen from the south-south-west, have been under the guardianship of the Office (and Ministry) of Works since 1929, and have been excellently excavated and displayed.

The original Norman church was never rebuilt, and the west front (not visible in the plate) even in its ruined state is one of the most graceful monuments of its period. The quire was extended with a square-ended presbytery early in the fourteenth century; the line of the Norman apse has been indicated in the turf and may with difficulty be distinguished in the plate, level with the second buttress from the east end. A Lady Chapel was added to the north of the presbytery in the fifteenth century, and a sacristy opening into the north transept.

The buildings follow the normal monastic scheme. Next to the transept lay the chapter-house, the apsidal end of which can be seen outlined in the turf; then came the undercroft of the dorter, still standing to first-floor level; then, crossing the south end of the dorter, the rere-dorter over a stream and drain. To the east of the dorter are the two halls of the infirmary connected by galleries with the church, with the cloister, with each other and with a garderobe over the stream. The small building alongside the passage near the presbytery of the church was the vestry. The frater lay parallel to the south walk of the cloister, with the warming-house between it and the dorter range. The original kitchen, with its four stone bases probably enclosing a hearth, lay immediately to the west of the frater; it was later superseded by a new kitchen lying to the south athwart the stream, and there were other buildings to the west. The ground floor of the western range was originally cellarage; above this were the guest-hall and prior's lodging (nearest to the church); additions were made to these in the medieval period and the whole was converted into a dwelling-house after the Dissolution. The high-pitched roof was a later construction, covering what had

been the prior's chapel and solar. In all this western complex a great deal of interesting remodelling, before and after the Dissolution, has taken place. The gatehouse (*c.* 1500) can be seen spanning the white drive due north of the prior's chapel beyond the belt of dark trees.

Plan and description in the *Guide* of the Ministry of Works, by F. J. E. Raby and P. K. Baillie Reynolds.

29

KELSO

TIRONIAN

THE ABBEY OF KELSO, at the centre of the small Roxburghshire town of that name, which lies on the north bank of the Tweed twenty-two miles upstream from Berwick, was founded by David, earl of Huntingdon, later King David I. The community came from Tiron, in the diocese of Chartres, an abbey of reformed black monks similar in its life and aims to Savigny and Cîteaux, and was the only foundation of this order in Scotland. The monks were first established in 1113 at Selkirk, and removed to Kelso by the king in 1128. The house, which was of a considerable size, suffered greatly, like its neighbours in the border valleys, from English invasions; it was burnt in 1344 and sacked by Lord Dacre in 1528 and by the invading armies of Henry VIII.

Scarcely any traces remain above ground of the conventual buildings, and most of the church has disappeared. The surviving part seen in the view from the north-west is the west end and western transepts, which date from 1175–1200. The church was of a shape very unusual, if not unique, in Great Britain, the west end resembling exactly the east end in plan and design. This arrangement, deriving ultimately from Byzantine architecture, is fairly common in surviving churches of the Carolingian period in the Rhineland and South Germany, and it is thought that the church at Kelso must have been copied from a German original, or (perhaps with less likelihood) from an Anglo-Saxon church of this shape which has perished.

There is a plan of the church and a short description in the *Archaeological Journal*, XCIII (1936), 328–9.

30

WAVERLEY

CISTERCIAN

THE ABBEY OF WAVERLEY in Surrey, two miles south-east of Farnham on the road to Godalming, was the first Cistercian foundation in England, the community coming from L'Aumône, in Burgundy, in November, 1128. Situated as it was in the woods and heaths of Surrey, 'hidden in a corner' as the patriotic northerner, Ailred of Rievaulx, put it, the abbey never won great fame among contemporaries, and there is a certain irony in the posthumous celebrity which its name achieved as the result of its adoption by Scott and its subsequent transference to numberless localities, institutions and objects of every kind. As the photograph shows, the ruins are in the state that all ruins were a century ago—they are indeed sadly neglected with trees shedding rainwater and branches on the walls, ivy forcing its way into crevices, and cattle stumbling into the undercroft (1949). They were, however, scientifically excavated by Harold Brakspear in 1899–1903, but were immediately re-covered, and to-day the turf shows scarcely a sign of disturbance. As the photograph was taken when the spring growth of rough herbage was at its height nothing is seen of the lines of masonry, which lie well below the surface, the level of the valley having silted up several feet since the first stone was laid.

The original church was long and narrow; it was replaced by a large building of the normal Cistercian type, begun in 1203 but not finished till 1278. In the photograph, taken from the south, the considerable remains of the walls are almost entirely masked by trees; a portion of the south-west angle can be seen below the tree immediately to the south of the bridge, and the masonry of the north-east corner of the presbytery is visible immediately above the round, dark tree near the ditch; the trees between hide the transept, but the end of the wall of the chapter-house can be seen to the right of foliage. From this spot the dorter extended southward in the usual position to within a few feet of the River Wey which, hidden by trees in the photograph, flows silently and unobtrusively, like so many rivers of Surrey and Sussex, below the south gable of the dorter, which is just hidden by the branches of a small tree.

The building standing free is the end of the lay-brothers' dorter, the undercroft of which was used as their frater. The lay-brothers' wing extended beyond the west wall of the church, while its south end was flush with that of the frater. Of the infirmary range and abbot's lodging to the east, and the guest-house and extensive offices to the west of the cloister nothing remains above ground, though all have been uncovered

and planned. The long stretch of water seen in the photograph is artificial and modern, and lies between a Regency mansion and the ruins. The ditches traversing the meadow are likewise modern, though hidden conduits abound on the site. The Wey was used for drainage, but the abbey's water-supply came from a spring on the hillside to the north-east.

Description and plans by Harold Brakspear, *Waverley Abbey* (Surrey Archaeological Society), 1905.

31

MELROSE

CISTERCIAN

The Monastery of Mailros (Old Melrose) was founded *c.* 650 by St Aidan with monks from Iona, but had ceased to harbour a community for some centuries when King David I, *c.* 1133, gave the place to the Cistercian order. This new foundation was made in 1136, on a site within a bend of the Tweed, where traces of a Romanesque church have been found, but conditions proved unsuitable, and a move was soon made to a new site two and a half miles to the west, a short distance from the river. The abbey was founded from Rievaulx; the second abbot was King David's English stepson, St Waldef (abbot 1148–59), the friend of St Ailred. Melrose soon acquired and long maintained wealth and celebrity; it had large flocks, and gave many abbots and bishops to Scottish churches, and later many ministers to the royal service. Pillaged by Edward II in 1322 and by Richard II in 1385, it regained its earlier external splendour for a time, but the brutal treatment meted out to it by the earl of Hertford in 1524 was fatal; the abbey never recovered, and soon fell into the hands of Commendators. The community ceased to exist shortly after 1570.

Melrose, though lying in a district second to none for natural beauty, cannot rival some of its sister abbeys in its immediate surroundings, though when seen from the south or, as Scott advises in oft-quoted lines, by moonlight, it presents an unforgettable spectacle. Architecturally, however, it has no rival in Scotland. The site has been in national custody since 1919, and has been carefully excavated as more and more land became available. Since the photograph was taken (1945) the Ministry of Works has acquired and demolished the large Abbey Hotel to the west of the kirk.

The original church, seen in the plate from the north-north-east, was of the normal Cistercian type, with aisled nave, transepts with three eastern chapels, and a short presbytery, and the first frater lay parallel to the north walk of the cloister. The church was rebuilt almost entirely, largely on the old foundations, after its destruction by fire at the hands of the English in 1385. The style adopted was very similar to that of the almost contemporary reconstructions at York and Beverley, and the master-mason may well have been a Yorkshireman. In particular, the tracery of the windows and the lines of the arcading have a lightness and a richness rarely found north of the Border.

The cloister lay to the north of the church, possibly for reasons of drainage. In the eastern range, after a small sacristy, came the large, rectangular chapter-house of the thirteenth century, to the east of which the dorter subvault extends beyond the north walk of the cloister across the present walled lane. The end of the dorter can be seen between two trees, spanning the great drain which passes beneath it on its way to the rere-dorter; the foundations of this are visible south of the lane at right angles to the eastern range. In the northern range the rebuilt frater stood at right angles to the walk of the cloister; just opposite its entrance the base and surrounding walls of

the lavatory are outlined in the turf of the garth. The unusually long western range housed the lay-brothers. Their frater, originally in the undercroft alongside the cloister, was later transferred to the northern part of the subvault. Their rere-dorter lay at right angles to the range, between its end and the present roadway; near it, and partly under the roadway, is the probable site of their infirmary. That of the monks lay east of the chapter-house on the site of a modern dwelling.

Water for the mill and for domestic purposes was obtained by damming the Tweed to supply a mill-lade, whence the water for the great drain was drawn. The dark channel of the lade can be seen in the left-hand bottom corner of the plate. The house between the lade and the drain is a fifteenth-century building adapted as a residence by the last of the Commendators, and is now used as a museum. The foundations further to the east are those of the abbot's hall.

Description and plan in the official *Guide* of the Ministry of Works, by J. S. Richardson. A detailed account will appear before long in the *Roxburghshire Inventory* of the Royal Commission on Historical Monuments.

32

DUNDRENNAN

CISTERCIAN

THE CISTERCIAN ABBEY OF DUNDRENNAN, five miles east-south-east of Kirkcudbright and one and a half miles inland from the Solway Firth, was founded by David I in 1143. It was one of the daughter abbeys of Rievaulx, and as such was often visited by St Ailred, whom Abbot Sylvanus of Dundrennan succeeded at the mother-house in 1167. At the other extreme of its history the house, in the person of its last commendatory abbot, gave shelter to Mary, Queen of Scots, for the last night that she spent on Scottish soil. The buildings, at first preserved after the change of ownership, gradually disappeared in the sixteenth and seventeenth centuries, but part of the abbey kirk was preserved as kirk of the parish till 1742.

The abbey is situated in a small and secluded glen with a good stream nearby and a small harbour on the Firth at Abbey Burnfoot. The church was of moderate size with aisled nave, transepts with three eastern chapels, and a short aisleless presbytery. It was never rebuilt, but a short western porch, still standing, was added.

The domestic buildings were normal in plan. The cloister lay south of the church; next to the transept was a narrow sacristy and book store, then the large rectangular chapter-house, rebuilt in the late thirteenth century; the arched door of this and the flanking windows can be seen in the plate. The long dorter on its subvault ran south to where the barn now stands; the rere-dorter, its site obscured by trees, stood at right angles half-way down the range. The frater lay perpendicularly in the centre of the southern range; its foundations, and those of the southern part of the western range lie under the garden of the adjacent manse. The western or lay-brothers' range, of which fragments remain, was refashioned as a series of cellars on the ground floor when the lay-brothers became extinct. The infirmary and abbot's lodging lay to the east of the cloister; the foundations visible above the trees in the photograph may be connected with them.

Description and plan in the *Guide* of the Ministry of Works, by J. S. Richardson.

33

SWEETHEART

CISTERCIAN

THE CISTERCIAN ABBEY OF SWEETHEART lies six miles due south of Dumfries, some two miles west of the estuary of the Nith, near the Glensone Burn or Abbey Pow. It was founded in 1273 from Dundrennan, a daughter-house of Rievaulx, and was the latest of the Scottish group of Cistercian abbeys. The foundress was Devorguilla, widow of John Balliol, who a few years later (1282) endowed her husband's foundation at Oxford. It takes its name, Dulce Cor, from the embalmed heart of Balliol which his widow kept with her until her death, when it was buried with her in the presbytery of the abbey kirk.

The church, of which the walls remain standing to roof level, is in the early Gothic style and dates from the years immediately following the foundation. The nave was aisled; the transepts had each two eastern chapels; the presbytery was aisleless. The crossing was surmounted by a battlemented tower rising some feet above the apex of the roof. The tower itself was crowned by a gable.

The conventual buildings to the south of the church followed the normal Cistercian plan. Along the eastern walk of the cloister are visible sacristy, chapter-house, treasury, parlour and warming-house and the range, with the dorter on first floor, continued for an equal distance beyond its junction with the southern range. The frater, which stood at right angles to the southern walk, was for long used as the parish kirk, but has now disappeared. The western or lay-brothers' range, which was equal or even greater in length than the eastern range, has vanished save for the doorway giving access to the cloister from the outside world; the dark shadow thrown by this doorway in the cloister garth can be seen in the plate.

The precinct was bounded to the south by a moat, and on the other three sides by a wall, some 12 ft. high, composed of massive boulders of granite from the neighbouring Criffell, no doubt collected when the land was cleared; it can be seen in the plate near the top; the walls enclosing the graveyard are not medieval. Beyond the wall, in the top left-hand corner, dark trees line the bank of the Abbey Pow.

Description with plan in the *Guide* of the Ministry of Works, by J. S. Richardson.

34

PLUSCARDINE

CISTERCIAN

THE PRIORY OF PLUSCARDINE lies six miles south-west of Elgin in Moray. It was founded in 1230 by King Alexander II and colonized directly from the Val de Choux, the mother-house of a small congregation resembling the Carthusians, situated in the forest not far from Chatillon-sur-Seine. Val de Choux later adopted the Cistercian constitutions, as did Pluscardine also. In 1454, when only six monks remained, it became a dependency of the Benedictine abbey of Dunfermline. The last monastic prior died in 1560, but some monks still lingered on under Commendators in a district tenacious of the ancient faith; the last monk died shortly after 1585; the last Commendator in 1622.

The ruins, which in the eighteenth century were more considerable than at present, stand in the beautiful valley of the Black Burn, sheltered by pine woods on the north and surrounded by fruit trees said to have sprung from those that stocked the monastic orchard. The eastern limb of the church, seen in the plate from the north-west, stands to roof level. In design it somewhat resembles Hexham; it has a large presbytery, to the north of which lies the later so-called 'Dunbar vestry' named after the prior who built it. The transepts have eastern chapels. The south wall of the nave remains but it is not certain whether it was ever completed. Adjoining the south transept and parallel to the presbytery is the large Lady Chapel; its eastern portion, which projects from the range, is in ruins, but the western half runs under the dorter which, with the rest of the range, is complete and roofed. The chapter-house adjoins immediately the Lady Chapel, then comes a parlour-passage and then the undercroft of the south part of the dorter, used, at least in the latter states of the priory's existence, as a warming-house, and in modern times fitted up as a church. South-east of the range the ruins of the prior's house can be seen. The frater, which stood on a sub-vault, demanded by the sharp fall of the ground, was on the level of the cloister. Nothing of the western range remains above ground. The precinct wall, with its two fine entrances, can be traced, but is not visible in the plate. The mill stood not far from the prior's house, and the meadow just visible in the plate to the south of the site was in medieval times under water as a small lake. In 1943 the priory was presented by the marquess of Bute to the Benedictine monks of Prinknash.

Description, with plates and rough plan, in *The Religious House of Pluscardyn*, by the Rev. S. R. Macphail (Edinburgh, 1881); cf. also *Old Moray*, by R. G. Cant (Elgin Society, 1948), pp. 18–19.

35

BALMERINO

CISTERCIAN

THE CISTERCIAN ABBEY OF BALMERINO stands on the southern (Fife) shore of the Firth of Tay, overlooking the Firth, two and a half miles west of the Tay Bridge. It was founded from Melrose in 1229.

The church, which was excavated in 1896, and is now flanked by a grove of trees, is seen from the north-west; it had originally an aisleless nave, transepts with eastern chapels, and a short presbytery. A southern aisle was soon added to the nave, but the cloister prevented a corresponding addition to the north. The cloister, as at Melrose, lay to the north of the church and much of the ground floor of the eastern range remains, including the vestibule to the chapter-house and the chapter-house itself, a large and magnificent building dating from the early sixteenth century and possibly never completed with vaulting. On the first floor of the range were the dorter and rere-dorter, and the whole block was converted into a mansion in the late sixteenth century. There are no remains of the frater or the western range, but a medieval barn is embodied in the modern farm buildings; it is the one lying nearly east and west, and higher than its fellows, of which the roof-ridge adjoins its eastern neighbour at right angles.

Description and plan in the *Fife, Kinross and Clackmannan Inventory* of the Royal Commission on Historical Monuments (1933), pp. 33–7. The probable source, 8 miles S.E. of the abbey, of the stone of which the fabric is built, and the route by which it was conveyed to the site, have been discussed in a recent paper in *Proceedings of the Society of Antiquaries of Scotland*, LXXXIII (1951), p. 62.

36

NEWMINSTER

CISTERCIAN

THE CISTERCIAN ABBEY OF NEWMINSTER, near the Wansbeck, two-thirds of a mile west of Morpeth in Northumberland, was one of the three daughters whom Fountains, herself an abbey of only seven years' standing, sent forth 'at a single birth' in 1139. The house had as its abbot a monk of Whitby who had joined the exodus from St Mary's, York, and who became celebrated as St Robert of Newminster. The abbey in its turn became a mother of three daughters, Pipewell, Roche and Salley, two of which figure in this volume.

The site which, as the photograph shows, is open and admirably suited for exploration, was excavated as a private enterprise a number of years ago, but most unaccountably no description or plan of the results found its way into print, while the excavator may have confused visitors by erecting fragments of masonry somewhat capriciously on old foundations.

So far as can be seen, a large church and small cloister are distinguishable, with the frater parallel to the south walk. Further interpretation would be hazardous, and the plate is given in the hope that it may attract Northumbrian antiquaries to reopen the investigation of these strangely neglected ruins of one of their most notable monastic houses.

37

CALDER

CISTERCIAN

THE CISTERCIAN ABBEY OF CALDER lies between the fells and the sea, some four miles south-east of Egremont, three miles from the Cumberland coast. It was originally founded from Furness, a Savignac house, in 1135; the monks suffered from want and from the Scots and, being refused admittance at Furness, crossed the great moors to found Byland. Furness sent a second band *c.* 1140, and thenceforward the abbey had an unbroken existence.

The view is taken directly from the west of the church, the west end of which, with its attractive western doorway, is hidden by foliage. The eastern end apparently remained as built, with short presbytery and transepts with eastern chapels, but the nave was rebuilt with aisles, and was of considerable width. The chapter-house, also the result of rebuilding on a large scale, adjoined the south transept; the eastern bay still retains its vaulting, as can be seen in the photograph; it is approached by a vestibule, entered from the cloister by the two middle arches; the easternmost arch gives access to a book room, that to the south leads to the undercroft of the dorter. The frater lies north and south at right angles to the southern walk. Part of it is preserved in the modern house, and its roof can be seen with a skylight to the north and a modern curved addition to the south. Nothing now remains of the western range. The stream of water that once flushed the offices still flows under the modern house and grounds, and no doubt portions of the lower walls of the conventual buildings could be discovered in the basement. The site of the infirmary and abbot's house has not yet been identified; the photograph shows foundations in the meadow to the east of the site.

Unsatisfactory description and plan in *Transactions of the Cumberland and Westmorland Archaeological Society*, VIII (1886), 467–504.

38

FURNESS

CISTERCIAN

THE RUINS OF THE ABBEY OF ST MARY in Furness lie in a narrow valley near the extremity of the Furness peninsula, less than a mile from the outskirts of Barrow. The valley is traversed by the railway, with a station adjacent to the great gateway, and some of the minor physical features have in consequence been disturbed, but time and the growth of trees have done much to smooth and mask the scars, and, as the photograph shows, the essential character of the site remains. The warm reddish tones of the local sandstone give a strong individuality to the ruins, which are remarkable also for the beauty of much of their architecture, for their extent, and for a number of idiosyncrasies of plan.

The house was originally a daughter of Savigny, and was founded at Tulketh near Preston in 1123; it was moved to Furness by Count (later King) Stephen in 1126. Transferred, though not without protest, along with her Savignac sisters to Cistercian allegiance in 1147, Furness claimed premier rank in the group and was herself the mother of a numerous family in England, Man and Ireland. The abbey had great estates, with prosperous sheepwalks and corn-granges, and remained wealthy to the end. The house was surrendered in 1537, in the aftermath of the Pilgrimage of Grace.

The first permanent buildings were erected before the merger and resembled in plan the Savignac or traditional Benedictine type. The church was planned with an aisled nave (not completed), short presbytery and transepts each with two apsidal eastern chapels. Shortly after becoming Cistercian the church was rebuilt with longer transepts having chapels in their eastern aisles. At the same time the frater, which had previously lain in the traditional monastic position parallel to the south walk of the cloister, was rebuilt in the Cistercian mode at right angles, but as the other building schemes were cramped by the narrow limits of the original cloister, the area was enlarged by the total destruction of the first frater, thus leaving the garth oblong in shape. The church did not attain its present shape till the early fifteenth century, when the presbytery was enlarged. Last of all, probably from about 1500 onwards, the construction of a large tower was begun at the west end, but possibly never completed (cf. Bolton, p. 199, and Fountains, p. 94). Meanwhile, the main conventual buildings had been remodelled with the church early in the thirteenth century. The eastern range was rebuilt on a somewhat unusual plan. Instead of the normal sacristy-cum-library alongside the transept, a sacristy was provided along

the south wall of the presbytery, and a magnificent chapter-house, 60 by 40 ft., adjoined the transept. This was approached through a short vestibule, which was one of three apartments entered through the broad archways from the cloister that are visible in the plate; those on either side of the vestibule were used as book-stores. The two smaller archways to the south led to the parlour and passage normally found in this position.

At first-floor level over the whole range ran the dorter. This was of great length—in fact, the longest in England—and the rere-dorter was situated somewhat abnormally parallel but not contiguous to the range half-way down its length; the two buildings were connected by a covered bridge. The foundations of the rere-dorter can be seen to the right of the broken eastern wall of the dorter. The course of the stream, seen in the plates as a dark line, is modern; its medieval bed lay much nearer to the trees, with a branch to the rere-dorter; these two streams joined a third, which had served the western range, at a point just above the larger of the two detached trees south of the dorter range.

To the south and south-east of the dorter were large groups of buildings which can only be distinguished by a visitor on the spot or a reader with an elaborate plan. That to the east in the space between trees near the cliff was the original infirmary, later converted into the abbot's lodging. As rebuilt the structure needed support, and the large bases of three of the buttresses can be seen on its western side. This block was connected by galleries with the dorter range and with the new infirmary; the wall supporting the latter gallery is that pierced by an archway on the smaller photograph. The new infirmary, a great hall with a chapel, ran east and west from the south end of the dorter range to the south-east corner of the lay-brothers' range; its eastern wall stands almost to full height, and the walls of the chapel can be seen to the right of the large detached tree.

The frater underwent an unusual number of transformations. Originally parallel to the southern walk, as has been noted, it was rebuilt in the Cistercian position *c.* 1150, and enlarged in 1170 and again in 1220. Finally, in the late fifteenth century when numbers had dwindled, the large frater was pulled down altogether and rebuilt as a smaller hall of two storeys, the lower of which was probably used as a meat-eating room. Some of these changes can be noted in the plate. As the eye passes southwards from the middle of the garth the lines visible are: inner margin of the original cloister; north wall of original frater; inner margin of new cloister; and south wall of original frater, coinciding with the north wall of all subsequent rebuildings. Further still to the south is the line marking the south end of the latest (shortened) hall, and beyond this again the southern ends of the earlier rebuildings.

The western range, devoted as always to the lay-brothers, was not as long as the dorter range in continuous roof-line, but was considerably prolonged to the south-west by the lay-brother's rere-dorter and infirmary. The pillar bases of their frater can be clearly seen in the smaller plate.

The precinct was large and strongly walled, enclosing 70 acres. A section of the wall can be seen crossing the field beyond the wooded slope to the east. The great gateway of the abbey court is, as has been said, extant, forming part of the building, now a hotel, at the top left-hand corner of the larger plate. A little beyond it to the north the externs' chapel (*capella ad portas*) still stands.

Lengthy description and plan by W. H. St J. Hope in *Transactions of the Cumberland and Westmorland Archaeological Society*, XVI (1900), 221–302. There is a simplified plan in the *Guide* of the Ministry of Works, by S. J. Garton, but the description there is less satisfactory than is usual in the series.

39

RIEVAULX

CISTERCIAN

THE CISTERCIAN ABBEY OF RIEVAULX, in the North Riding of Yorkshire near Helmsley, takes its name from the River Rye, which flows through the valley near its site. It was not the first plantation of the white monks in England (see Waverley, p. 62), but, founded as it was directly from Clairvaux by St Bernard's own monks, under the patronage of both Henry I and Thurstan, the zealous archbishop of York, it became at once in general esteem the premier abbey of the order in England, and its reputation was enhanced still further by the prestige of its third abbot St Ailred (1147–66), the 'Bernard of the north'. Its numbers rose in consequence, and under Ailred, only some thirty years after its foundation in 1131, it housed a community of 140 monks and 600 lay-brothers. How these numbers were accommodated in buildings smaller than the present remains is a problem to which the early documents give no solution; it must be remembered that many of the lay-brothers spent their time on the granges, and were only at the abbey by relays or on great feasts; there is also contemporary evidence from Ailred's day that when all were present the church was packed with them 'like bees in the hive'. We can only suppose that, in early days at least, there was a great quantity of temporary wooden structure outside the permanent stone buildings.

The ruins of the abbey lie near the foot of a sloping hillside which forms a wide arc of turf rising, at a little distance from the site, steeply through woods of beech and other trees to a terraced crest, whence the eye looks across the narrow valley to another wooded slope on the western side. Seen on a spring morning, or an autumn afternoon—or indeed at any time or season—it is one of the most exquisite views in England, rivalled among monastic sites only by Fountains, which indeed it may be judged to surpass in the beauty of its architecture.

The sloping confined site set a number of problems of design and construction. These were triumphantly overcome, but at the expense of one almost universal convention—the church had of necessity to be orientated almost exactly south and north, with the consequent swing of ninety degrees round the compass of the whole complex of buildings. In what follows the practice of other writers has been adopted in retaining 'east', as if the layout were normal.

The church as completed, was very large, some 370 ft. in length. The nave, which is the earliest large Cistercian nave of its kind to leave any remains, dates from the earliest years (1135–40); it was plain Romanesque, and the whole of the first church was of the normal Cistercian type with transepts with eastern aisles and a short,

square-ended presbytery. In this church the monks' quire extended through the crossing and included the first bay of the nave. About 1230 the beautiful new quire and presbytery, with eastern ambulatory and chapels, were added. This part of the fabric, even in its ruined state, is one of the most superb examples of Early English Gothic.

Next to the south transept came the usual narrow vestry and book-room. Then came the great chapter-house of most unusual plan. Oblong, with an eastern apse, it had a vestibule to the west which was continued as an aisle round the whole room. The gravestones of early abbots are seen in the middle; there also, near the west wall and invisible in the photograph, is the elaborate shrine of St William, St Bernard's secretary, the first abbot. Next to the chapter-house comes the narrow parlour, with the day-stair to the dormitory which occupied the first floor of the range. Then, after a narrow passage, comes the long undercroft of the dorter, used originally as the warming-house and later as novices' quarters. The dorter originally extended more than 300 ft. from the transept over the falling ground to the true west, but the further part gave trouble, as can be seen from the bases of the flying buttresses in the grass on both sides and at the end (cf. Byland), and when numbers decreased the building was reduced in length and the dorter now ended at a new wall flush with the high wall running east, which flanked the great drain of the rere-dorter.

The buildings further to the east are unusually regular in plan. The space of which the dorter and the rere-dorter form two sides was the infirmary cloister, and the long building still standing on the east was the infirmary hall; the infirmary chapel has not yet been identified. When numbers decreased, this infirmary, only some forty years before the Dissolution, was converted into the abbot's hall and lodging. The reduced space now needed for the invalids may have been found in the long range completing the infirmary cloister to the north. This, known as the Long House, was a building ultimately fitted up within as a series of private apartments, possibly first used by the students and senior monks.

South of the cloister the great roofless frater is seen, occupying the normal position for the frater in the fully developed Cistercian abbey. It replaced an earlier one parallel to the cloister and gave room for a new warming-room to the east and kitchens to the west. The western range, devoted to the use of the lay-brothers, is, as Sir Charles Peers observes, 'singularly small and inadequate', and should be compared with the magnificent western ranges at Fountains and Furness. As has already been noted, there were 600 lay-brothers at Rievaulx in Ailred's day (*c.* 1160), and no doubt they were accommodated in wooden quarters intended to be temporary. The present range, built *c.* 1200, may have been part of a larger scheme obliterated by post-medieval buildings now covering the site, or it may be an indication that before the end of the twelfth century permanent devolution to granges and some reduction in the number of lay-brothers had already taken place.

The second plate, taken from a point above the Rye valley upstream from the ruins, shows well the characteristics of the site, when allowance has been made for the fall of the ground on both sides of the valley. In the distance, the more level uplands can be seen sloping down towards Helmsley, and beyond the woods are the grounds of Helmsley Castle, once the possession of the dukes of Buckingham, and later the seat of the Duncombe family. The cramped site of the great abbey, which made necessary the various architectural expedients that have been mentioned, was not due to any lack of foresight. For more than seven centuries the Rye has flowed in its present bed, close to the western slope and hidden in the plate by trees. Originally, however, its course lay down the centre of the valley a little west of the furthest extension of the frater.

This stream formed the boundary between the lands of Walter L'Espec, founder of Rievaulx, and Roger de Mowbray; hence the necessity for the abbey to lie on its left bank. The situation was soon rendered still more delicate when Mowbray allowed the wandering Savignac monks from Calder to settle on his lands near Rievaulx; the

two abbeys were a disturbance to each other, and ultimately the more recent arrivals migrated to Byland. Previously, however, they had shown a brotherly feeling by allowing the monks of Rievaulx to divert the Rye and to become owners of the land now on its left bank—the fields seen in the plate. Rievaulx still, however, made use of the old stream to turn the abbey mill and flush the great drain, and by a system of dams and canals they used the old channel to float down the building stone they required from the quarry of Penny Piece, a short distance upstream, and a wharf was constructed for the purpose not far from the western end of the site.

Plan and description in the *Guide* of the Ministry of Works (1938) by Sir C. R. Peers. See also the account (with map of the valley) by W. H. St J. Hope in *Victoria County History of Yorkshire: North Riding*, I (1914), 494–502.

40

BYLAND

CISTERCIAN

The Cistercian Abbey of Byland lies at the foot of the southern slope of the Hambleton hills in the North Riding of Yorkshire, some four miles in a direct line from Rievaulx Abbey, two miles west of the present Ampleforth Abbey and four and a half miles from the site of Old Byland. The abbey had an unusual origin. The first monks were a colony from the Savignac house of Furness who had been sent in 1134 to found Calder. Driven out by the marauding Scots, they took to the road and after lengthy wanderings and three previous temporary settlements finally came to rest, where the ruins now stand, almost a different body of men, and now owing allegiance to Cîteaux. The final settlement was not made till 1177, but the reputation of the community was already high, and in the last quarter of the twelfth century Byland, Fountains and Rievaulx ranked as the three luminaries of the North. Though the abbey cannot compare with her two sisters either in beauty of surroundings or in the distinction of such architecture as survives, the ruins of Byland, as excavated and reconditioned by the Office of Works, are of great interest owing to their compact completeness on an open site which presented few problems to the original planners and none to the excavators.

The church was built by slow stages, but without change of plan or remodelling, since it was not begun till the neighbouring Cistercian abbeys had evolved the type of great church best suited to their changing outlook. The fabric at Byland is of noble proportions, being 330 ft. in length, and had the presbytery been of the size of that at Rievaulx the two churches would have been roughly equal. In contrast, however, to Rievaulx and Fountains the arcading has disappeared, and the remains of the relatively plain exterior walls are low. This, and the open site, make it a far less impressive building than the churches of the two sister abbeys; the most distinctive feature is the west wall of the nave with its broken half-circle of window, here (p. 87) seen set off by its own dark shadow in the low sunlight of a summer evening.

The interior arrangements of the church can be clearly seen on p. 89. A somewhat unusual feature is the western aisle of the transepts, which are in consequence broader than in most Cistercian churches. The east end was terminated by five chapels; then came an ambulatory; then the presbytery enclosed by a stone screen. The site of the high altar is marked by a modern stone; the original *mensa* is in use for its true purpose in the neighbouring abbey of Ampleforth. West of this the line of the wide footpace can be seen level with the next pier. The monks' quire ran from the centre of the crossing and occupied the two eastern bays of the nave. It was closed

to the west by a screen which has disappeared, but the line of stone substructure beneath the northern row of stalls is clearly distinguishable. There is no sign in the photograph of another screen, which stood two bays further down the nave, nor yet of the site of the altar which stood on its western side and was used for the lay-brothers' Mass. One bay to the west of this is a line which probably marks the limit of the lay-brothers' quire. In the bays of the south aisle west of the monks' quire the arrangements for chapels containing altars can be clearly seen. The medieval paving of glazed tiles still exists in several places in the crossing and transepts; it appears as a white area in the second photograph.

Passing from the church to the cloister (which lay in its normal position to the south) we can see, after the usual narrow room divided by a partition into book-room and vestry, the large chapter-house, which was roofed by vaulting springing from corbels and columns; the base of one of the latter can be distinguished. Then came the parlour and the passage to the cemetery and eastern buildings. The long and narrow enclosure between two walls to the east of the range is the great drain; above it on the first floor was the rere-dorter, standing at right angles to the dorter half-way along it and not, as was more usual, at the end furthest from the church. The sub-vault of the dorter continued the eastern range to the south; this subvault had on its eastern side a line of open arches, of which the piers are visible. In early days these may have been boarded up; later, a partition was run up along the length of the subvault, and a series of small rooms running through the arches was provided, as can be seen in the photograph. The flat oblong of masonry in the grass to the east of the east wall of these rooms is the base of a flying buttress that strengthened the wall of the dorter, weakened by the arches below. A similar expedient was found necessary at Rievaulx and Kirkham. The enclosure to the east of the dorter is not (as might be supposed) the infirmary cloister. Its southern range was a post-Dissolution structure; that to the north-east is the abbot's lodging; this is comparatively small, but it must be remembered that the abbot's house in English Cistercian abbeys never attained the size and magnificence of the quarters provided for the abbot in the great black-monk houses. Through the undercroft of the abbot's lodging runs another wide drain, shown in the photograph (p. 89). To the north-east again from the abbot's house is the enclosure used as the monks' cemetery.

South of the eastern range was the infirmary, standing free in an unusual position. The long foundation walls are those of the hall; the square walls at the east end are those of the crypt of the infirmary chapel. West of the infirmary the small isolated building is the meat-kitchen, where flesh-meat, forbidden to be served in the frater, was prepared for the sick and for guests, and in later centuries for all the monks in turn. North of this, opening out of the cloister, is the square warming-house adjoining the long frater, the east wall of which still stands to a considerable height.

The frater stood five feet above the level of the cloister, resting on a subvault used as cellarage; the bases of the supporting columns can be seen. Next to it, to the west, came the kitchen, the partition in which is not medieval, and to the south, beyond the kitchen court, the rere-dorter of the lay-brothers. The shed in this court has no antiquarian significance. The long western range devoted to the lay-brothers is well preserved on ground level, with the 'lane' or lay-brothers' cloister parallel to the west walk of the great cloister. Flying buttresses were found necessary all along its length.

Description and plan by Sir C. R. Peers in the *Guide* of the Ministry of Works; see also the account in *Victoria County History of Yorkshire: North Riding*, II (1923), 10–19.

41

JERVAULX

CISTERCIAN

THE CISTERCIAN ABBEY OF JERVAULX lies, as its name indicates, in the valley of the Ure in Wensleydale, four and a half miles north-west of Masham on the Leyburn road, in the North Riding of Yorkshire. Unlike many Cistercian abbeys, it does not lie in a narrow valley and is at some distance from the river. The house was originally founded at Fors, higher up the valley, by Savignac monks, and adopted as a daughter by Byland. This was in 1150; six years later, made desperate by the poverty of the land at Fors, the monks moved to Jervaulx. Here, as at New Byland, and for like reasons, the main buildings of a great abbey were put up on a virgin site without the necessity for rebuilding, during the last decades of the twelfth century. Jervaulx ranked among the greater Yorkshire abbeys, and escaped suppression in 1536, but in the following year its abbot was implicated in the Pilgrimage of Grace and subsequent disturbances, and was beheaded at Tyburn; his abbey in consequence escheated to the Crown and was immediately dismantled. Sir Arthur Darcy wrote to Cromwell on arriving to view the place that it was 'wholly covered with lead and there is one of the fairest churches I have seen, fair meadows, and the river running by it, and a great demesne'. The buildings were never used as the nucleus of a mansion, and were excavated by W. H. St J. Hope and H. Brakspear in 1905.

The church, 264 ft. long, seen in the plate from the west, was of the normal Cistercian type, with a short, aisled, square-ended presbytery, transepts with eastern chapels and aisled nave. The high altar, the site of which lay within and towards the east end of the white oblong in the photograph, was 25 ft. west of the eastern wall, along which were five altars. On the east walk of the cloister, after a narrow vestry, came the chapter-house; this was a large room, with vaulting springing from the walls and from two rows of columns, some of which are visible in the photograph. Then, after the parlour, comes the subvault of the dorter, used originally as the novitiate and later, as elsewhere when numbers fell, reconditioned as a series of private rooms. Over it, as also over the chapter-house, extended the great dorter, the western wall of which stands to roof level. At right angles to the dorter, running eastwards, the walls can be seen which enclosed a wide corridor on the ground floor and the rere-dorter at first-floor level. At the east end of this, walls running south at right angles are visible; this was the abbot's lodging, and beyond this again to the east lay the infirmary. This was of unusual design, and the plan and details can be seen clearly by visitors; in the photograph they are indistinguishable.

Along the south walk of the cloister, the lines of the foundations of the frater can

91

be seen running southward, in the position typical of the second stage of Cistercian building, which here was the original one. Between it and the dorter, opening out of the cloister, was the warming-room; the raking weathering of its roof is visible in the wall of the dorter. To the west of the frater lay the monks' kitchen. The walls joining the south end of the frater to the south end of the dorter are those of the misericord, or meat-eating refectory. This was a fifteenth-century addition to the buildings, served by a meat-kitchen between it and the abbot's lodging.

The long western range, extending from the church to a line flush with the ends of frater and dorter, was taken up on the ground floor as to its northern half by cellarage, and as to its southern half by the lay-brothers' frater. On the first floor, along the whole length, was their dorter. This range is the earliest in date of any of the buildings, and, as in some other abbeys, was probably put up to house the lay-brothers engaged in constructing the abbey, while the choir monks still remained at Fors. This may well be the reason why the north wall of the dorter is entirely detached from the church; in the narrow space between ran the stairs from the dorter to the lay-brothers' quire in the nave. The foundations of the lay-brothers' rere-dorter can be seen running west of the subvault of the dorter and at right angles to it immediately north of the light-foliaged tree; it will be noted that the line of this rere-dorter, if prolonged eastwards, passes through the monks' rere-dorter and along the south wall of the infirmary: this was in fact the line of the great drain. North of the lay-brothers' rere-dorter, near the bush in the photograph, a visitor to the site can see the lines of foundations of the guest-house; south of this, in the shadow of the light and dark trees, stood the lay-brothers' infirmary. The markings in the meadow to the south of the site are perhaps those of the convent garden.

There is a full account of the excavations, with a large plan, by W. H. St J. Hope and H. Brakspear in the *Yorkshire Archaeological Journal*, XXI (1911), 303–44.

42

FOUNTAINS

CISTERCIAN

THE CISTERCIAN ABBEY OF ST MARY by the springs (*ad fontes*), probably the best known of all monastic ruins, had no ordinary origin. Unlike all other Cistercian houses, which were founded by a colony from an existing Cistercian abbey, it originated (like the original Cîteaux) in a group of Benedictine monks who, reacting against the laxity of their own abbey, St Mary's at York, withdrew in the last days of 1132, under the patronage of the reforming Archbishop Thurstan, to what was then a remote and wild spot under a great elm by some hillside springs in Skeldale, whence they appealed for support and counsel to St Bernard at Clairvaux. The saint replied with encouragement, and despatched a monk of his own to guide them; they adopted the Cistercian customs and ranked as a daughter of Clairvaux. The abbey soon became populous and wealthy, with great flocks and wide lands.

Fountains is some three miles south-west of Ripon, in the West Riding. The ruins lie on the level floor of a narrow and shallow valley, the steep slopes of which are now covered with timber; the swiftly flowing moorland stream of the Skell washes the southern edge and traverses the site. Extensive and well preserved, the buildings, especially when the vista opens upon them from the east, give the beholder a sudden shock of beauty that has something almost magical in its illusion of life; in the mists of a summer's morning the abbey seems to sleep rather than to be dead.

The first permanent buildings were begun *c.* 1135 on normal Cistercian lines under the guidance of St Bernard's architect, Geoffrey of Clairvaux. The church was planned on a large scale with an aisleless presbytery, transepts with eastern chapels and a long aisled nave of eleven bays. This long, narrow building received its principal modifications, as so often, in its eastern limb. They were accomplished by three abbots of the name of John, who ruled in succession from 1203 to 1247. The first two remodelled the presbytery; this now had a length of five bays with aisles. The third was chiefly responsible for the most notable feature of the church, the eastern transept or 'nine altars', built, as its name suggests, primarily to accommodate in more spacious surroundings at least a small number of the many private Masses. While an eastern transept is not uncommon in great English churches (e.g. Canterbury, Lincoln, Beverley), such a transept actually forming the eastern end of the church finds a parallel only at Durham, built at almost the same time. The interdependence is clear, but authorities differ as to which was the original. The rectangular platform at the east end of the presbytery is probably not the medieval footpace of the high altar, but the work of an eighteenth-century owner who did much to clean up the ruins. The large marble gravestone at the east end of the quire is probably that of Abbot Swinton (1471–9).

The monks' quire included the easternmost bay of the nave, where fragments of a stone screen can be seen. Then, after a retro-quire with altars occupying another three bays came another screen, to the east of which stood the rood altar with the lay-brothers' quire beyond. The aisles of the nave which, as often in Cistercian churches, were walled off from the nave, contained numerous chapels and altars. The tower to the north of the north transept was the work of Abbot Huby (1494–1526). It is an unusual feature in a Cistercian church, specifically forbidden by the original statutes. Beautiful in itself, it does much to transmit the peculiar quality of 'surprise' to the well-known view from the east, but it has a curious effect from the north, where its uppermost stage is seen emerging from the narrow valley as if from underground.

The cloister, 125 ft. square, was originally built before 1147, when it and the domestic buildings were burnt out in a raid by the partisans of the deposed Archbishop William of York, who took this revenge upon the reforming Abbot Henry Murdac, William's successor in the see. The conventual buildings followed the normal plan. To the east, after a narrow sacristy-library adjoining the south transept, came the noble vaulted chapter-house, where numerous grave-slabs of abbots can be seen, among them that of Abbot John III who built the room. Then, after a parlour and passage, comes the subvault of the dorter; the dorter itself extended over the whole range. At right angles to this at the end, and running eastwards, was the rere-dorter, under which flowed the Skell. The range returning northward at right angles to the rere-dorter was the abbot's lodging. Beyond this again eastward lay a great complex of buildings, the plan and construction of which were rendered still bolder and more ingenious by the presence of the swift and often flooded river and the steep southern bank of the valley. Abbot John of Kent dealt with both these obstacles. The hillside was excavated and the site levelled and the river was taken underneath the buildings in four parallel stone tunnels which drained off refuse of all kinds.

Immediately over the river lay the infirmary; the area of the large pillared infirmary hall is clearly visible, running almost north and south; the long narrow passage giving access to the cloister can also be seen; this carried the abbot's gallery and private way to the church at first-floor level. The buildings still further to the east are (from north to south) the infirmarian's lodging, the infirmary chapel and the infirmary kitchen. The room abutting on the infirmary to the west, immediately over the mouth of the tunnel, is the misericord, or meat-refectory, whence a passage led to the abbot's lodging.

In the southern range of the cloister, the roofed warming-house with its chimney lies between the dorter subvault and the frater. The latter is a fine room 110 ft. in length; adjoining it to the north-west was the kitchen. The splendid western range,

which is such a notable feature in views of the abbey from this side, was devoted principally to the lay-brothers. The subvault contained cellarage in its northern part and the lay-brothers' frater to the south. It was erected in the late twelfth century and the vaulting, which rests on plain ribs that join without capitals to form the supporting columns, is in perfect condition and is extremely beautiful. On the first floor was the lay-brothers' dorter; the staircase leading to their quire in the nave can be seen. The small building abutting on the range to the west half-way along its length is the cellarer's office or checker; the larger building at the end was the lay-brothers' rere-dorter, with their infirmary west of it straddling the river. The small complex of buildings to the north-west of this infirmary contained the guest quarters. Not the least interesting feature of the whole plan is, as has been said, the mingled boldness and ingenuity with which the swiftly flowing and incalculable waters of the Skell are utilized, controlled and obliterated in their long traverse of the site.

The precinct was large, embracing the whole valley and its slopes as seen in the second plate, together with the pastures in the foreground. The massive stone ring-wall is still extant for much of its ancient course; it is visible running eastwards to the wood on the extreme right of the photograph. The only gateway lay up the valley to the west, just off the plate. A mill race led to the abbey mill, embodied in the long gabled building in the foreground; the bakehouse and brewhouse lay across the river from the guest-house, in the open space seen in the photograph. The great gate to the outer court of the abbey lay west of the western range, approximately at the base of the tapering shadow cast by a conifer. Still further to the west, and outside the plate, stands Fountains Hall, a mansion constructed in the early seventeenth century largely from material taken from the monastic buildings on the south-east of the site.

Public interest was recently directed to Fountains by the announcement that the site, once the property of the Catholic marquess of Ripon, was to be acquired by a syndicate of which the duke of Norfolk was chairman, and that it was proposed to to hand the ruins over to a Benedictine community who would rebuild them, or at least make the church usable for liturgical purposes. As was natural, the announcement gave rise to an animated debate, in which protests and proposals of every kind were made. In the event the matter went no further, and the present proprietor of Fountains will retain ownership.

There are numerous accounts of Fountains. The best is a long article with elaborate plans by W. H. St J. Hope in the *Yorkshire Archaeological Journal*, XV (1900), 269–402.

43

ROCHE

CISTERCIAN

THE CISTERCIAN ABBEY OF ROCHE (de Rupe), so called from the outcrop of rock in the valley nearby, lies in south-east Yorkshire between Rotherham and Bawtry. It was founded in 1147 from Newminster in Northumberland, a daughter-house of Fountains, and the site and lay-out of the buildings of Roche are not unlike those of her Yorkshire grandparent. As the photograph shows, the abbey is beautifully situated in a valley at the foot of a low cliff masked by trees, and the buildings straddle a considerable brook from which, as at Fountains, conduits were led under the offices to carry away the sewage and kitchen refuse. The site has been excavated by the Ministry of Works and the lines of the buildings stand out in perfect clarity, relieved by the dark shadows thrown by the masonry and trees as the sun verges towards noon on a summer's morning.

The plan is that normal to English Cistercian abbeys in the period of the order's greatest prosperity in the second half of the twelfth century. The church, of which the east end alone stands to any height, has the typical plan with long nave, transepts with chapels in the eastern aisle, and short square-ended presbytery. The architectural nave was divided internally at the fifth pier from the west by a stone wall or *pulpitum*, east of which were the stalls of the monks. West of this was the retro-quire, closed by another screen; west of this again was the altar where Mass was said for the lay-brothers who worshipped in this part of the church.

Adjoining the south transept were the sacristy and book-room, originally separated by a partition; then came the chapter-house with columns to support the vaulting. Next, after a passage-room, came the long subvault of the dorter, possibly used as novices' quarters; the rere-dorter extends eastwards at right angles athwart the stream. At right angles to the east end of the rere-dorter is part of the infirmary, possibly the infirmary chapel, and returning from it and running askew from south-east to north-west towards the cloister is the abbot's lodging. Adjoining it, the square room with one corner of masonry standing was the kitchen of the abbot and infirmary, and this and the abbot's lodging were served by a tributary stream, the conduit of which appears out of the trees as a dark oblong. At the bottom right-hand corner of the plate the large hall, in which four column-bases remain, was probably the lay-brothers' infirmary, and may have been used as a guest-house when the intake of lay-brothers ceased.

On the south side of the cloister the long frater is seen; it extends over the stream, into which a section of the floor has collapsed. The greater thickness of the wall exactly over the stream on the west side carried the stairway to the *pulpitum* or reading desk. The frater was flanked as usual by the warming-room to the east and

the kitchen to the west. The latter is comparatively small, but its annexes run back to the stream or drain. The west range was, as usual, devoted to the lay-brothers' quarters. Their frater was on the ground floor between the stream and the tree-top in the photograph; their dorter ran the whole length of the range on the first floor. Roche, unlike Fountains, Rievaulx and some other houses, appears to have kept something of a balance in early days of plenty between choir monks and lay-brothers, and their range in consequence did not extend notably south of the cloister. The fine gatehouse is substantially complete; standing north-west of the church a little beyond the margin of the plate.

Roche, as we know from the reminiscences of an Elizabethan writer who had heard the story from witnesses, was looted and demolished by the neighbours immediately after the Dissolution—a fact which makes the far more complete disappearance of other great abbeys all the more remarkable. The existing balance of turf and foliage in the precinct was achieved by Capability Brown.

Description and plan in the *Guide* of the Ministry of Works, by A. Hamilton Thompson.

44

SAWLEY

CISTERCIAN

THE CISTERCIAN ABBEY OF SALLAY (or Sawley, as it appears on modern maps) lies on the left bank of the Ribble some thirteen miles north-east of Blackburn and four miles from Clitheroe in Lancashire. The house was founded from Newminster, itself a recent foundation from Fountains, in 1147. Though never wealthy or unusually large, Sallay had a somewhat distinguished history. Stephen of Eston, abbot 1224–33, was a spiritual writer of note with a reputation for sanctity, and in the next century William of Rymyngton, later prior, was chancellor of Oxford in 1372–3; while about the same time an unknown monk of the house translated into English verse a popular work of Robert Grosseteste. Sallay was suppressed in 1536, but the monks were restored in the same year by the leaders of the Pilgrimage of Grace—for which the abbot, Thomas Bolton, was executed.

The church, which is seen from the north, was in its final state of an unusual shape. Originally designed on the primitive Cistercian model, it had an aisleless nave, transepts with eastern chapels, and short aisleless presbytery. The latter was greatly enlarged with aisles, but the nave was never enlarged to match—the position of the early cloister would indeed have made a south aisle impossible—and in the later Middle Ages, possibly after destruction at the hands of the Scots, when the lay-brothers had become extinct, the western part of the nave was left derelict and a wall thrown across it at the western end of the monks' quire.

Beyond the south transept in the eastern range lies the usual sacristy-book-room, then the small chapter-house, never rebuilt, and then, after a parlour and passages, the subvault of the dorter. The rere-dorter met the south end of the range at right angles; the great drain is clearly visible. The infirmary, and possibly also the abbot's house, may have lain to the east of the eastern range. The frater can be seen standing perpendicularly to the southern range, flanked by the warming-house (east) and kitchen (west). The western range, originally the quarters of the lay-brothers, may later have become partially the guest-house; the small house at right angles to the south end is on the site of the lay-brothers' rere-dorter or infirmary. The square building with a chimney near the south-west angle of the nave is probably post-Dissolution. The ruins of the gateway, astride the western half of the modern road, lie 250 ft. north of the church, and do not appear on the plate.

The site was excavated after a fashion by Lord de Grey in 1848; as can be seen it has become overgrown, and a careful fresh investigation is much to be desired.

Description and antiquated plan in *Yorkshire Archaeological Journal*, XX (1909), 454–60.

45

WHALLEY

CISTERCIAN

THE CISTERCIAN ABBEY OF WHALLEY lies by the River Calder, one and a half miles above its junction with the Ribble, some thirteen miles from Preston and six miles north of Blackburn. It was founded in 1296 by a community which had originally been settled in 1178 at Stanlaw, an inhospitable site on the south bank of the Mersey estuary, not far from the present entrance to the Ship Canal. In consequence, all the buildings date from the fourteenth century or later; the great period of building was between 1330, when the church was begun, and 1444, when the main plan was completed.

The view, taken from the north-north-west, shows the foundations of the church outlined in the turf. The plan is of a normal early fourteenth century type, with aisled nave and presbytery. The transepts have each three eastern chapels, but the north transept alone has a western aisle. The site of the high altar is indicated, as is also the base of the stone screen surrounding the presbytery and the stone grooves west of the crossing into which the woodwork of the quire stalls fitted.

Next to the south transept came the sacristy; then the vestibule of the chapter-house. This was octagonal (cf. Margam, Bolton and Thornton), a shape here explained by the late date of its construction. Then, after a parlour and a passage, the southern undercroft of the dorter, which extended over the whole eastern range. The building at right angles to the eastern range at its southern end is the passage to the rere-dorter, which here stood at some distance from the range.

In the southern range are the warming-house (standing to roof level) and kitchen, separated by the frater. Although the current plan shows this as parallel to the walk in the cloister, it is not clear that this has been established by excavations, and it is more probable that it ran perpendicularly to the south. The western range was built last and still stands. At the date of its completion (1415) there can have been few, if any, *conversi* to occupy it, and the upper storey may have been used from the beginning for hospitality.

To the east of the eastern range a large complex of buildings existed. The foundations visible in front of a tree are those of the abbot's house. Beyond this was a large infirmary block with chapel and hall. This last was incorporated into a long gallery built by Sir Ralph Assheton in 1664–5 and now itself in ruins. Assheton was responsible also for destroying the church, abbot's house and part of the eastern range, in order to give clearance for his lawns and garden. The Assheton mansion, now used as a Warden's House and Conference House, has a Tudor and Jacobean nucleus, lying between portions of a (pre-monastic) chapel belonging to the old

manor-house at the north-east corner (the ruins are just visible in the plate) and the monastic infirmary to the west.

Whalley saw a recrudescence of building in its last phase. In 1480 the great north-eastern gateway (partly visible at the left margin of the plate) was constructed, and the last abbot, John Paslew (1507–37) rebuilt the abbot's house and constructed a Lady Chapel. Paslew, who became a monk in 1487, was an old man in 1536, when he and his community were sworn to the Pilgrimage of Grace a few days before its collapse. For this he was tried and hanged at Lancaster, and the abbey fell by attainder.

The whole site came on the market in 1922, and was sold in two lots; the western range came into Catholic hands, and now contains a chapel; the larger portion was acquired by the Anglican diocesan authorities of Manchester, and on the erection of the diocese of Blackburn the Assheton mansion was adapted as a Diocesan House. It was the first warden of this House, Canon Lumb, who conducted excavations in 1930–4 and gave to the site its present orderly appearance.

Description and plan in *Whalley Abbey*, by Archdeacon Lambert (no date).

46

CROXDEN

CISTERCIAN

The Cistercian Abbey of Croxden lies in a fertile valley of north-east Staffordshire, between Cheadle and Uttoxeter, to the west of the River Dove. One of the later English foundations, the house was a settlement of a colony from Aunay-sur-Odon, which had arrived in 1176 at Cotton and moved two years later to a more propitious site. The church, built when the days of early severity were over, has a more elaborate plan than most English Cistercian abbeys (cf. Beaulieu, another late foundation), and a chronicle of the house allows of fairly exact dating for the buildings.

The site, here seen from the south-east, is unfortunately bisected by a modern road which passes over part of the nave, crossing and south transept. Nevertheless, the whole abbey was excavated in the first decade of the present century and, though subsequently covered up, can be plotted from the plans then made. The church, 240 ft. long, and built between 1180 and 1250, consisted of an aisled nave, transepts, each with two eastern chapels, and an apsidal presbytery surrounded by a chevet of five radial chapels; the whole was copied from Aunay. Of this the west end and the south wall of the south transept remain to some height, and part of the south wall of the nave. Of the chevet, only a fragment of the northernmost chapel remains, and can be seen north of the road to the left of a dark tree. In the eastern range, after the normal sacristy-bookroom, came a square chapter-house, of which the entrance arches and part of the northern wall-arcade can be distinguished. Then came parlour, passage and the undercroft of the long dorter with rere-dorter at right angles to its southern end; the southern wall of this can be seen in front of the south wing of the farm buildings. East of the farm-yard a large infirmary has been excavated, lying partly under the present trees and road, with its north end near two may trees in blossom by the road. South of the farm-yard, fragments of the abbot's 'new house' (1325–6) are visible.

The southern range contained warming-house, frater (perpendicular to the cloister) and kitchen. The position occupied by the fireplace in the south wall can be seen. This south wall of the warming-house is continued by a later one (*c.* 1500) which cuts across the original frater and may have provided a smaller dining-place when numbers fell (cf. Furness). The lay-brothers' range has disappeared and the site is covered by a farm dwelling, but the walls adjoining the church remain. A stream runs south of the abbey; to the north-west, at the bend of the road, lies the

millpond, whence water was conducted for drainage. Beyond the bend, on the east side of the road, is the *capella ad portas*, now used as a church; the gatehouse lay south of this where the road is hidden by trees. There was a large precinct of 70 acres, and traces of the medieval wall can be seen; it is that running east from the road beyond the church to a large elm.

Short description, with excellent plan, photographs and drawings in *St Mary's Abbey, Croxden*, by C. Lynam (1911). There is a short account also, with plan, in the *Guide* of the Ministry of Works, by F. K. Baillie Reynolds.

47

BUILDWAS

CISTERCIAN

The Abbey of Buildwas lies on the right (south) bank of the Severn, some eleven miles below Shrewsbury in the direction of Bridgnorth, where the river skirts the southern slopes of the Wrekin. The house was founded from Savigny in 1135, and was aggregated with its sisters to Cîteaux in 1147. The site is bounded to the north by private grounds, but the shell of the church stands clear and almost intact, and the regularity of its design and the simplicity of the arcading give beauty to the ruins.

The church is of the normal early Cistercian plan, with aisled nave, transepts with eastern chapels, and a short aisleless presbytery. It was probably begun before the merger of 1147 and completed by 1170. The foundations to the south of the south aisle are those of a chapel added *c.* 1400 under unknown circumstances.

Owing to the position of the river and the lie of the land the cloister was sited to the north of the church to obtain adequate drainage, but the arrangement of buildings was otherwise normal. In the eastern range lay sacristy, chapter-house and parlour, with dorter above. The rectangular, almost square chapter-house, of which the dark roof appears in the photograph, retains its vault rising from four pillars. The rere-dorter, the lower part of which can be seen, stood at right angles at the north-east corner of the range. Beyond this to the east lay the infirmary; two arches of the arcade of its hall can be seen spanning the entrance to the offices of the dwelling-house, which embodies parts of the infirmary and abbot's lodging. The northern range no doubt contained the warming-house, refectory (at right angles to the cloister) and kitchen, of which foundations remain. The western range contained, as usual, cellars and lay-brothers' quarters, but owing to a fall in the levels the ground floor is considerably lower than the west walk of the cloister, which itself is lower than the south walk and the church. The western range was probably of three storeys; cellars on the ground floor, storage and lay-brothers' frater on the first floor, and lay-brothers' dorter above. The rooms of this range had no direct access to the west walk of the cloister, but were separated from it by a long passage or 'lane' by which the lay-brothers passed from their dorter to the church.

Description and plan in the *Guide* of the Ministry of Works, by A. Hamilton Thompson.

48

BASINGWERK

CISTERCIAN

THE RUINS OF BASINGWERK ABBEY lie near the estuary of the Dee one and a quarter miles north-east of Holywell in Flintshire. The original beauty of the situation has been lessened in modern times, and the ruins are hemmed in by the branch line of railway to Holywell to the south and the main coastal road to the east; beyond this again runs the main line of railway to Holyhead.

The abbey was founded originally for monks of the order of Savigny in 1131. It passed in 1147, with the other Savignac houses, into the family of Cîteaux. Lying as it did on the main road from Chester to Caernarvon its allegiance could not be disguised, and though originally Welsh in sympathy it became definitely English from the reign of Edward I onwards. The site is now under the guardianship of the Ministry of Works, and has been fully cleared.

The church, which lies with almost exact orientation, was relatively small, having short transepts with two eastern chapels and a short square-ended presbytery which was never enlarged. In the view, which is taken from the north-west, the bases of the columns between nave and aisles can be seen in the turf, as also the line where the monks' quire ended. The sacristy, chapter-house, passage and subvault of the dorter are visible in the usual order. The large room still further to the south is the thirteenth-century warming-house; this is in an unusual position and presumably replaced an earlier and smaller one demolished when the frater was rebuilt in its new position at about the same time. This again is unusual; the rebuilt Cistercian frater normally lay in the centre of the southern range, but here it lies alongside the dorter. The range of ruined walls running east from the end of the warming-house is probably not medieval, but may cover the site of the infirmary. West of the frater the foundations of the kitchen can be seen, and to the north of this traces of the vanished western range of the lay brothers.

Description and plan in the *Guide* of the Ministry of Works, by A. J. Taylor.

49

VALLE CRUCIS

CISTERCIAN

THE CISTERCIAN ABBEY OF VALLE CRUCIS lies very beautifully in a tributary valley of the Vale of Llangollen, one and a half miles north-north-west of the town. Its name was taken from Eliseg's Pillar, an ancient memorial cross four or five centuries older than the abbey, and the house was one of a small late group of white monk foundations in Powis; its existence began in 1201. Contrary to the opinion of George Borrow, who referred to it in *Wild Wales* as 'a place of great pseudo-sanctity, wealth and consequence', it was a small and poor house; the conventual buildings were on an unusually minute scale, the nave of the church being almost as wide as the cloister garth and considerably longer than its walks. The church as completed had a short presbytery, transepts with eastern chapels, and an aisled nave broad in proportion to its length. Immediately in front of the east end is a large pool, in which, for an observer on the ground, the triple lancets of the eastern wall are mirrored. The eastern range is intact, and was long used as a farm-house. On the ground floor are sacristy, chapter-house (with fine vaulting) and parlour; on the first floor is the dorter, with rere-dorter to the south. This range has several small idiosyncrasies of planning and design. Elsewhere nothing exists above ground and there have been no systematic excavations.

Description, with plan reproduced from *The Builder*, by M. R. James in the Great Western Railway book *Abbeys* (1925), 22–3. There are some interesting photographs of details in R. L. Palmer, *English Monasteries in the Middle Ages* (1930).

III

50

CYMMER

CISTERCIAN

The Cistercian Abbey of Cymmer or Kymmer in Merioneth, founded in 1198–9, and not to be confused (as in the *Monasticon* and elsewhere) with its mother house, Cwmhir in Radnorshire, lies at the head of the Mawddach estuary near the confluence of that stream with the Wnion (Kymer deu dyfyr = 'the meeting of waters') one and a half miles north-west of Dolgelly. The ruins are in the heart of what, to the eyes of to-day, is one of the most beautiful regions of water, wood and mountain in the British Isles, but on a site which was, till recent years, remote and which is still wild.

The Cistercians did not reach Gwynedd (north-western Wales) for seventy years after their arrival in England, and Cymmer was from the beginning a small and poor house at the periphery, so to say, of the Cistercian circle. It is for this very reason of interest, as its remains show a small Cistercian plan which was never remodelled from its first design. The church is a small, plain aisled building exactly east and west, and, as can be seen in the photograph (taken from the east) stops a little short of the eastern line of the cloister wall. From this it seems certain that the structure was designed to be no more than the nave of a larger church which was never built. A small square western tower was added *c.* 1350. The lines of the cloister can be seen, but the chapter-house, foundations of dorter and rere-dorter are concealed by farm buildings. The frater lies in the normal monastic position parallel to the south walk and not (as in most of the great rebuilt white-monk abbeys) standing out at right angles. The buildings of the western range were probably never completed. The line of a drain can be seen crossing the floor of the frater and continuing outside, but this, so the excavators say, is not medieval, as the water supply was not taken from the river but from springs at the foot of the hillside below the so-called 'Precipice Walk', and the drainage therefore ran into the Mawddach to the south. The shingle of the river's bed can be seen along the top of the photograph.

The farm-house immediately to the west of the church has medieval work at its base, and has been identified with the monastic guest-house. Between it and the neighbouring cottage (also medieval in origin) ran the old road which here forded the Mawddach some distance above the modern bridge on the Dolgelly-Barmouth road. This in medieval times (as also its successor before the construction of Barmouth railway bridge) carried all the traffic between central and north-western Wales. The abbey therefore must often have been a place of enforced halt when the river was in spate.

There is a description, with a plan, in the *Guide* of the Ministry of Works by C. A. Ralegh Radford.

113

CYMMER: PANORAMIC VIEW

The panorama, taken almost above the western saddle of the Cader Idris range where the old coach road from Dolgelly to Towyn crosses the watershed, shows the valley of the Wnion (centre right) and that of the Mawddach (left centre). The tide is out; at high water the mud flats are covered to a point slightly above the junction of the two rivers. The bridge over the Mawddach carrying the Dolgelly-Barmouth road is visible; Kymmer lies in the trees immediately above the bridge on the left bank of the river above the bend. To the right, immediately above the wing of the aircraft, is the small town of Dolgelly. In the distance is Lake Bala, with the hills of Clwyd beyond to the left and the Arenigs bounding the view on the extreme left of the plate. To the right of the lake, in the distance, are the Berwyns; on the extreme right, nearer to Dolgelly, the slopes of Aran Mawddy and Aran Benllyn.

51

STRATA FLORIDA

CISTERCIAN

THE PRESENT APPEARANCE of the site and surroundings of Strata Florida give little indication of the size of this once-celebrated abbey or of the place it held in the national life of Wales. The great church, surrounded by conventual buildings and gardens, then stood near the trackway which was the principal thoroughfare over the high moorlands between the valleys of Cardigan and Rhayader. To-day the main road runs ten miles to the north; the valley is a cul-de-sac, and the abbey, of which little remains save a fine west doorway, lies in a rarely visited and somewhat cheerless valley which gives access to a few lonely farms. Like so many others, the house did not find its final resting-place at once, but lay first near the River Flur, which gave it its name, some two miles to the south-west, where foundations on a considerable scale have been discovered. The final site was by the River Teifi, some fourteen miles south-east of Aberystwyth.

The abbey was founded on its first site in 1164 by Robert FitzStephen, a Norman baron of Cardigan, but within a few months the Normans were driven out of the district by the Welsh under Rhys ap Gruffydd, who patronized the monastery, and the place soon became a centre of the national and literary activities of Dinefwr. It was here that Gerald of Wales left and lost his library, and here also, in all probability, that the principal annals of Wales, *Brut y Tywysogion*, were composed. The house at this epoch had wide and scattered lands and great flocks, but by the Dissolution its prosperity had passed.

The church was a large building, which took almost a century to complete. It had a long aisled nave, transepts with three eastern chapels, now roofed over, and a short presbytery which before long was enlarged to the east; this eastern end was used to house two chapels behind the high altar. These arrangements can be seen in the plate, with the dark rectangle marking the site of the high altar. It was usual in Cistercian churches for a wall of some height to separate the nave (the lay-brothers' quire) from the aisles (often used as chapels); at Strata Florida a further step was taken and the piers of the nave arcade stood on walls some five feet high, of which the foundations can be seen—an arrangement unique in England and Wales. Screen walls also blocked all sides save the eastern of the space beneath the crossing, where the monks' quire lay. The church, therefore, large as it was in dimensions, must have presented an unusually confined appearance to one standing within.

The conventual buildings, so far as is known, followed the usual plan. The narrow sacristy can be seen next to the south transept, and the chapter-house next to it in the shadow of a tree. To the east is a group of medieval tombstones. Beyond, to the south, some mounds mark the end of the dorter. The frater and southern walk are beneath farm buildings, but there are some remains of the western range beneath the trees. The great court occupied the site now filled by the large vegetable garden. To the north of the church is the parish graveyard, where the imperishable slate headstones, casting each a black shadow, seem here, as often in Wales, to indicate a population far greater than that which in fact occupies the district.

Description and plan in the *Guide* of the Ministry of Works by C. A. Ralegh Radford. For a fuller account of the history and excavations of 1887 see S. W. Williams, *Strata Florida* (1889).

52

STRATA MARCELLA

CISTERCIAN

THE CISTERCIAN ABBEY OF STRATA MARCELLA or Ystrad Margel (sometimes known as La Pole) lay some two and a half miles north-east of Welshpool in Montgomeryshire. It was founded in 1170 by Owen Cyfeiliog, a prince of Powys and a celebrated bard; the founding community came from Whitland in Carmarthenshire, the mother of so many Welsh houses. The buildings have disappeared entirely, as has also a farm-house built upon the site, and when excavations were undertaken in 1890 under the direction of S. W. Williams, the excavator of Strata Florida, the position of the church and cloister was unknown.

The photograph shows the site from the south-west; it lies between the Severn and the Welshpool-Oswestry road, here bordered by the Shropshire Union canal. The position of the church, which was no less than 270 ft. in overall length, is marked by extensive traces of buried foundations south-west of the transverse hedge near the centre of the plate. The larger of the two dark objects seen in the area is a bush growing upon a pile of carved stones unearthed by the excavators; it is (or was) surrounded by a fence enclosing part of the nave of the church. The smaller black object to the south-east is near the site of a grave, conjectured to be that of the poet-founder, who became a monk of the abbey. The cloister lay to the south of the church, but neither it nor the conventual buildings have been excavated. It was, however, ascertained that the nave ran westwards for four bays beyond the western range—an unusual feature in a Cistercian house, possibly due to a late addition. South of the site can be seen the course of the main drain, a leet from the river; traces of other buildings are visible, some of them doubtless connected with the farm and its outbuildings.

Account and rough plan in *Montgomeryshire Collections*, XXV (1891), 149–96.

53

MARGAM

CISTERCIAN

THE CISTERCIAN ABBEY OF MARGAM lies some two miles from the coast of Swansea Bay at a point three and a half miles south of Port Talbot on the Bridgend road. The abbey stood at the foot of a steep hillside, once covered by oak trees, and the dark waters of the stream and fishpond supplying the monks can be seen in the plate. The church, which was large, has almost entirely disappeared save for part of the nave embodied in the modern parish church. The original nave was aisled, with eight bays, six of which form the existing church. The transepts had eastern chapels and there was an aisled presbytery.

The cloister lay to the south of the church, with its southern walk just short of the celebrated orangery, the eastern portion of which must cover the site of the frater. The chief remaining feature of the ruins, which alone suffices to render them remarkable, is the twelve-sided chapter-house, approached by a vestibule. The vaulting was supported by a central column which still stands, and was uninjured until its collapse in 1799; the clustering shafts now break off a few feet above the capital. This building dates from *c.* 1200, and besides being a very early example of a polygonal chapter-house (the earliest being that at Worcester *c.* 1170), is all but unique among English Cistercian chapter-houses, the small room at Dore in Herefordshire being scarcely comparable. Cistercian chapter-houses were as a rule rectangular, and the typical plan of the order, as well as the prohibition against elaboration, was traversed at Margam. The subvault of the dorter and part of the rere-dorter can be seen to the east of the orangery.

Plan and description by H. E. David in *Archaeologia Cambrensis*, 6th ser., LXXXIV (1929), 317–24. Consult also W. de Gray Birch, *Margam Abbey* (1897), where an engraving is given of the chapter-house before the fall of the vaulting.

54

TINTERN

CISTERCIAN

TINTERN ABBEY, the ruins of which yield to none in purity of architectural style and in the perfection of their setting in a deep valley framed by river and hanging wood, and which have been rendered familiar, wherever English literature is read, by Wordsworth's poem, was nevertheless throughout its history a comparatively undistinguished house. It was an early Cistercian foundation from the Burgundian abbey of L'Aumône, one of the 'elder daughters' of Cîteaux, and was in existence in 1131, but the church and most of the conventual buildings were rebuilt, more elaborately than early Cistercian sentiment would have permitted, from *c.* 1220 onwards in the Early English style. The large nave, the last part to be rebuilt, was begun *c.* 1270 and not finished till the beginning of the fourteenth century.

The buildings follow the normal Cistercian plan, save that for some reason, possibly connected with problems of water and drainage, the cloister and conventual buildings lay to the north of the church. The smaller view, an almost vertical photograph, would not be readily identifiable by anyone who was not familiar with the plan of Tintern. It shows the walls of the church which, save for the north wall of the nave, are almost intact; the eastern aisle of the transept is visible. The chapter-house is separated from the north transept by a narrow vestry and book-room; beyond it, after the parlour and passage, comes the undercroft of the vanished dorter, used as novices' quarters. The foundations of the rere-dorter, running east from the end of the dorter, formed one side of the small infirmary cloister, and the infirmary hall can be seen beyond to the east. A passage joins the infirmary cloister to the north aisle of the presbytery. The long refectory lies at right angles to the north walk of the great cloister, with the warming-house to the east and the kitchen to the west. Beyond the kitchen is the western or lay-brothers' range with their refectory parallel to that of the monks. Their dorter was above on the first floor. The line of the main drain can be seen between the kitchen and frater, between the frater and the eastern range, and again passing under the rere-dorter.

The second photograph is more easily recognizable, though no view from the air can show the familiar background of dark woods behind the east end. The plan of the infirmary buildings can be clearly seen, with the Wye beyond.

For plans and description, see the *Guide* (1934) of the Ministry of Works by Sir Harold Brakspear.

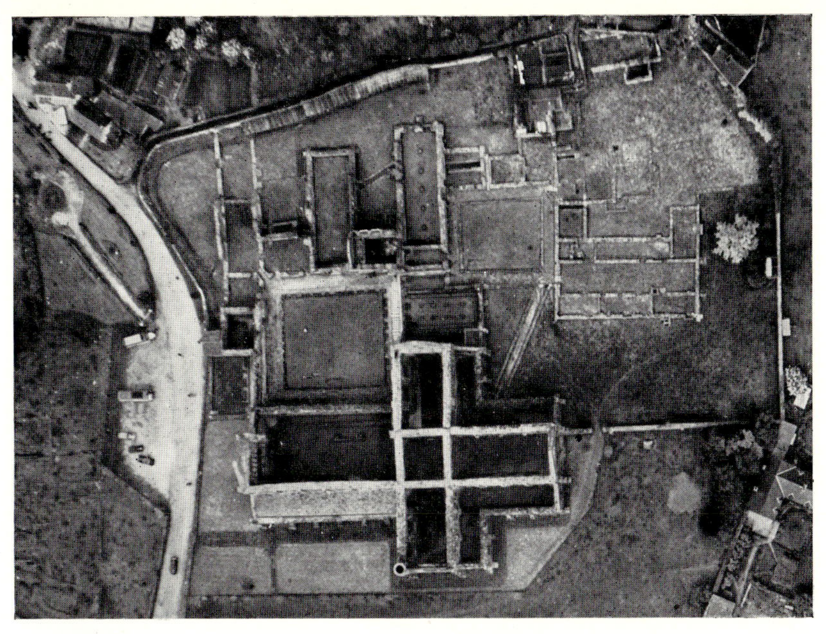

55

HAILES

CISTERCIAN

THE SITE OF THE CISTERCIAN ABBEY OF HAILES lies at the foot of the steep green slope where the Cotswolds fall to the vale of Evesham between Winchcomb and Broadway. It was a late foundation, made in 1246 by Richard Earl of Cornwall with monks from Beaulieu, and its consecration in 1251, when King and Queen and all the notables of the land were present, along with Grosseteste and twelve other bishops, was one of the great social occasions of the time. When in 1270 Edmund of Cornwall presented to the abbey a relic of the Precious Blood, the place became one of the most celebrated goals of pilgrimage in the country.

Designed when the Cistercians had ceased to trouble about conforming to pattern, the church differs from most English white-monk churches, not excluding Beaulieu and Netley. The first plan was of a large church with aisled nave, transepts with three chapels and a large aisled presbytery with an ambulatory at the east end; beyond this were chapels under a low eastern roof, as on a smaller scale at Abbey Dore. When, however, the relic was presented the east end was rebuilt to accommodate the shrine behind the high altar, and the new work terminated with an apsidal ambulatory and five radiating eastern chapels. The site of both the high altar and the shrine can be seen in the photograph. The conventual buildings conformed to the normal Cistercian type, with large rectangular chapter-house, and frater at right-angles to the south walk of the cloister, between warming-house and kitchen.

The site, which had long lain derelict and overgrown, was excavated by Harold Brakspear in 1899; it then lay fallow again for a number of years, after which a tenant, the eminent physician Sir J. Fowler, tricked it out in 1928 with yew, cypresses and flowering chestnuts as seen in the plate. It is now under the care of the National Trust. The view is taken from the east.

Plan and description by Harold Brakspear in *Archaeological Journal*, LXIII (1906), 261.

56

KIRKSTEAD

CISTERCIAN

THE SITE of this once important Cistercian abbey lies near the east bank of the River Witham between Lincoln and Boston, a mile south-west of Woodhall Spa and three miles north of Tattershall Castle, which can be clearly seen from the precinct. Kirkstead was one of the three first daughters of which Fountains became mother 'at a single birth' in 1139, the other two being Louth Park and Newminster; she had as her first two abbots Robert and Walter, two of the group who had seceded from St Mary's, York, and herself became a mother in 1147, when she sent a colony across the North Sea to found Hovedö on an island in the fjord near Oslo.

The view shows the site from the south-east; as with other fenland sites the network of water channels is confusing, and it is not clear whether the precinct was co-extensive with the large field in the centre of the plate; there may have been an inner moat, such as that shown by the antiquary Stukeley (1726) on his largely imaginary 'ichnography'. In any case, the field track crossing the site is modern and the medieval gateway may have been near a wide gap in the hedge west of the site, with a secondary entrance to the south near the chapel of St Leonard.

The tall fragment of masonry, visible from afar, is part of the south wall of the south transept. The masonry on its southern face presents several problems as to the elevation of the eastern range, but the outline of the large church, with short transepts and presbytery, and a long and narrow nave, can be distinguished by visitors on the ground, as can also the site of the cloister garth to the south, some 60 ft. by 75 ft. in area, and the surrounding ranges with outlying buildings to the south-west, possibly infirmary and abbot's quarters.

South of the site, and at a little distance, is the exquisite Early English chapel of St Leonard, which was used by dependants of the abbey as well as by externs; it was the so-called *capella ad portas*. Large depressions to the south-west of the precinct were probably fishponds, and another system of narrow parallel ditches or stews can be seen in a field to the north of the site where the road turns at a right angle.

The last abbot of Kirkstead, like his fellow at Barlings, was swept into the Lincolnshire rising when the insurgents proceeded from Horncastle to Lincoln. He was subsequently executed at Lincoln, and his abbey fell by attainder to the Crown.

The site has recently passed into the possession of the University of Nottingham.

There is no plan or full description, but there are a few notes in the *Archaeological Journal*, XL (1883), 296–302.

57

REVESBY

CISTERCIAN

THE CISTERCIAN ABBEY OF REVESBY, a daughter house of Rievaulx, lay some eleven miles north of Boston in Lincolnshire. Founded in 1143, the house had as its first abbot St Ailred, who left it in 1147 to be abbot of Rievaulx. Nothing now remains above ground, but the site is clear and would repay excavation; a very partial beginning, almost a century ago, revealed a little of the church and cloister. In the view, looking a little west of north, the white object surrounded by a wall is a tomb before the high altar. The position of the church can be seen, with the cloister garth to the south. The eastern range is fainter, but the southern end of the long dorter, with the rere-dorter at right angles, can be distinguished, with what appears to be an infirmary court further east. In the southern range the east wall of the frater can be traced. The western range has the appearance of forming a side of a smaller court; if this is medieval, it has no Cistercian parallel in England, but more probably the square enclosure was a post-Dissolution house or farmyard. The precinct, which was surrounded by a moat, and a mound or wall, can be traced throughout its circuit, with fishponds at the south-west angle.

There is no full account or plan of Revesby. For the excavation of 1869 see *Associated Architectural Societies' Reports and Papers* (1869), x, i, 22–6.

58

TILTY

CISTERCIAN

THE SITE OF THE CISTERCIAN ABBEY OF TILTY in Essex, founded in 1153, lies seven and a half miles north-east of Bishop's Stortford. The buildings have been completely destroyed and pillaged, and the only fragments above ground are parts of the west wall of the cloister and kitchen. Part of the plan has been recovered from excavations in 1901 and 1942, and still more is visible in its main lines in the plate.

The church, seen in the view from the east, was relatively small (174 ft. in length) and was of the normal Cistercian type without additions. It had an aisled nave, transepts with eastern chapels and a short presbytery. The cloister lay to the north owing to exigencies of drainage. Part of the outline of the church is visible, with the bases of the pillars showing, immediately above a patch of dark vegetation near the centre of the plate. The north transept is followed in the eastern range by the sacristy, chapter-house, and subvault of dorter; this last extended to the north of the cloister, and still further north the foundations of the rere-dorter can be seen by the bushes lining the bank of a stream. From the north-east angle of the cloister a long passage is visible, leading to a rectangular building on a different orientation; this may have been the infirmary. There is no apparent trace of the abbot's lodging, which should normally have lain between this and the church. The northern walk gave access to the frater and kitchen; on the west the lay-brothers' range is visible, with disturbances in the ground that suggest that their frater lay in an unusual position at right angles to the range. Some distance to the west of the church traces have been seen on the ground of a large building which was probably the guest-hall, converted to a dwelling-house after the Dissolution. South of the abbey, and beyond the limits of the plate, the chapel of the externs (*capella ad portas*) now forms the chancel of the parish church. To the east a field-name still perpetuates the site of the abbey vineyard.

Descriptions and sketch plans in *Trans. of the Essex Archaeological Soc.* (new ser.) XVIII (1928), 89–93, and *Essex Review*, LVIII (Oct., 1949), 169–79.

59

COGGESHALL

CISTERCIAN

THE CISTERCIAN ABBEY OF COGGESHALL lay a quarter of a mile south of the small town of that name, well known in the later Middle Ages as a centre of East Anglian cloth manufacture. Coggeshall lies nine miles west of Colchester on the river Blackwater; the stream here flows in two channels, the broader one, visible as a dark sheet of water in the foreground of the plate being the leat to the abbey mill, while the true channel is hidden by trees. The abbey, an early foundation from Savigny in 1140, became Cistercian in 1147. Early in the thirteenth century it had as abbot Ralph, writer of a valuable chronicle.

All that remains of the medieval fabric forms part of the irregular group of buildings immediately beyond the mill-leat; they are seen from an angle slightly south of east. They consist of four parts: (1) a fair-sized, L-shaped dwelling-house with prominent chimney stacks; (2) a narrow building, little more than a corridor of two storeys, joined to it and running north and south; (3) a larger building, running east and west from the south end of the corridor; and (4) near this, at its south-east corner, but not actually joined to it, another small building. The first of these, now known as the 'Abbey' and in earlier documents as the 'abbey house', was built soon after the Dissolution (*c.* 1582) partly on the site of a lodging leased from the monks and said to occupy part of the infirmary hall; the east wing was added almost a century later. The corridor connected a medieval building, of which some fragments remain in the 'Abbey', with a two-storeyed medieval block which ran eastwards from the southern end of the dorter range; this may have housed the infirmary on its upper floor, with the chapel at its eastern end. The small detached building of early thirteenth-century date has not been satisfactorily identified; it may have been a kitchen or a guest-house. The remains of these medieval buildings are interesting as showing an extensive use of brick as early as *c.* 1220.

The whole complex so far described, lay outside the cloister at its south-east angle. All the main conventual buildings, together with the alleys of the cloister, have wholly vanished. The church has likewise vanished entirely, but the outline of its walls can be clearly seen in dry seasons and is visible in the plate. The marks show an edifice of the normal early Cistercian type, with short transepts and presbytery. The outline of a large chapel adjoining the nave to the north-west is just visible. The half-circle in the grass has nothing to do with the fabric of the abbey, nor has the oblong depression still further north at the right-hand margin of the plate.

A little over a hundred yards west of the west end of the church stands the *capella ad portas*, dedicated to St Nicholas, an unusually fine specimen of the chapel of the externs (cf. Furness and Kirkstead, pp. 81, 126), which was restored by Bodley in 1897, when it was transformed from its previous use as a barn. The gatehouse probably stood where the clump of trees hides the road.

Excavations were begun at the west end of the nave by W. H. St J. Hope in the summer of 1914; they were abandoned at the outbreak of war. Recently further attempts have been made to explore the site, which is certainly one that would repay a thorough investigation.

Description by G. F. Beaumont, in *Transactions of the Essex Archaeological Society*, new series, XV (1918), 60–76; description with plan, independent of Beaumont's article, in the *North-East Essex Inventory* of the Royal Commission on Historical Monuments (1922), pp. 165–8.

60

ROBERTSBRIDGE

CISTERCIAN

THE CISTERCIAN ABBEY OF ROBERTSBRIDGE, the only house of the order in Sussex, lay on the south bank of the Rother (in medieval times navigable to this point), ten miles inland from Hastings. It was visited by several kings, including Henry III and the first two Edwards. The remains of the abbey have been incorporated in, or obscured by, the Abbey Farm, its gardens and outbuildings, and have never been excavated on a large scale.

In the view, which is taken from the south-east, the outline of the abbey church is clearly marked by lines of parched grass which indicate the position of wall foundations. It appears to have conformed to the normal Cistercian type for small abbeys. The cloister lay to the south of the church; the chapter-house has disappeared, though its entrance has been excavated by Mr L. F. Salzman, but the south end of the undercroft of the dorter can be traced. The south walk gave access to the warming-house (once used as an oast-house and now in ruins) and to the frater, parallel to the walk and never rebuilt in a perpendicular position; the walls of the frater exist in a broken and ivy-covered condition. There are traces of the south-west portion of the lay-brothers' range. At right angles to the western range stood the building now used as a farm-house (with white gable end); this was erected *c.* 1250 and is usually described as the abbot's house, though the normal site of the abbot's lodging in Cistercian houses was east of the eastern range. It has a vaulted undercroft on the ground floor. The moat to the north may have delimited the precinct, and the parallel depressions to the north-west, at the top of the plate, were probably fishponds.

Description, with no reference to the church, in *Victoria County History of Sussex*, IX (1937), 219–20; cf. also *Sussex Notes and Queries*, V, 206–8, for Mr Salzman's excavations.

61

NETLEY

CISTERCIAN

THE CISTERCIAN ABBEY OF NETLEY lay near the eastern shore of Southampton Water, some three miles south-east of the town of Southampton. Founded from Beaulieu, only a few miles away across the estuary, by Peter des Roches, bishop of Winchester, in 1238, with Henry III as co-founder, it was dedicated, at the king's wish, to Edward the Confessor, but in spite of royal patronage it never became large or distinguished in any way. At the suppression in 1536 it passed to Sir William Paulet, who converted the nave into his hall, the south transept and eastern range into living-rooms, and the southern range into apartments with a gatehouse in the middle. The cloister garth was used as a courtyard.

The church, built as it was in the mid-thirteenth century, did not conform to the early Cistercian type. Both nave and presbytery were aisled, and the presbytery was longer than was customary in earlier Cistercian churches. The transepts had two eastern chapels. The chapter-house was relatively small; next to it, to the south, came the parlour, and the dorter extended over the whole range. The building running east from the south end was the rere-dorter on the first floor, and possibly part of the infirmary on the ground floor; it does not lie at right angles to the range, but returns slightly, presumably owing to the alignment of the great drain. The detached building at some distance to the east was the abbot's lodging. The lines of a wall visible in the turf between it and the eastern range are not monastic, but are the remains of the terraced gardens of the mansion. The frater, which ran southward from the southern walk, was demolished to clear the approach to the post-Suppression gatehouse, and almost all traces of the western range have disappeared.

Description and plan in the *Guide* of the Ministry of Works, by A. Hamilton Thompson.

62

BEAULIEU

CISTERCIAN

The Cistercian Abbey of St Mary de Bello Loco Regis lies deep in the New Forest at the head of the tidewater of the Beaulieu River, some four miles from the Solent and an equal distance west of Southampton Water. One of the latest Cistercian plantations in England, it was founded by King John in 1204, possibly as a satisfaction for the vexations and mulcts the order had previously suffered at his hands. The community came directly from Cîteaux, and the abbey within a few decades became herself the mother of Netley and Hailes. After the surrender in 1538 the place went to Thomas Wriothesley, later earl of Southampton, and remained with his descendants, ultimately passing by marriage to the Montagus, dukes of Buccleuch; a cadet branch of this family was ennobled with the title Montagu of Beaulieu. The superfluous abbey buildings were used as a quarry for stone for Hurst Castle. A thorough investigation of the site was made in 1900 by W. H. St John Hope and Harold Brakspear, and the outlines of the foundations were marked with white gravel in the turf.

The abbey lies on the left bank of the Beaulieu River where the stream, after flowing into a large mill pool, swells into a tidal inlet. The only approach was from the river at the foot of the mill pool, where the small outer gate and elaborate great gate still exist; the latter is now connected with Palace House, the residence of Lord Montagu of Beaulieu. The mill lay by the outer gate. Water for drainage did not come from the river, but was provided by a stream of which the course can be traced near the right-hand margin of the plate. It broadened into two fishponds, the one now converted into a pleasure ground immediately east of the infirmary range, the second due south of the abbey, distinguishable as a weed-grown pool in the pasture in the foreground of the photograph. A conduit from the upper pool led a stream of water under the offices and back into the river.

The church which, owing to its late date, exhibits none of the successive developments and extensions so common in Cistercian abbeys, was the largest in area of all the white-monk churches in England, owing chiefly to its unusual width. The plan was unlike any other English Cistercian church, though very similar to that of Clairvaux. The presbytery, which ended in a semicircular apse, was surrounded by an aisle around which in turn lay a ring of eleven chapels. The north transept had aisles to the east and west, and its northernmost bay was apparently formed into a porch or galilee; the foundations of the inner wall of this can be seen. The south transept had an eastern aisle only, and was not so wide as the northern one; the night stair to the dorter was in the thickness (here 12 ft.) of the western wall. The sacristy and library, as in the normal Cistercian plan, adjoined the south transept, and since their foundations correspond to those of the galilee in the northern transept it is probable that they were included structurally within the south transept. The nave had north and south aisles.

In the eastern range the sacristy was followed by the chapter-house, the roof of which was carried by a double row of columns; next came the parlour and the subvault of the dorter, which ran at first-floor level along the whole range. The foundations of the southern end of the dorter and of the rere-dorter which stood out at right angles to the east have been obliterated by the parish cemetery. The

frater lay in the normal Cistercian position at right angles to the south walk of the cloister; it is in perfect preservation owing to its conversion, soon after the Dissolution, into a parish church for the people previously dependent upon the abbey. It lay between the warming-house and kitchen, both of which have been lost to the graveyard.

The western range contained as usual the cellarage and lay-brothers' frater on the ground floor, and their dorter above. Here the northern half has been converted and the southern destroyed. There are some indications that when the recruitment of lay-brothers ceased, their quarters were used as the abbot's lodging and guest-house.

To the south-east of the church the plan of the infirmary range has been recovered and indicated. The large apartment was the infirmary hall, the small parallel annexe the misericord; the building projecting at right angles was the chapel. The line of foundations across the hall, with indented fireplace, marks a conversion in the fifteenth century, when the infirmary hall was divided into a number of rooms.

There is an admirable description with a large plan by W. H. St John Hope and H. Brakspear in *Archaeological Journal*, LXIII (1906), 139–86. See also the *Guide* of the Ministry of Works.

63

STANLEY

CISTERCIAN

THE CISTERCIAN ABBEY OF STANLEY was situated in Wiltshire, three miles east of Chippenham, and half-way between that town and Calne, only a short distance north of Bowood, the seat of the marquess of Lansdowne. The house, a daughter of Quarr, was originally founded in 1151 at Lockswell, not far distant, but as so often with Cistercian houses, the first site proved unacceptable and a move was made in 1154 to Stanley, where permanent buildings were erected. The site, here seen from the north-east, lies in the wide valley of the small River Marden between the stream and the Calne branch of what was the Great Western Railway. Though it is recorded that the domestic water supply was piped from Lockswell, the locality abounds in streams and in addition to the monastic trenches the abandoned activities of another era are visible in the disused Wilts and Berks canal which, with its feeder channel, appears in the lower right-hand corner of the plate and again winding across the right-hand top corner. The monks used water to surround their precinct, and the elaborate system of channels and sluices can scarcely be grasped without a plan. The stream, which flows away from the camera, was tapped below its second bend in the foreground; one channel formed the moat to the north of the precinct, another fed the main drain, and the third, after supplying a fishpond, crossed the railway to feed the millpond, of which the retaining banks can be seen on the near side of the road; the abbey mill occupied the site of the present New Abbey Farm at the apex where road and railway converge.

The entrance to the abbey was by a causeway running on top of the retaining bank between the millpond and the mill leat, and the great gateway of the abbey lay at the foot of the pond where the earthwork meets the dark line of trees. The abbey itself lay between the L-shaped moat and the farm buildings on the same side of the railway. The site of the cloister garth can be recognized by the small detached shed in the pasture, which protects an expanse of tiled pavement uncovered by the excavators in the west walk of the cloister.

The whole great complex of buildings has disappeared almost to the last stone, and the mounds and hollows do not cover masonry, but mark the pits of the stone-robbers' delvings. The person responsible for this thorough-going slighting was apparently Sir Edward Baynton, the original grantee in 1537, who transported the material to build a large house at Bromham near Devizes. During the excavation of

the site, evidence was forthcoming that the abbey church, like that of Lewes, was brought down by a demolition gang, one of whom was crushed by a fall of stone.

The general arrangement was normal; but the cloister lay to the north of the church owing to a rise of the land to the south; the level expanse of the garth can be seen in front of the shed, with the church to the spectator's left, the eastern range in front, and the frater to the right. The whole was scientifically excavated by Harold Brakspear in 1905–6, and with the aid of his plan the lay-out can be readily discerned by the visitor *in situ* or the reader with the annexed plate. The church in its final form had aisles in nave and presbytery, and both dorter and frater were of ample proportions.

Description and plan by Harold Brakspear in *Archaeologia*, LX (1907), 493–516.

64

CLEEVE

CISTERCIAN

The Cistercian Abbey of Cleeve in West Somerset, some two miles south-west of Watchet and the Bristol Channel, was founded from Revesby in Lincolnshire in 1188. Although the church has disappeared, the remainder of the buildings are unusually complete and (what is still more unusual) roofed; they present several features of great interest, showing more clearly than any other Cistercian house the process of refashioning that went on after the disappearance of the lay-brothers.

The precinct seen from the west-south-west occupies the greater part of the plate. It was bounded on the west by a wall on the bank of a stream which flows behind the roadside trees, and on the other sides by a moat, fed by the stream; the moat, after enclosing the rectangular meadow north of the church, turned south alongside the present track of a disused mineral railway, finally joining the stream below the lower margin of the plate. A leat from the stream served the mill, which stood on the site occupied by the modern mill, near the group of farm buildings. Two fishponds lay between this point and the abbey. The main entrance to the precinct was over a bridge into a small court visible to the extreme left of the plate towards the top. Between this court and the great court lay the great gateway, still extant, which was rebuilt by the last abbot shortly before the Dissolution.

The plan of the church has been recovered by excavation, and can be seen. It consisted of a nave of seven bays, aisled; transepts with eastern chapels, and a short presbytery. The original conventual buildings followed the normal plan. In the eastern range, after a narrow sacristy, came the rectangular vaulted chapter-house, then a parlour and a passage and the dorter subvault. On the first floor lay the dorter, still extant and roofed along its whole length. The rere-dorter ran eastwards at right angles to the southern end. As the abbey was founded comparatively late, it is probable that the first frater stood in the normal mature Cistercian position perpendicular to the centre of the southern range; the south foundations and magnificent tiled floor of this building have been discovered. The western range, the abode of the lay-brothers, was also originally of normal design. In the south wall of the church the niche still stands (barely visible in the plate) marking the seat of the president at certain duties in the north walk of the cloister.

The remarkable feature of Cleeve is the evidence of wholesale rebuilding in the last phase of the abbey's life, and of the growing attention to domestic comfort. Some of this, being detailed or interior, can be examined only on the spot. The principal

change however, is visible. This is the new and beautiful frater rebuilt in the fifteenth century in the old monastic position parallel to the south walk (compare and contrast Furness, p. 80). This stands on an undercroft, apparently of two living-rooms, but as this wing has been inhabited and reconditioned from time to time on the ground floor, a closer examination is desirable. The frater proper is reached by stairs from the cloister; it has the normal 'hall' design of buttery, screens and great fireplace; this last was on the south side and the chimney-stack, visible in the plate, fills a whole bay. The hall is covered by a magnificent wooden roof, and bears on its eastern wall above the dais a sadly deteriorating painted crucifix. Shortly after this piece of conversion the south-west part of the western range was rebuilt as the abbot's lodging; this was probably completed only a year or two before the suppression.

There is no full recent description or measured plan. There is a good account (for its date) with sketch plans in the *Proceedings of the Somerset Archaeological Society*, XXXV (1889), 83–120. In the same journal, LXXVII (1931), 37–47, are some valuable notes on more recent excavations.

65

FORDE

CISTERCIAN

THE CISTERCIAN ABBEY OF FORDE lay in a detached parish of Devon (now transferred to Dorset) some three miles south-east of Chard, near a ford on the upper Axe, in a valley which would still be secluded if it were not traversed by the main line of railway from Salisbury to Exeter. The founding community came from Waverley in 1136 and had settled at Brightley near Okehampton; the site was unpropitious, the founder died, and the monks were on their way back to Surrey in despair when, like their brethren from Calder a year or two previously (see Byland), they fell in with a benefactress who gave them a new home; they began life at Forde in 1141. The house prospered, and within a few years welcomed its most distinguished recruit, Baldwin, archdeacon of Exeter, who soon became abbot and then in turn bishop of Worcester and archbishop of Canterbury. The subsequent history of the place was uneventful, but its very latest years were marked by an almost feverish activity in building under Abbot Chard, who lived to surrender his unfinished work. The abbey then suffered partial demolition, but the decay was arrested and a new shape given by Sir Edmund Prideaux, who took possession in 1649 and employed, if not Inigo Jones certainly his pupil John Webb, who rebuilt and redecorated a large part of the conventual buildings. That, and later additions within and without, made Forde one of the most remarkable houses of the West Country.

Despite its appearance, the place retains a considerable amount of medieval work, some of it without a parallel in England. The view is taken from the south-west, showing the front of the mansion, of which the main axis runs from east to west along the line of the north walk of the monastic cloister, which lay to the north of the church. This latter has disappeared to the last stone; its site has never been excavated, and the view from the air is not informative. It lay where now is lawn on the near (south) side of the wide drive, its west end flush with the low projecting building, and the high altar lying in the neighbourhood of the tall light-foliaged tree which casts a long shadow in the formal garden. Consequently, the sacristy in the eastern range would have coincided with the drive. The rectangular building (now converted into a domestic chapel) is in fact the original twelfth-century chapter-house modernized, and the long gabled roof stretching north beyond it is the monks' dorter standing on an undercroft. As has been said, the north walk of the cloister is standing, with the old frater perpendicular to it; this has two floors—a late medieval remodelling found elsewhere, carried out when numbers had shrunk and a second frater for meat-eating was needed. To the south-west of this frater the medieval kitchen still exists as the kitchen of the mansion.

The western or lay-brothers' range has disappeared save for fragments of its central portion, but west of the western range is the most unusual feature of the medieval abbey—a great new abbot's hall, which must have seen few social occasions of the kind it was designed to serve. This was erected from *c.* 1520 onwards by Abbot Chard, the last abbot; the great windows of four of its bays are visible in the plate and, advancing from its south-eastern corner, the great and splendid gatehouse, one of the richest monuments of late autumnal Gothic, constructed in the lovely, durable Ham stone, with Perpendicular ornament set off with a frieze of Renaissance motifs. One of the most beautiful creations of its age, it can have been in use for only a dozen years or so before the surrender; the cloister, which Chard was rebuilding with fan vaulting, was unfinished when the end came. When the house was remodelled, the westernmost bays of the great hall were converted to two floors of rooms, and still more drastic changes were made to the block further to the west, which had been intended by Chard for the abbot's lodging. In the left-hand bottom corner the large fishponds can be seen.

Small plan and description in *Country Homes of Dorset* (1935), pp. 54–8, by A. Oswald. A full account is about to appear in the *West Dorset Inventory* of the Royal Commission on Historical Monuments.

66

BUCKLAND

CISTERCIAN

THE CISTERCIAN ABBEY OF BUCKLAND in Devon, four miles south of Tavistock, was founded in 1278 by Amicia, widow of Baldwin, earl of Devon. Save for the abnormal foundations at Oxford and London, it was the last house of the white monks to be founded in England, as it was also the most westerly; the Cistercians gained no foothold in Cornwall. The house lies in a valley enclosed on all sides save the west, upon a stream which flows down to the Tavy. It is perhaps unique among English Cistercian remains by reason of the disappearance of all the monastic complex save the church, which was ingeniously converted into a dwelling-house in Elizabeth's reign, probably by Sir Richard Grenville. Shortly after it passed into the possession of Sir Francis Drake, and it still contains relics and portraits associated with him.

The photograph, taken from the north, shows the church, orientated east-north-east and consisting of a short presbytery, crossing with south transept, and nave. The tower has been utilized for domestic purposes to the top, and the arches of the crossing are visible in an upper room. The north transept, together with the cloister and conventual buildings, which lay to the north of the church, have disappeared. The only other remains of medieval construction above ground are a small turreted building among the stabling in the foreground, and the fine barn, more than 100 ft. in length, which can be seen to the south-east of the mansion. It is now the property of the corporation of Plymouth, and is used as a museum.

There is no adequate plan or recent description. An excellent account for its date (1875) was contributed by the antiquary J. B. Rowe to the *Transactions of the Devonshire Association*, VII, 329–66.

67

MOUNT ST BERNARD

CISTERCIAN

THE MODERN CISTERCIAN ABBEY OF MOUNT ST BERNARD lies some eleven miles north-west of Leicester, on igneous rock near the summit of the high ground of Charnwood Forest, in a bleak and dusky landscape. The abbey was founded in 1835, three hundred years after the first Dissolution, by Ambrose Phillipps (later de Lisle) an enthusiastic pre-Tractarian convert to Catholicism. Phillipps, whose family owned land in Leicestershire, was born at Garendon, once a Cistercian abbey, and he conceived the project of re-introducing the white monks to England. The community of reformed Cistercians (Trappists) came from Melleray in France, and Phillipps presented them with exactly the kind of land that was given to the white monks of Garendon seven hundred years before—230 acres of rough moorland, of which only 40 acres were under cultivation. It was characteristic of the donor that he should have raised the funds for the purchase of the land by means of a loan from the Vicar Apostolic of the Midland District. As before, the desert blossomed as the rose of Sharon, and the abbey has long been surrounded by fertile fields and gardens, with trees to break the wind, and sheds and byres that house prize stock. Besides giving the land, Phillipps persuaded his friend John, the 'good earl' of Shrewsbury, to subscribe towards the fabric, and the monks erected an abbey in the years 1835–44 to the designs of A. W. Pugin. Pugin and his patrons, though fanatical Goths, did not aim at reproducing the primitive Cistercian plan—which in fact had not then been reconstructed by antiquarians—and the complex of buildings, with its chimneys and turrets and the absence of large halls, may be contrasted with some of the Yorkshire sites. Moreover, the abbey was designed for a community of about thirty and remained for almost a century small and at times dwindling. Between the two world wars, however, there was a revival of life, and the numbers were more than doubled, with a consequent straggling growth and adaptation of buildings.

The church, of which the nave and tower (the latter not a primitive Cistercian feature) are recent work, is in the traditional position, but its internal ritual arrangements are quite out of tradition, the monks occupying the nave and crossing, and the architectural presbytery being given up as a lay church. The minute cloister is south of the nave, and the octagonal chapter-house, with its pointed roof, is in the traditional position, but Pugin set the refectory in the old monastic position along the south walk, with the dormitory above it, and the confused tangle of buildings does not therefore show the long lines of dorter and frater to which the Cistercian views

have accustomed us. Actually, Pugin's refectory is now the library, and a new refectory (with another dorter above) has been adapted out of farm buildings in the long composite building forming the eastern range. The abbot's lodging is in the western claustral range, and the wing extending to the south-west of the original refectory is the infirmary. The large block north of this and south-west of the west end of the church is the guest-house for visitors and retreatants. The lay-brothers' quarters are in the eastern part of the original refectory range. The monks' cemetery can be seen immediately south of this block. If the whole design is, architecturally speaking, more huddled and domesticized than a medieval abbey would have been, the layout of gardens, hedges, farm-buildings and the rest warns us that such a site as Byland would, in its heyday, have looked very different from its present aspect of smooth greenery.

68

DRYBURGH

PREMONSTRATENSIAN

The Premonstratensian Abbey of Dryburgh lies in rich, well-wooded parkland at a bend of the River Tweed; it is in Berwickshire, three miles east-south-east of Melrose and eight north-north-west of Jedburgh. Like Melrose, it is in the heart of exquisitely beautiful country, the scene of more than one episode of border history famed in ballad, and, in modern times, the landscape which more than any other formed the mind of, and was beloved by, Sir Walter Scott.

The house, the first Premonstratensian foundation in Scotland, was settled by canons from Alnwick in 1150; they came at the invitation of David I or his Constable, the Norman Hugh de Moreville. Within a few decades Dryburgh housed a spiritual master of distinction, Adam, who, though elected abbot, chose to become a Carthusian and migrated to Witham in Somerset, where he became the friend of St Hugh of Lincoln and the counsellor of Hubert Walter. Dryburgh, with its neighbours, suffered greatly at the hands of marauding English armies, and was ravaged by Edward II in 1322 and by Richard II in 1385. The house never wholly recovered, and early in the sixteenth century fell, like other Scottish abbeys, into the hands of Commendators, while in 1544 it was twice raided, once by the earl of Hertford and a second time by a band of Northumbrians. On the latter occasion both abbey and burgh were burnt out, and neither was rebuilt, though the community dragged on a tenuous existence till 1600.

The abbey was constructed of local stone of an unusually pure and rich texture and tint, and the architecture in general, like that of Melrose, was lighter and more English in character than that of more northerly churches. Little remains of the abbey kirk, which would appear to have retained its original dimensions throughout its history. The view, seen from the north-west, shows the aisled nave, somewhat wide for its length, and the transepts, each with two eastern chapels, those alongside the presbytery being longer by a bay's length. The presbytery was unaisled and relatively long. Within the church, the canons' quire, as can be seen, extended two bays west of the crossing. The claustral buildings owe their partial preservation to their occupation as a dwelling-house. The ground falls from north to south, and the unusual expedient was adopted of stepping the buildings at different levels; the cloister garth is lower than the church, and the floor of the eastern and southern ranges is 5 ft. below cloister level. Next to the transept came the library and vestry, then a parlour (these two rooms being now family burial places), then the large chapter-house, beyond which to the south lay the undercroft of the dorter, used as a warming-house and noviciate. The rere-dorter probably stood at right angles to the end of the range, where the well-marked channel of the leat from the Tweed can be seen.

Along the south walk lay the frater. This stood on two vaulted chambers which, like most of the eastern range, lay below the level of the cloister, the frater itself being approached by stairs and having screens at the west end with kitchens beyond. There was originally no western range, merely a wall, but later some cellars were constructed here. From the south-west angle of the frater a bridge led across the watercourse, with a small gatehouse on the further bank. The infirmary and prior's house have not been excavated; the former probably lay east of the southern part of the dorter range.

In a chapel on the north side of the presbytery lies the tomb of Sir Walter Scott, whose ancestors, the Haliburtons, had right of burial here; nearby in the transept is the vault of the Haigs of Bemerside, where the first Earl Haig is buried.

Full description, with photographs and plan, in *Berwickshire Inventory* of the Royal Commission on Historical Monuments (1915), pp. 132–48. There is a shorter account, with plan, in the *Guide* of the Ministry of Works by J. S. Richardson.

69

ALNWICK

PREMONSTRATENSIAN

THE PREMONSTRATENSIAN ABBEY OF ALNWICK lay on the left (north) bank of the River Aln, less than a mile above the town. The only building remaining above ground is the great gatehouse. The abbey was founded from Newhouse in 1147.

The precinct, which is seen from the east, was semicircular, with the river, which lies just off the plate to the left, as circumference and the precinct wall as diameter. A small portion of this wall is visible in the plate to the east of the gatehouse, between it and a dark tree. The gatehouse itself stands at the centre of the circle. The site was carefully excavated by W. H. St John Hope in 1884, at which time it was 'a perfectly level green field'. Since then, as can be seen, the 'ingenious application of concrete' employed by the sixth duke of Northumberland to mark the lines of the walls has somewhat suffered, but the main outlines can be distinguished. The plan presents several unusual features. The church consisted of a long aisled nave (the plinths of many of the columns are *in situ*), short and narrow transepts with eastern chapels, and a short presbytery. The canons' quire extended two bays westward of the crossing, and the lines of the foundations supporting the stalls, including the western return stalls, are visible.

Next to the south transept came sacristy and parlour, side by side, and then a chapter-house (earlier than 1184) of unique design, a rectangular apartment opening into a circular one. Hope declared that he could find no trace of the completion of the circle across the opening to the west, but it is possible that in fact a circular chapter-house was approached by a wide vestibule. To the south of the chapter-house was the warming-house, with the infirmary, and perhaps the abbot's house, to the east. The frater lay parallel to the south walk and, as often with the white canons, was on the first floor. The west walk of the cloister existed, but no trace of a western range was found, nor are there any traces of parched lines in the grass in this position. The guest-hall and offices were ranged round an outer court to the west. Lines of parched grass disclosing the outline of ranges of small rooms are visible to the south-west of the gatehouse; no doubt they formed the west and northern (return) ranges of this court. The line of wall-foundation touching the north-west angle of the nave is not medieval.

Detailed plan with description in *Archaeological Journal*, XLIV (1887), 337–46, by W. H. St J. Hope; reprinted in *Archaeologia Aeliana*, 2nd series, XIII, 1–10. The plan is reproduced on a smaller scale by A. W. Clapham in *Archaeologia*, LXXIII (1923), 130.

70

SHAP

PREMONSTRATENSIAN

THE REMAINS OF THE PREMONSTRATENSIAN ABBEY OF SHAP lie a mile to the west of the village of that name and some three miles north of the point where the main road and west coast main line of railway to the North cross the watershed of the fells at Shap summit. The Premonstratensians, particularly in England at the end of the twelfth century, chose of set purpose remote and wild situations for their abbeys, and this site in an upland valley on the left (west) bank of the Lowther not far from its source, must have satisfied their demands to the full. Indeed, it seems probable that it was in search of greater solitude that they left Preston, near Kendal, where they had been established shortly before their migration *c.* 1180.

The only notable part of the abbey to remain above ground is the western tower of the church, but the ruins were excavated by the young W. H. St John Hope in 1885. The church, as so often with the white canons, was of irregular plan. In its original form it had a short presbytery with a southern chapel or vestry alongside; transepts with two eastern chapels; and a nave with a northern (but not a southern) aisle. Fragments of the walls of nave and transepts, near the crossing, can be seen in the plate. The western tower, which stands to parapet height, was an addition *c.* 1500 (cf. the towers at Bolton and Fountains). The cloister lay in the normal position to the south; in the eastern range, after a narrow vestry or passage, came the large rectangular chapter-house, adjoining which to the south was the large warming-house; the southern end of this lay near the present north wall of the farm-yard. Over the whole range ran the dorter. At the end, running eastwards at right angles towards the river was the rere-dorter; some distance along this, at right angles to the south, the infirmary branched off under the present trees to the east of the pens of the sheepfold. The frater lay along the southern walk on an undercroft which still exists in large part beneath the farm-yard. The western range, containing guest-rooms over cellarage, ran from the north-east corner of the farm-house to the church; a large fragment of its eastern wall is visible. No trace remains of the buildings of the outer court or of the great gateway, which probably lay north-west of the church, but the wall seen in the plate above the wood to the east of the river is probably part of the medieval precinct-wall.

Description and plan by W. H. St J. Hope in *Transactions of the Cumberland and Westmorland Archaeological Society*, x (1889), 298–314: see also the *Westmorland Inventory* of the Royal Commission on Historical Monuments (1936), pp. 207–8, with a good plan.

71

BLANCHLAND

PREMONSTRATENSIAN

The Premonstratensian Abbey of Blanchland, and the modern village of that name, lie in a remote part of the valley of the Derwent, and on the left (north) bank of the river, which here forms the boundary between Northumberland and Durham. High moorlands surround it on every side, and in the Middle Ages it must have been one of the most isolated religious houses in the country. The abbey was small and poor, but it did not escape the ravages of the Scots shortly before 1327, when it was visited by Edward III. Though a lesser house, its remoteness allowed it to continue its existence till 1539. The church and most of the buildings were subsequently dismantled, but after lying in ruins for two centuries the presbytery and transepts were in 1752 reconditioned for service as the parish church, and have since received several alterations. The site has never been systematically excavated.

The buildings, as often in small Premonstratensian houses, do not conform to a typical plan. The quire, the earliest part of the fabric of the church, is small and aisleless; in the early thirteenth century a northern transept was built (or rebuilt), and later the existing tower, largely for defensive purposes. There is no evidence that a south transept was ever built. The nave was narrow and aisleless, at least on the south side. The cloister garth lay south of the church, where the lawn of the inn now lies, and the chapter-house and dorter no doubt lay along the east walk, while the frater occupied the site of the row of cottages to the south. The western range was early converted into a dwelling-house, and in modern times became the Crew Arms; its plan and interior preserve several medieval features; it was probably the guest wing. The medieval gatehouse, now separated from the western range, spans the roadway opposite the inn. The Shildon Burn bounded the precinct on the west, turning the abbey mill on its way to the Derwent, visible in the plate to the south of the site. The river formed the southern boundary.

Description, with plan by W. H. Knowles in *Archaeological Journal*, LIX (1902), 328–41.

72

EGGLESTON

PREMONSTRATENSIAN

THE PREMONSTRATENSIAN ABBEY OF ST MARY and St John the Baptist at Eggleston stands in surroundings of great beauty overlooking the dark waters of the Tees where they are joined by those of Thorsgill Beck. The district is peculiarly rich in romantic and literary associations. Eggleston lies midway between Barnard Castle and Rokeby, immortalized by Scott; Brignall Banks are only a few miles distant and nearby is Scargill, the home of Macaulay's exiled Jacobite. The ruins of Eggleston itself, seen from the river, were the subject of a well-known study by Turner.

The house was a relatively late foundation, in 1195–8, a daughter of the neighbouring St Agatha's. The buildings seen in the view from the west were comparatively small in scale, and, like so many Premonstratensian houses, show many minor deviations from the typical plan. The original church, built immediately after the foundation, was a small aisleless structure with a short presbytery. Rebuilding began within fifty years, when a longer and wider east end was constructed; next, the transepts were rebuilt, receiving eastern chapels, and the nave was widened. As the existing cloister prevented extension to the north, the widening was all on the south side, and the south transept is thus considerably longer than the northern. As for the nave, though widened, it was lengthened by only a few feet, and in consequence does not extend along the whole walk of the cloister. As can be seen, there are a number of grave slabs in the church.

The cloister was placed to the north of the church, no doubt as more convenient for the water supply and drainage. The eastern range, with the chapter-house and dorter, was converted into a Tudor dwelling-house, as the surviving windows and chimney show, and this in turn into a row of tenements which remained in occupation till about the beginning of the present century. When they were abandoned, much of the medieval masonry was taken for use elsewhere. At the end of the dorter and at right angles to it lay the rere-dorter; its subvault is extant and visible. The frater lay parallel to the north walk; at its north-west angle can be seen a fireplace of the kitchen. The western range presumably contained guest-rooms and cellars; as can be seen it lay considerably west of the west end of the church. No traces of the infirmary range and prior's lodging survive; if prevented by the lie of the land from being in the typical position east of the cloister, they may, as in other Premonstratensian houses, have lain either west of the cloister or south of the church beyond the transept. The ruins are now in the custody of the Ministry of Works.

There is a description, with plan, in *Victoria County History of Yorkshire: North Riding*, I (1914), 113–16; neither is wholly adequate.

73

EASBY

PREMONSTRATENSIAN

THE PREMONSTRATENSIAN ABBEY OF EASBY, or St Agatha juxta Richmond, lies on the left bank of the Swale one mile below Richmond in the North Riding. It was founded in 1152 and had an uneventful and undistinguished history till its suppression in 1535. The site was thoroughly investigated by W. St J. Hope in 1886 (one of his earliest major ventures) and is now in the custody of the Ministry of Works.

The plan is interesting on account of several unusual features. The inner precinct, covered with mown grass, is clearly distinguishable from the rough pasture surrounding it. The outer precinct, bounded by the river to the west, included the mill (obscured by the wing of the aircraft on the larger plate) and the triangle of land between the two roads and the river to the south. The parish church, which antedated the abbey, forms with its churchyard an enclave in the site. To the east of this lies the gatehouse.

While the position of the river, with its facilities for drainage, no doubt conditioned the eccentric position of the dorter, it is not clear why the church, on an unembarrassed site, was placed so far to the south, thus cramping all buildings beyond it in the direction of the parish church.

The church lies at the centre of the complex, with the cloister to the south and the infirmary range to the north. It originally consisted of a short aisleless quire, transepts with eastern chapels and aisled nave. The line of the original east end can be seen very faintly in the turf (larger plate), a little short of the higher walls of the late thirteenth-century presbytery; the sacristy to the south is also of later date, and the large chapel, with portions of its walls still standing, in the angle between the north transept and nave, dates from *c.* 1340.

The cloister lies to the south of the church. Instead of the normal rectangular plan, its shape is trapezoidal, the dimensions being: north side 98 ft., east 63 ft., south 82 ft. 6 in., west 100 ft. No obvious reason can be assigned for this, save the general consideration that Premonstratensian planning was very frequently unmethodical, and that there may have been an original error of judgment in siting the church too near the parish cemetery. Along the eastern walk of the cloister, beyond the transept, came a narrow sacristy and library, then a large chapter-house, of which the walls are still standing, and beyond it a square parlour, near which lay the entry to the cloister from the outer world. Owing partly, perhaps, to the lack of space but probably still more to considerations of drainage, no attempt was made to build the dorter in its usual place on the first floor of the eastern range; in its stead, in the fifteenth century, a set of well-appointed living rooms was constructed, and the

square chimney-like erection, which trespasses on the ground level on the floor space of the parlour, is the pit of a first-floor garderobe.

The fine two-storeyed building to the south is the frater, standing on a subvault. Its position is unusual in that it extends beyond the south walk of the cloister to the east, and terminates the eastern range at the point whence normally access was provided under the dorter to the infirmary and abbot's lodging. These as will be seen, are sited elsewhere. In the second bay from the east on the south wall of the frater the pulpitum or reader's desk can be seen (larger plate). In the north wall of the frater the two small doors led into the subvault; the large door in the seventh bay was the entrance to the frater, which was reached by a broad internal flight of steps giving access to the first floor outside the 'screens'. The kitchen ran south from the frater at right angles; the foundation of its southern wall can be seen in the grass in the smaller view.

The western range was long and lofty. On the ground floor to the south came the guest-hall, then cellarage and last (next to the church) the warming-house. Above, in the northern portion, lay the canons' dorter; to the south of this were private rooms for guests and canons. The building to the west of the western range still stands: it was of three storeys, viz., servants' hall, guests' solar, and private rooms: at all three levels access was provided to the three-storeyed rere-dorter which served the dorter also; it was flushed by the mill-race, which ran in a tunnel from the mill, under the rere-dorter and modern road, and emerged in an open channel, now concealed by bushes to the left of the dwelling-house at the top of the larger plate.

Owing to the eccentricities of plan already mentioned, the infirmary and abbot's lodging formed a large group to the north of the church and cut off by it from the cloister. Access from one side to the other lay either in an outdoor route round the west end of the church, or through the north transept, whence a door led to the infirmary. The long hall of the infirmary can be seen running eastwards from the range; at its west end, and at right angles, was the infirmary dorter, and at the far (north) end of the block, the kitchens. The abbot's lodging lay on the first floor between the infirmary and the north transept; the flues of two chimneys can be clearly seen. This whole block, of which other members can be traced in foundations, is perhaps unique in arrangement among excavated sites.

There is a description with plans by W. H. St J. Hope in *Yorkshire Archaeological Journal*, X (1887), 117–58; the plan is reproduced in *Archaeological Journal*, LXX, 332. The *Victoria County History of Yorkshire: North Riding*, I (1914), 53–9, recapitulates Hope's article with a plan.

74

COCKERSAND

PREMONSTRATENSIAN

THE SITE OF THE PREMONSTRATENSIAN ABBEY OF COCKERSAND is in striking contrast to those of the majority of its sisters. The house stood on the extreme seaward edge of the flat, salt-sodden moss between the estuaries of the Lune and the Cocker six miles south-south-west of Lancaster, where

'the bleak winds
Do sorely ruffle: for many miles about
There's scarce a bush.'

Founded in 1190, the house had an uneventful existence, and in spite of its remote situation, has disappeared more completely than most. Much of its masonry went to make a strong sea-wall that now borders the shore nearby, and other fragments have been traced in scattered farm-houses of the district. If the tradition is accepted that the quire-stalls in Lancaster church come from the abbey, this lonely group of buildings once housed what Francis Bond has called 'the *chef-d'œuvre* of English woodwork, wonderful alike in design and execution'.

The view shows the site, which is on the extreme left of the plate towards the foot, from the west. The only building intact is the hexagonal chapter-house, of unique design, which owes its preservation to its function as mausoleum for the Dalton family; it is indeed piled thick and deep with burials. The chapter-house is the isolated structure half-way between the farm-house and the foreshore, where two field-walls converge. The narrow church lay to the north (i.e. left) of the chapter-house, and a few fragments of the transept can be seen at the extreme edge of the plate. The west end lay a few feet short of the present foreshore, which in the Middle Ages was somewhat further west. The southern wall of the cloister, with fragments of the frater wall, have been traced; beyond them at the very edge of the herbage, is a piece of the building, formerly part of the guest-house, known as 'King John's Hall'. Just to the right of this, in the bank above the foreshore, the outlet of the great drain can be seen. The site has never been fully excavated.

Description and plan in *Transactions of the Lancashire and Cheshire Antiquarian Society*, XL (1922–3), 163–93.

75

WELBECK

PREMONSTRATENSIAN

THE PREMONSTRATENSIAN ABBEY OF WELBECK in Nottinghamshire, founded 1153–60, lay some four miles south-south-west of Worksop in the heart of Sherwood Forest. It had a peaceful and undistinguished existence, and its modest buildings at the Dissolution gave no hint of what was to come. Although the church and eastern range were soon destroyed, the southern range and the southern end of the dorter remained recognizable till the mid-eighteenth century, when modern Welbeck began to take shape at the direction of Lady Oxford, widow of the second Harley earl. It was not long before all landmarks were obliterated by the rising splendours of the dukeries. When the architect and landscape gardener had done, not a trace remained externally of the medieval past, though in fact a few vaults remained embedded like fossils in the great pile on which, with its hot-houses, its ballrooms, its stables, its covered equestrian exercise hall (of which the circular skylights can be seen in the plate) and its miles of underground passages several million pounds were spent in the mid-nineteenth century by the fifth earl of Portland.

The view looks towards the south-east angle of the mansion, of which the great east front stands along the line of the western range of the cloister; it is here that part of the vaulted undercroft still survives on ground level, in what is architecturally the basement of the modern house. The lawn in front of the east wing is roughly coincident with the cloister garth, which the abbey church closed to the north at the base of the present narrow plantation. A fragment of the west wall of the church is still in place in a basement room. The terrain of the precinct has been as thoroughly remodelled as the fabric; in addition to woods, terraces, gardens and subterranean adits the sight-screen of a cricket field can be seen to the south.

There is a partial plan in A. Hamilton Thompson's *The Premonstratensian Abbey of Welbeck* (1938), but the work is chiefly historical.

76

CROXTON

PREMONSTRATENSIAN

THE PREMONSTRATENSIAN ABBEY OF CROXTON in Leicestershire, founded *c.* 1150, lay near the crest of the ridge of high land eight miles south-west of Grantham on the road to Melton Mowbray, and four miles south of Belvoir Castle, from which a wide belt of parkland stretched to a hunting-box near the site of the abbey. The buildings above ground have disappeared to the last stone, but the site was excavated by the late duke of Rutland *c.* 1922, and a plan was drawn up by Sir A. W. Clapham. Like most Premonstratensian abbeys, it was of irregular plan, showing signs of more than one rebuilding. The cloister lay to the north of the church, and an extension of the north transept led to a transference of the dorter to the western range, where it lay over the warming-room, itself in an unusual position.

In the plate which shows the terrain from the east, the site of the abbey, which cannot be recognized by any markings, lay west of the long fence in the direction of the lakes, beyond the house with the high-pitched roof. The lines and mounds in the foreground have no connection with the conventual buildings, and may indicate the site of a medieval village displaced by the monks. The site of a large tithe barn is indicated here on the large-scale Ordnance maps.

Plan and short description by Sir Alfred Clapham in *Transactions of the Leicestershire Archaeological Society*, XXII, pt. iv (1945), 289–91. The description is reprinted from *Archaeologia*, LXXIII (1923), pp. 131–5.

77

BARLINGS

PREMONSTRATENSIAN

THE PREMONSTRATENSIAN ABBEY OF BARLINGS was the northernmost of the chain of religious houses which stood along the eastern margin of the fen that bordered the Witham in its course between Lincoln and Boston. The site, approachable from only one direction, lies at the end of a lane that diminishes to a farm-track some seven miles east of Lincoln. The abbey was founded from Newhouse in 1154.

The precinct, here seen from the south-south-east, is bounded to the east by a considerable stream; it was probably co-extensive with the large open area seen in the plate, around the greater part of which the course of a moat is visible, though here, as on many fenland sites, traces of dykes and ponds form a complicated pattern that defies interpretation. The entrance to the courtyard of the abbey probably lay at the end of the farm-track near the centre of the plate, where two cottages, partly built of ashlar and fragments of chiselled stone, stand among trees. The land is level and low-lying all around, but the church stood upon what is the highest point in the neighbourhood and even now the fragment of masonry is a landmark on every side, while from the site the towers of Lincoln cathedral are visible to the west and a wide horizon of fen to the south.

The masonry still remaining is part of the north wall of the nave, west of the crossing. As late as 1727, when Buck's drawing was made, a square pinnacled tower stood over the crossing; the masonry of the south-west pier is still visible in the turf, and the site of the other two angles is marked by heaps of debris. The tower had already fallen when Nattes made his drawing for Sir Joseph Banks in 1796. The cloister garth can be seen by visitors on the ground as a depression surrounded by mounds, and the excavation of the whole, which has never been attempted, would doubtless reveal the complete plan. As the plate shows, a deep channel penetrates the site to within a few yards of what may have been the kitchen to the south of the frater, but its date and function are uncertain. The long oblong depression parallel to the southern moat was doubtless a fishpond.

The last abbot of Barlings, Matthew Mackerel, for twelve years a suffragan of the bishop of Lincoln with the title of Chalcedon *in partibus*, was swept into the Lincolnshire rising of 1536 and was subsequently arrested with four of his canons. He was executed at Tyburn, and Barlings suppressed by attainder.

There is no plan or recent description.

78

TUPHOLME

PREMONSTRATENSIAN

The Premonstratensian Abbey of Tupholme in Lincolnshire, founded from Newhouse shortly before 1190, lay only some five miles distant in a direct line south-east of its sister Barlings. Half-way between the two Premonstratensian houses lay the large Benedictine Abbey of Bardney, which must have been in full view of Tupholme and within sound of its bells.

The view shows the site from the north-east. The precinct, which included a large part, if not all, of the wide central field, has certain clear limits, but, as at Barlings, the several channels are difficult to interpret and may be in some cases post-Dissolution.

The only fragment of the abbey now standing is the south wall of the frater, which forms a link between two small dwellings and serves as the northern side of a farm-yard. It contains the stairway and two graceful arches which gave access to the reader's *pulpitum*. The site of the cloister, barely distinguishable in the photograph, can be seen clearly on the ground to the north of the wall, as can also the main outline of the church, which is in the usual position north of the cloister. The moated site to the south-west, surrounded by trees and bushes, had no connection with the abbey and may be of later date. Beyond it to the south are several depressions, some still holding water, which may have been fishponds or millponds fed from a water-course which bounds the site to the south and flows into the Witham. Stukeley in 1726 gave an engraving of a gate-house, which has since entirely disappeared.

There is no plan or adequate description; some notes with a drawing are in *Lincs. Notes and Queries*, III (1892), 97–101, 153–5.

79

LEISTON

PREMONSTRATENSIAN

THE SITE OF THE PREMONSTRATENSIAN ABBEY OF LEISTON is some two miles from the Suffolk coast, five miles north of Aldeburgh and three and three-quarter miles east of Saxmundham. The house was founded by Ranulf de Glanville in 1182 nearer the sea, and was transferred hither and rebuilt in 1363, the structure incorporating considerable portions of the earlier buildings. A few years after the move, in 1389, the abbey was partially destroyed by fire. Considerable fragments remain, embodied in a farm-house and its outbuildings, and standing free.

Of the large church, which had an aisled nave and presbytery, with large chapels to north and south of the east end, only the transepts and eastern limb remain; they are seen in the plate from the north-west. The position of the west end of the church is marked by the site of the farm-house that faces the road. The cloister lay to the south; its site is now occupied by a kitchen garden. A sacristy adjoined the south transept; then came a large chapter-house and further down the range a warming-house; the dorter lay above. A portion of the rere-dorter is concealed by the elder bush in bloom in the plate. The frater, standing on an undercroft, lay along the whole of the south walk of the cloister; its west end containing a large window stands to roof-top height. The western range contained the cellar with guest quarters and abbot's lodging above. The turreted porch giving access to this and to the cloister is hidden by trees.

Plan and short description by Sir A. W. Clapham in *Archaeologia*, LXXIII (1923), 137–41.

80

BAYHAM

PREMONSTRATENSIAN

THE PREMONSTRATENSIAN ABBEY OF BAYHAM (Begham) was established on its present site shortly after 1207, having originally been settled at Otley (*c.* 1180), whence it had made a first move to Brockley. It was one of the houses suppressed by Cardinal Wolsey to augment the revenues of his new colleges in 1524.

The ruins are beautifully situated on the Sussex side of the Kent-Sussex border some four and a half miles south-east of Tunbridge Wells; the small river Teise flows nearby to the north (its bed hidden by bushes just off the plate) and formed the boundary of the precinct in this direction. The great gateway, partially extant, was approached by a bridge over the river (off the plate to the right); it now forms the entrance to a house formerly the residence of the owners of the property.

Bayham is notable for the size and unusual design of its church. It was originally planned and built after the normal Premonstratensian pattern: a long nave, possibly with north aisle, transepts (of which the northern one, if ever built, has left no trace above ground) and aisleless presbytery. Adjoining the church in the usual position to the south of the nave was the cloister. Late in the thirteenth century, however, the church was enlarged to the east by the addition of a second transept (with eastern chapels) and a presbytery ending in a semi-hexagonal apse (lying between the two trees in the photograph); aisles were also added connecting the two transepts. These additions gave the church an overall length of 257 ft.

The conventual buildings followed the normal arrangement. The eastern range, continuing the line of the original south transept, contained the sacristy, chapter-house and subvault of dorter. What appears in the plate as a dividing wall in the chapter-house is in reality masonry resting on an arcade of three arches. The frater, raised on a subvault, was entered from the cloister at its south-west angle; its south wall, with a single lancet remaining, can be seen in front of the dark trees. The western range formed the guest-hall. The infirmary and prior's lodging have disappeared; traces of what may be their foundations are visible in the grass to the south-east of the semicircular path.

Description and plan in *The Builder*, July 3, 1897; the plan is reproduced by Sir A. W. Clapham in *Archaeologia*, LXXIII (1923), 131.

81

ST RADEGUND'S

PREMONSTRATENSIAN

THE PREMONSTRATENSIAN ABBEY OF ST RADEGUND or Bradsole lay on high ground between Folkestone and Dover, two miles in a straight line from the coast. It was founded directly from Prémontré in 1191. It was excavated in 1880 by W. H. St J. Hope, being his second venture in this field (the first was at Dale Abbey, Derbyshire), but little care has been given to the ruins, and they still present the forlorn, ivy-bound appearance deplored by Hope. All the existing buildings (according to Hope's account) date from the first decades of the abbey's history. The church, which is seen in the plate from the north-east, is somewhat unusual in plan. The unique feature was the flint tower with elaborate buttresses, which has in the past been erroneously taken for a gatehouse; this stands in the angle between the nave and north transept. A long presbytery, of which the eastern part, visible in outline in the grass, east of the tower, was used as a Lady Chapel, was flanked by aisles shorter than itself; there were transepts with eastern chapels and a short, aisleless nave. Of the conventual buildings many walls remain to a considerable height, covered with a luxuriant growth of ivy. The chapter-house adjoined the south transept, and was followed in the eastern range by a parlour and warming-room; the infirmary hall projected eastwards, and a piece of its wall can be seen; over these ran the dorter; it is noteworthy that the same stairway in the south transept was used both by night and by day for access to the church and cloister. The frater, built on an undercroft, remains along what was the south walk of the cloister, though it has been converted into a farm-house. The western range appears to have contained guest-rooms. The large barn along the south side of the farm-yard is medieval. There are the remains of two gateways in what was the precinct wall—one beside the road in the foreground of the plate, near a tall tree, the other half-way up the plate on its left margin by an isolated tree near a well worn cart-track. The course of the precinct wall and ditch, and of other walls and water-courses, can be traced in the photograph for portions of their length.

Plan and description by W. H. St J. Hope in *Archaeologia Cantiana*, XIV (1882), 140–52.

82

TITCHFIELD

PREMONSTRATENSIAN

TITCHFIELD, an abbey of Premonstratensian canons near the Solent in Hampshire, two and a half miles from Fareham on the road to Southampton, was founded in 1231 and had a normal but uneventful life. At the suppression in 1537 it was immediately granted to Thomas Wriothesley, afterwards earl of Southampton, who proceeded forthwith to build a great mansion in and about the monastery, exploiting to the full all the possibilities of the church, though he found it necessary to pull down the great central tower to ensure that his chimneys should draw. Wriothesley's house was in its turn pulled down in 1781 by the then owner of the land, save for the great embattled gateway which still survives as a striking, if roofless, memorial to its builder. As the photograph shows, taken from the north-west, the site, in the midst of a plantation of fruit trees, has been partially cleared, and the lines of the buildings indicated.

The church, relatively small in scale (it was 190 ft. in length), was of a plan very similar to that of the early great Cistercian churches—an aisleless nave and presbytery; wide transepts with an eastern aisle containing chapels. Wriothesley's great gateway stands athwart the nave exactly in its midst; the bays to east and west were used as lodges. To the east of this the plan of the church can be seen with the position of the high altar marked. The cloister, which lay to the north, became the court of the Tudor mansion; the lines of the parlour, chapter-house (with the bases of columns) and warming-house can be seen. The subvault of the dorter continues the line of the eastern range under the trees, with the rere-dorter running east at right angles. The frater lay parallel to the north walk, and the cellarer's building completed the square.

There is a plan (by C. R. Peers) and a description of the Tudor mansion by W. H. St J. Hope in *Archaeological Journal*, LXIII (1906), 231–43.

83

TALLEY

PREMONSTRATENSIAN

The Premonstratensian Abbey of Talley in Carmarthenshire, some seven miles north of Llandilo, lies in a remote and beautiful landscape at the head of two lakes, from which the Welsh name of the abbey is derived. It was the only house of its order in Wales. Founded at an uncertain date towards the end of the twelfth century by Rhys ap Gruffydd, it was regarded with jealous eyes, if Gerald of Wales is to be believed, by the neighbouring Cistercians at Whitland, who succeeded in ejecting the canons *c.* 1200; when they won their way back in 1208 it was with reduced resources—a story that has found interesting confirmation in the course of recent excavations. The site came in 1933 under the care of the Commissioners of Works, who straightway carried out extensive excavations and consolidations, and purchased parcels of land on which some of the ruins lay.

The church, seen from the south-west, consisted of an aisleless presbytery, transepts, each with three easterly chapels, and a central tower over the crossing. Much of this still stands, and much more was standing at the beginning of the nineteenth century. The nave as originally planned was to have north and south aisles, and to extend to the edge of the road seen in the plate. The bases of the piers together with foundations of the south wall and part of the west wall exist. Excavation, has, however, shown that the north wall was never constructed, and a medieval cross wall, together with a blocking wall along the northern nave arcade, restricted the nave to less than half its proposed area, and left it with a south aisle only. As the masonry of the whole is of a single epoch, it seems clear that the reduction in scale of building was due to the early exile and misfortune already mentioned. A similar change of plan is apparent in the cloister. Foundations of the original western wall can be seen, together with the opening for a doorway in the south wall of the nave west of the cross-wall; further east, another wall can be traced, with an entrance to the nave east of the wall. The cloister in its final and reduced shape lay south of the reduced nave. Some of its area, and the site of the conventual buildings to the south and south-west of the garth, are still covered by farm buildings. One of the lakes can be seen beyond the modern parish church, and there appear to be traces of buildings or gardens in the pasture east of the ruins.

Description with plan of church by B. H. St J. O'Neil in *Archaeologia Cambrensis*, XCVI (1941), 69–108. An abbreviated version of this forms the *Guide* of the Ministry of Works.

84

BARDSEY

AUGUSTINIAN

THE AUGUSTINIAN ABBEY OF BARDSEY lay on the island of that name, separated by two miles of tide-race from Braich-y-pwll, the headland in Caernarvonshire that forms the northern limit of the bay of Cardigan. Though lying open to all the winds, which prevent the growth of any vegetation higher than thorn and short-cropped willows, the more level part of the island is fertile and, unlike so many of the western isles of Britain, still supports an industrious and contented community. The high (548 ft.) hill which forms a bastion to the north-east of the island gives an effective shelter against the bitter north-eastern *tramontana* of winter and also serves as a cushion against the sou'-wester.

From the earliest times of Celtic Christianity (fifth century) the island, like so many others, was a gathering-place of the culdees or Celtic monks, and, as its name suggests, many of them—many thousands, according to legend—found their last resting place there. At some unspecified moment in the thirteenth or early fourteenth century the culdees adopted the Rule and external style of Augustinian canons, but how far this implied a change in their traditional way of life is quite uncertain. Nothing of the abbey, which was probably small and irregular in design, now remains save the ruins of the base of a thirteenth-century tower, which stands near the modern chapel and school-house towards the north of the island, at the foot of the slope of the hill.

In the photograph the island is seen from the south-west, with the promontory of Caernarvonshire beyond. In the first bay to the east of the point (to the right on the plate) is the little haven of Aberdaron, whence pilgrims of old, and the motor-boat to-day, pass over to Bardsey when weather permits. The hills in the extreme distance are the Rivals, beyond Nevin. To the right, just off the plate, is Pwllheli.

There is a historical account of Bardsey in *Archaeologia Cambrensis*, 7th ser., VI (1881), 340 ff.; for a vivid description of the island in recent years, with map, see R. M. Lockley, *I know an Island* (London, 1938), pp. 110–26.

85

CAMBUSKENNETH

AUGUSTINIAN

THE AUGUSTINIAN ABBEY OF CAMBUSKENNETH lies three-quarters of a mile east of Stirling, beyond and within a bend of the River Forth, which can be seen in the foreground of the plate. It was founded by King David in 1147 for Arrouasian canons, and had a distinguished place in Scottish church history; in particular, some of its latest abbots, such as Patrick Panter (*ob.* 1519) and Alexander Milne (*ob.* 1542), were eminent figures in political and diplomatic life. It was destroyed in the religious rivalry of 1559.

Nothing of any importance remains above ground save the detached bell-tower, which stood at the north-west angle of the nave. The church, 178 ft. in length, consisted of a nave with northern aisle, transepts with eastern chapels, and a short presbytery. The canons' quire extended into the nave and the foundations of the quire screen are visible in the plate. The railed enclosure in the presbytery contains the medieval tomb of James III before the high altar; the monument erected by Queen Victoria to the king in 1865 lies alongside to the north.

The cloister is unusually small, and as a result the transept, sacristy and chapter-house occupy the whole of the eastern range; the foundations of the refectory can be seen along the south walk. Between the abbey and the river are numerous traces of buildings as yet unexcavated. Those east of the cloister in the middle of the meadow are probably infirmary and abbot's house; those to the south, with eastern wall standing, may represent the guest-hall.

There is no recent description or plan. For an old account see *Proceedings of the Society of Antiquaries of Scotland*, VI (1866), 14–33.

86

JEDBURGH

AUGUSTINIAN

THE AUGUSTINIAN ABBEY OF JEDBURGH stood within the medieval town, on a site sloping southwards to the Jed Water. Modern alterations to the road, and the establishment of a large rayon works, have deprived the ruins of the amenities afforded elsewhere by a spacious and peaceful precinct.

The house was founded in 1138 by that great benefactor of the Church, David I, near his castle, and transferred to the site of the present kirk *c.* 1145. A church, built *c.* 1080, was already in existence, and the foundations that have been discovered of the canons' first cloister show that it was considerably smaller than that constructed later. The present kirk, which is almost exactly orientated, is roofless, and its east end is incomplete, but much of the rest stands as a fine example of the Anglo-Scottish style of architecture which distinguishes the great churches of the Tweed basin. It has a long aisled nave, used for a time as the parish kirk, but abandoned in 1875; the presbytery is flanked with chapels and may originally have ended in an apse. Some of the work in presbytery and crossing is pure Norman, while much of the rest is transitional. In the ground plan the transepts scarcely project beyond the outer walls of the nave, but externally short transepts of a single bay would have appeared. The building visible on the north side is not, architecturally speaking, part of the transept, but a self-contained mausoleum of the Catholic Ker family (marquess of Lothian).

In the cloister garth the beds as laid out represent the first cloister. The west wall of the later cloister ran west of the isolated oblong bed, and its south walk was bounded by the second of the southern walls, reckoning from the church. The ground falls steeply here, and the foundations lie in terraces. It seems clear that the frater, parallel to the south walk, extended considerably to the south of the first undercroft. The chapter-house, in the eastern range, was apsidal. Any buildings, such as the infirmary block, which may have existed to the east of the eastern range, have been partially covered by the roadway and the ramp upon which the War Memorial stands.

Plan of church and brief description in *Archaeological Journal*, XCIII (1936), 329–30. The Royal Commission on Historical Monuments of Scotland is shortly to publish a volume on Roxburghshire.

87

BRINKBURN

AUGUSTINIAN

BRINKBURN, a priory of Austin canons, stands within a sharp bend of the River Coquet, some eleven miles south-south-west of Alnwick in Northumberland. The situation is beautiful in the extreme, as the photograph, which has something of the texture of a painting, shows well. Indeed, the exterior of the church and its roof, the result of energetic, not to say ruthless, reconditioning in 1858, are somewhat flattered by the camera, appearing less hard and toneless than when seen by the spectator on the ground.

The house was founded *c.* 1135, but the church, which resembles Hexham in plan, was not rebuilt till 1195–1220. The interior remains in essentials as then completed; it is a beautiful example of late transitional architecture. The cloister was in the normal position, but the only walls visible are those of the vestibule to the chapter-house. The undercroft of the frater, which was parallel to the south walk of the cloister, is embedded in the cellarage of the modern mansion.

The intake of the mill-race, which passed underground south of the frater, can be seen near the corner of the house; it doubtless served as the main drain. The cottages in the wood downstream mark the site of the priory mill. As the canons had the pastoral care of a small district, their church escaped destruction at the Dissolution and remained a chapelry until recent times.

Plan and description by J. C. Hodgson in *History of Northumberland*, VII, 478–87.

88

LANERCOST

AUGUSTINIAN

THE AUGUSTINIAN PRIORY OF LANERCOST lies some eleven miles north-east of Carlisle, on the right bank of the River Irthing, and a little south of the line of Hadrian's Wall. The house was founded *c.* 1160, but the church and other extant buildings are almost entirely of a single period, viz. the early thirteenth century. Lying near the Border, and near the main west coast route to Scotland, Lanercost attracted both distinguished travellers and marauding Scots. It was raided in 1296 and still more severely in 1346. Shortly before the first raid in 1280, Edward I and Queen Eleanor were its guests, and in 1306 the same king, now mortally sick, stayed there for six months, leaving only to go to his death at Burgh. At the Dissolution the nave of the canons' church was preserved for the parish, the rest being dismantled, and part of the monastic buildings was converted into a residence by the grantee, Sir Thomas Dacre. The site, seen in the view from the south-west, has recently passed into the control of the Ministry of Works, who have excavated the eastern range.

The church, which retained its original form without alteration, had a presbytery flanked by two short aisles opening out of the eastern aisle of the transepts. The nave, as often in Augustinian houses, had an aisle to the north only. The western front is a composition of notable, if severe, beauty. The eastern range of the cloister originally contained the chapter-house and subvault of the dorter, but in the fifteenth century a large and presumably lofty new chapter-house was built clear of the range to the east. The rere-dorter and infirmary, which probably extended to the east of the dorter, have left no traces above ground; the lines of the vegetable garden should not be mistaken for foundations. Along the south walk the undercroft of the frater is in perfect preservation. The western range, which contained cellarage on the ground floor and the prior's lodging above at the southern end, was remodelled by Thomas Dacre, who converted the first floor into the long and splendid Dacre Hall, and added the so-called Dacre tower at the south end. West of this range at its northern end, and now without physical connection with it, is a tower of Edwardian date, which may well have been the king's lodging on his second visit; it now forms part of the vicarage. The outer court lay to the north-west of the church, and was bounded by the road. The base of a cross, visible in the open space north of the west front, marks the site of a privileged market or fair held in the precinct. The remains of the beautiful medieval gatehouse, now giving access to the church by a drive across the meadow, are not included on the plate.

There is a long historical account with remarkably good photographs in the *Transactions of the Cumberland and Westmorland Archaeological Society*, I (1870), 95–137; there is a short account *ibid.*, New Series, XXVI (1926), 255–61; and a still shorter notice, by A. Hamilton Thompson, in the *Archaeological Journal*, XCVI (1939), 323, with a good plan.

89

KIRKHAM

AUGUSTINIAN

KIRKHAM, a priory of Austin canons some twelve miles north-east of York on the road to Malton, was founded *c.* 1122 by Walter L'Espec, soon to become founder also of Rievaulx. Kirkham speedily became and long remained one of the most important houses of canons in the North, but in its first decades it felt the pull of the newly arrived Cistercian way of life, and all but transferred itself bodily to the new order. In the event, no change of allegiance was made, though Waldef, the saintly prior, half-brother to King David of Scotland, joined Rievaulx, together with some companions, and later became second abbot of Melrose.

The site, excavated and controlled by the Ministry of Works, lends itself excellently to aerial photography; the present view is taken from the west-north-west. It is bounded on the south-west, beyond the precinct wall, by the River Derwent. The plan abounds in abnormalities, great and small, some explained by the architectural history of the place, some perhaps due to difficulties of site; not all of these can be seen in the photograph.

Entrance to the precinct was by a large and beautiful gatehouse, seen in the view above the river-meadow and opposite a large farm. The unusual appearance of the plan of the church is due to successive rebuildings. The original church of 1140 had an aisleless nave, broad transepts, each with two eastern chapels, and a short presbytery. The nave was rebuilt in 1180, but almost the only important addition was the doorless west front with two towers; part of the wall of the southern tower can be seen. Fifty years later rebuilding on a grand scale was undertaken, beginning from the east, and the short aisleless presbytery was replaced by a great aisled choir and presbytery, with an ambulatory and chapels at the square east end, suggesting the architectural influence of Fountains, which embarked upon a similar scheme about the same time, or of Durham, the ultimate parent of the plan. This new work, which in area was roughly equal to the original nave and transept combined, was not carried further than the west end of the quire, but large piers were constructed (of which that at the north-east angle of the crossing can be clearly seen in the photograph) to carry a great central tower, which was never constructed. This would have necessitated the realignment of the east walk of the cloister; in consequence, the chapter-house, built at the same time as the quire, was set some ten feet to the east of the

original wall of the cloister. The cluster of small rooms to the north and west of the north transept were later additions, giving accommodation to the sacrist and the like.

The cloister has several irregular features, some of which are visible in the photograph; in particular, the slightly oblique angle at which the frater and south walk are set. The original small chapter-house and dorter along the east wall were demolished as obstructing the site of the great new chapter-house, and traces of the line of the original east wall of this dorter can be seen crossing the floor of the chapter-house. The new dorter was built in a somewhat abnormal position running south at a slight angle (perhaps due to the sharp fall of the ground) from the south-east angle of the cloister. As a cross-piece to it, but again not exactly at right angles, stands the two-storied rere-dorter, the walls of which, still standing, are clearly distinguishable. In a north-easterly continuation of this, and forming the arc of a large circle, are the foundations of the prior's lodging (excavated) and infirmary (visible under herbage). The building jutting out westwards towards the chapter-house was the misericord, where meat was provided on certain occasions and to certain classes in the later centuries of the Middle Ages. Returning to the cloister, the long frater is seen parallel to the south walk and standing on a subvault. The large square room external to it at the south-west angle is the kitchen, with the guest-house, half hidden in shadow, running back towards the rere-dorter. The western range, if ever built, has disappeared. The wall seen in that position in the photograph is post-medieval.

There is a plan and description of Kirkham in the *Guide* of the Ministry of Works, by Sir C. R. Peers.

90

BOLTON

AUGUSTINIAN

THE AUGUSTINIAN PRIORY OF BOLTON was situated some six miles from Skipton on the road to Harrogate, in the West Riding of Yorkshire; it has been for centuries, and still is, popularly known as Bolton Abbey, though never of abbatial rank. It lies among surroundings of exquisite beauty beside the River Wharfe, a little below the spot where the stream, issuing from the high moorland about Great Whernside, and escaping from the narrow wooded valley through rocks which approach one another to form the Strid, flows swiftly but smoothly with amber waters over a wide and stony bed. Across the river a cliff, rising steeply above the eastern bank, frames an expanse of verdant parkland. The scene, with its associations of religion and romance, has been immortalized by Girtin, by Ruskin and by Wordsworth.

The house was an early plantation of regular canons, founded from Huntingdon in 1121 at Embsay near Skipton, and transferred to a more sheltered and fertile site shortly after 1154. Though never distinguished by wealth or numbers or fervour, the canons, on several different occasions, commanded the services of master-masons of unusual talent, and the church takes a very high place among the monuments of Gothic genius.

As often, the existing fabric, here seen from the south-west, is the result of successive rebuildings. The original church was small, probably with a short presbytery and aisleless nave. The nave was partially rebuilt in the thirteenth century, with a north aisle, and in the fourteenth the spacious and beautiful presbytery was added, and the transepts reconstructed or at least refashioned. As a result, the church was larger than the original designers of the cloister had intended, and the south transept ran along almost the whole length of the eastern walk, thus thrusting the conventual buildings in this range to a site south of the cloister. To add to the irregularity, the axes of the transepts are not perpendicular to the main axis of the church, but have an easterly cant; this is emphasized in the south transept and is continued along the whole line of the eastern range. Next to the south transept is the vestibule leading to the chapter-house which is clear of the range to the east. This, a fourteenth-century building replacing one within the range, is of unusual design, octagonal in shape (cf. Thornton, p. 200; Whalley, p. 102, and Margam, p. 120), and must have been a very beautiful structure. Beyond to the south stretched the undercroft of the dormitory, with the rere-dorter at right angles. The dorter range is continued to the south by the new lodging for the prior, contemporary with the presbytery and chapter-house. In the photograph this is obscured by trees and their shadows. Beyond this again, slightly to the west, and now without physical connection with the

range, is a two-storied medieval building, known as the Boyle Room from its use as a school-room in the Boyle foundation. This, it is conjectured, may have been the infirmarian's lodging, the infirmary hall having been destroyed to make way for the adjoining house, now the rectory. The markings in the meadow to the south-east of the eastern range are the foundations of post-Dissolution cottages.

The south range was occupied by the frater, which stood above cloister level on an undercroft and was reached by stairs from the west walk. The western range, which was unusually lofty, contained cellarage on the ground floor and the original prior's lodging above. This range, as often in canons' houses, extended west of the original west end of the church, but the angle was later more than filled by the massive base of a western tower of excellent design begun by the last prior, Richard Mone, in 1520 and left unfinished at the suppression. The architect's intention was to incorporate the tower into the church by removing the original west end, but here again the suppression came too soon, and in consequence the original west front, itself an unusually successful composition, remains *in situ*. The nave is in use as the parish church.

Besides the buildings described, some other medieval appurtenances, not visible in the plate, are still extant. These include the magnificent gatehouse, which forms the nucleus and most imposing feature of Bolton Hall, and the abbey mill. The white objects in the river-bed are bathers.

For everything connected with Bolton Priory, see the monograph by A. Hamilton Thompson, *The Priory of St Mary, Bolton-in-Wharfedale* (Thoresby Society, XXX (1928)), which contains full historical and architectural accounts, in addition to a plan and numerous illustrations.

91

THORNTON

AUGUSTINIAN

THE AUGUSTINIAN ABBEY OF THORNTON, founded *c.* 1139 by William le Gros, earl of Albemarle, at the advice of his kinsman, St Waldef, later second abbot of Melrose, was colonized from Waldef's priory of Kirkham in Yorkshire. It was a house of some consequence and considerable wealth, lying four miles from the south bank of the Humber immediately south of Kingston-upon-Hull. The church and some of the conventual buildings, partially covered by those of a modern farm, have recently been excavated by the Ministry of Works.

The church, a large cruciform structure replacing a smaller one, was 282 ft. long internally with transepts of 127 ft. A Lady Chapel was added east of the presbytery *c.* 1400; this was of unusual size (70 ft.) and would have made of Thornton the largest conventual church in the county. Nothing now stands above ground save the south wall of the south transept and part of the adjacent chapter-house.

The almost vertical view, taken from the east-north-east, shows clearly the plan of the church, with the bases of the piers and the tomb-slabs, many of which have been identified. The wall behind the high altar is visible; the Lady Chapel was entered through a narrow doorway in the eastern wall of the church. The foundations north of the presbytery are those of the chapel of St Thomas. In the angle between the south transept and the chapter-house the small dark chamber was probably the treasury.

The cloister lay to the south of the nave, with the dorter at first-floor level in the eastern range. The octagonal chapter-house, of which two sides remain, was begun in 1282, and is one of a relatively small class of which other examples are at Worcester (p. 10), Margam (p. 120), Bolton (p. 197) and Cockersand (p. 164). The frater lay along the south walk; the site of the infirmary is probably occupied by the farmyard.

The oblique view, taken from a point slightly north of west, gives a good prospect of the surroundings of the site. Almost due west of the church, and more than 200 yards from it, stands the massive gatehouse, one of the finest examples of its type in England. Built soon after 1382, when licence to crenellate was obtained, it is one of the earliest large buildings in the country to be constructed of brick; it contained elaborate apartments used as the abbot's lodging, and was strongly fortified. The sixteenth-century brick barbican was probably added by an Elizabethan owner. A precinct wall and exterior moat, traceable in part in the photograph, enclosed a large area. The fields around the abbey show a multitude of markings which have not yet been interpreted. The four depressions surrounded by a ditch in the third field to the south-east of the site, at the top of the plate, were doubtless fishponds; the ground falls here to a brook beyond a field-road visible in the plate.

Short description by A. W. Clapham in *Archaeological Journal*, CIII (1946), 172–4; plan of gateway *ibid.*, LXVI (1910), 358–9. The *Guide* of the Ministry of Works (1951, but not brought fully up to date) covers both abbey and gateway.

92

NEWSTEAD

AUGUSTINIAN

THE AUGUSTINIAN PRIORY OF NEWSTEAD lay nine miles north of Nottingham in the southern limits of Sherwood Forest. It was one of the houses founded by Henry II shortly after 1170 in expiation for the murder of Archbishop Thomas. Like its neighbours in the Dukeries, Welbeck and Rufford, it became a great house, with parkland and formal gardens; it has a certain celebrity as the property and home for a short space of Lord Byron.

The mansion is seen from the west; the church has disappeared, save for the west front, but the cloisters and conventual buildings exist almost complete, woven with considerable skill and taste into a great country house in the nineteenth century. It is now the property of the City of Nottingham, and parts of it are let as flats.

The original church was narrow and aisleless, with short transepts and presbytery. A century later, 1280–90, the nave was rebuilt with a northern aisle and a remarkably fine west front. It will be noted that the west front contains three compartments, as if covering nave and aisles, whereas in fact the north walk of the cloister lay behind the south compartment. Whether the expedient was adopted to give balance to the composition, or whether it was intended to rebuild the cloister and provide a south aisle is not known. The east end was also enlarged, but as no excavations have been undertaken the dimensions of the new presbytery cannot be known. The monument with a circular base erected by the poet Byron to the memory of his dog, was said to cover the site of the high altar; more probably, it marks the line of the east end.

The south transept exists, divided into rooms; the ground floor was, till recently, used as a billiard-room; next came the parlour and then the fine rectangular vaulted chapter-house, long used as a domestic chapel. Then, after a passage to the infirmary, came the warming-house. The frater lay along the south walk on an undercroft of plain, almost severe vaulting; the floor of the undercroft was below ground level. The frater became the drawing-room of the mansion, and the undercroft the servants' hall. Beside the south-western angle the modern kitchen can be seen, with octagonal roof and central louvre clearly modelled on Glastonbury; it occupies the site of the canons' kitchen. The western range had cellarage on the ground floor with the prior's lodging above. The infirmary lay immediately to the south-east of the cloister, where is now a rose garden. The great outer court lay west of the church.

Description, with plan, by A. Hamilton Thompson in *Transactions of the Thoroton Society*, 23 (1919), 112–141.

93

HAUGHMOND

AUGUSTINIAN

THE AUGUSTINIAN ABBEY OF HAUGHMOND in Shropshire, some four miles north-east of Shrewsbury, stands on a site sloping gently from east to west and north to south below a rising wood; as the photograph shows, the ruins, beautiful in their architecture, are rendered still more attractive by the meadows and trees that surround them. The house was founded *c.* 1130–8, and was one of the relatively few houses of Augustinian canons of abbatial rank. It remained throughout comparatively well-to-do, and as one of the larger houses it survived till 1539, when it was surrendered by eleven signatories. The plan of the whole has been recovered by excavation, and has many features of interest.

The church, which is in the foreground of the view and lies almost exactly east and west, evolved by three main stages. The first building was on a very modest scale, and probably no more than presbytery and transepts had been finished when it was decided to make a more ambitious start; this first building lay alongside of the later church to the south, and traces of the foundation of the presbytery can be seen running from the cloister across the later south transept. The second church, long and aisleless with transepts having eastern chapels, was then built to the north and east; as the site sloped considerably from east to west the quire was six feet above the level of the nave, and the footpace of the high altar almost the same height above the quire. These changes of level can be clearly seen in the photograph. In the centre of the presbytery can be seen two grave slabs of the thirteenth century: they are those of John FitzAlan and Isabel de Mortimer. The nave, a late twelfth-century work, has vanished, save for the processional doorway opening into the west walk of the cloister; this, identifiable in the photograph by the white mortar over the arch to the right of the dark tree in the garth, is late Romanesque and richly ornamented. The grave visible in the centre of the nave is that of Ankeret, daughter of John Leighton (*ob.* 1528). In the thirteenth century an aisle was added to the nave on the north; the bases of three of the piers of the arcade can be seen in the grass; the existing cloister prevented a similar extension on the south.

The cloister was in the usual position south of the church. The chapter-house, separated from the transept by a vestry, is still in part standing, and the west front pierced by a triple Romanesque doorway, can be seen in the photograph. The other walls of the existing fabric are mainly those of a post-suppression building, covered by a wooden ceiling brought from some other room and surmounted by a modern roof. Continuing the range southwards at a slight angle was the warming-house and other rooms, of which the foundations remain, and the bases of the columns supporting the roof; over the whole was the canons' dorter. At the end of the range, at

a return angle, can be seen the foundations of the rere-dorter, with the stone channel enclosing the usual stream of water. This position of the rere-dorter is unique among known plans. The frater stood on cellarage slightly above cloister level and parallel to the south walk; the bases of the supporting columns can be seen; the west wall and part of the south wall are standing. Beyond the frater was an inner court, shut in by the dorter to the east and the kitchens to the west; one of the great fireplaces of the latter is visible, and above it, level with the top of the wall, the vents of the two flues. Along the south side of the inner court lies the great infirmary hall of the early thirteenth century, a noble building with a fine west window. The building adjoining it to the east is the abbot's lodging, with its southern wall standing to roof level. The wall beyond it is modern, and the medieval precinct wall does not survive above ground, though the meadows to the south-west show many markings, some of which may conceal foundations. After the Dissolution many of the buildings, including the infirmary hall and abbot's lodging, were converted into a mansion, which was, so it would seem, completely destroyed by fire during the civil war.

The whole site was methodically excavated by W. St J. Hope and H. Brakspear in 1907. It has recently passed into the custody of the Ministry of Works, and excavations were still being conducted when the photograph was taken.

There is a large plan and full description by W. H. St J. Hope and H. Brakspear in the *Archaeological Journal*, LXVI (1910), 281–310.

94

LILLESHALL

AUGUSTINIAN

THE AUGUSTINIAN ABBEY OF LILLESHALL lies some five and a half miles east-north-east of Wellington (Salop) on the road to Newport. It was founded *c.* 1144–8. The view, taken from the south, shows the ruins, which have not been excavated, in a picturesque but very overgrown condition. The walls still stand to a considerable height, especially in the eastern parts. The church was long (207 ft.), but aisleless from end to end. There was a tower at the crossing, and another, as frequently with the canons, at the west end; each transept had a chapel flanking the presbytery.

The plan of the eastern range can be made out by visitors on the ground, but in this case is not so clear from the air; the wall seen in the plate half-way along the range is the southern wall of the chapter-house. The frater is still above ground along the south walk of the cloister. There is a tradition that the fine carved stalls now in Wolverhampton parish church were taken thither from Lilleshall at the Dissolution.

Short description, without plan, by M. R. James in *Abbeys* (Great Western Railway, 1925), pp. 137–8.

95

LLANTHONY

AUGUSTINIAN

THE REMAINS OF THE AUGUSTINIAN PRIORY OF LLANTHONY in Monmouthshire lie on the north-eastern slope of a remote and beautiful valley which runs up into the heart of the Black Mountains some nine miles north of Abergavenny. The photograph, which is taken from the north, gives no impression of the steep gradient of the hillside or of the confined space of the valley, on either side of which rise spurs 2000 ft. in height. Remote as the site is, it can never have fully deserved the descriptions of twelfth-century writers, which would suggest a site resembling that of the Hospice on the Great St Bernard.

The house was founded in 1103 by a small group of hermits, whose fervour soon attracted others, and before long it had given to Hereford as bishop its saintly prior, Robert of Bethune. Fifty years later its religious observance and hospitality received warm praise from Gerald of Wales, who compared it with abbeys of the black and white monks, to their disadvantage. Before that, Welsh raids had driven the canons to Gloucester, where their temporary refuge, on the east bank of the Severn, just outside the city, became Lantony the Second (p. 210), which in time eclipsed the mother house in wealth and numbers.

Considerable portions of the church are still standing; there is an aisleless presbytery, flanked by chapels, and small transepts with a tower at the crossing; these have been dated *c.* 1180–90; also an aisled nave of *c.* 1210 with two western towers, both of which survive as to their base. The cloister lay to the south. In the eastern range, the apsidal chapter-house can be seen in part; to the south, a few fragments of the north wall of the frater which stood on an undercroft, are extant; the western range, consisting of cellarage and canons' dorter, is incorporated in the dwelling-house now used as the Abbey Hotel, a resort well known to anglers. South of the cloister, and lying beyond the approach to the hotel, are the infirmary and its chapel, now used as nave and chancel of the parish church.

Short description by M. R. James in *Abbeys* (Great Western Railway, 1925), pp. 133–4, with plan. For an architectural account, with plans and excellent photographs, by E. W. Lovegrave, see *Archaeologia Cambrensis*, XCIX (1947), 64–74.

96

LANTONY

AUGUSTINIAN

MONASTIC RUINS IN BRITAIN are for the most part situated on sites of considerable natural beauty; the remains of Merton (Surrey) and Lewes (Sussex) which have been disturbed by a line of railway, are exceptional. An example of a less fortunate house, Lantony priory, on the south-western outskirts of Gloucester, is included to show a site that has been hardly treated by modern industry.

Lantony *secunda*, as it was called, was founded *c.* 1134 by Milo of Gloucester as a refuge for the canons of Llantony in the Black Mountains (p. 208) who were being harassed by the Welsh; the two houses grew jointly till 1203, when a partition was made and both remained independent for the rest of their existence; *Lantonia secunda*, by reason of its situation and endowment, grew to be the more important of the two, and is familiar to antiquarians owing to the action of its last prior, who salved the conventual library at the Dissolution, the books ultimately accruing to the library of Lambeth Palace, where they remain.

The view, taken from the west, shows the gateway and ancient precinct wall bordering a road in the foreground. In the centre of the site is a house embodying medieval work, possibly the guest-rooms; to the right (south) is a roofless barn, containing some medieval work, while to the left (north) another and larger roofless barn is wholly medieval. The cloister and its buildings have vanished; the eastern walk probably lay almost along the line of the canal bank, partially under a large warehouse. What was thought to be the base of the walls of the quire of the church was discovered and removed during the construction of the Berkeley-Gloucester ship canal (1816–26); the east end would consequently lie in the bed of the canal at the north end of the warehouse. The priory had previously suffered during the siege of Gloucester in 1643, when the tower was destroyed.

There is no accurate description of Lantony, but there is an interesting account of the site as it was a century ago, with a sketch plan, in *The Priory of Llanthony*, by J. Clarke (Gloucester, 1853). Short notes in M. R. James, *Abbeys* (1925), pp. 134–5.

97

KENILWORTH

AUGUSTINIAN

THE AUGUSTINIAN PRIORY OF KENILWORTH in Warwickshire was founded *c.* 1125; it became an abbey *c.* 1450, and though never very wealthy or distinguished, derived a certain importance from the proximity of the royal castle of which the ruins lie one-third of a mile to the west. It is probable that the parish church of St Nicholas, seen to the right of the plate, was built by the canons shortly before *c.* 1280 to relieve their church of lay people; the parish graveyard lay north of the abbey church, and the progressive extensions of its area in 1840 and 1886–7 led to the first excavations, culminating in 1890 in the uncovering of the nave and north transept. The graveyard was then enclosed by a wall, the line of which was followed by a public footpath, both passing over the site of the frater, garth, crossing and quire of the abbey. Further investigation was thus seriously handicapped, and the careful work undertaken in 1922–3 was necessarily confined to the area on the hither side of the path.

The view, taken from the south-east, shows clearly the outline of the church. Originally built to a normal Augustinian plan with narrow nave and transepts and short presbytery, it was rebuilt gradually from the thirteenth century on a scale of some magnificence. The original presbytery was replaced by a quire with aisles and north and south chapels alongside, and later still a long and narrow presbytery (perhaps partly in ritual use as a Lady Chapel) was thrown out eastwards. The existing cloister prevented, and the provision of a parish church rendered unnecessary, a similar enlargement of the nave. There was no western tower, but foundations of an octagonal building, thought to be a campanile, were found in 1840 near the north-west angle of the nave.

In the eastern range, fragments of the wall of the apsidal Norman chapter-house are conspicuous, separated by a slype from the south transept. South of the chapter-house, foundations of the original dorter were found, and it was the opinion of the late Sir Harold Brakspear that the dorter was on the ground floor. A later southward extension of the dorter stood on a subvault, but as the ground falls steeply, the level of the new dorter was only a few feet above that of the cloister. A large rere-dorter was found at the extreme end of the range at right angles to the new dorter, and traces of an earlier one near the end of the old dorter; these and extensive foundations of the infirmary to the east of the range were excavated and covered in, and are invisible under crops. The east end of the frater, which stood on a subvault, was excavated as far as the footpath, but the remainder of the buildings to south and west were

inaccessible. At the south-west corner of the nave a room excavated in 1890 was identified as the outer parlour; west of this lay the outer court to which access was obtained through the great gatehouse at its north-west angle (visible in the plate as an ivy-clad ruin). At the south-west corner of the court stood another building, identified as the guest-house, which can be seen in the plate on the opposite side of the trees from the gatehouse.

Full description and plan, by E. Carey-Hill, in *Transactions of the Birmingham Archaeological Society*, LII (1927; published 1930), 184–228.

98

MAXSTOKE

AUGUSTINIAN

THE SITE OF THE AUGUSTINIAN PRIORY OF MAXSTOKE lies some eight miles in a direct line due east of the city centre of Birmingham, in the as yet unspoilt landscape of north Warwickshire. It was one of the very latest of the houses of canons to be founded, owing its existence to William de Clinton, an official of some importance in the early part of the reign of Edward III. He founded the priory in 1336, and also built the castle of the same name, which still stands about two miles away.

The precinct, which is here seen from the south-east, is almost square, but appears as a lozenge, with its acute angles touching the right and left margins. The site was abundantly supplied with water: the rectangular meadow west of the road and north of a large group of farm buildings in the plate was a large mere in medieval times, as was also the meadow in the corresponding position across the precinct just short of the white hayfield. The channel of the watercourse linking them can be seen, and from the eastern pond a conduit took a stream through the offices, with a branch to a millpond. The tall piece of building at the centre of the precinct is the remains of the central tower, with the chancel arch visible; the west end of the church lay just short of the inner precinct wall at the apex of the shadow cast by the ruins. The church had an aisleless presbytery and a nave, possibly with a south aisle, separated from the eastern limb by the central tower and transepts. The cloister, for no easily discoverable reason, lay to the north of the church. It has been excavated and, if the findings of seventy years ago may be trusted, it showed several features of interest, perhaps to be explained by the late date of the plan. Thus (1) the eastern wall of the cloister was not, as is usual, a continuation of the western wall of the transept, but followed the line of the eastern wall, and the entrance to the cloister was therefore through a door in the north wall of the transept; (2) the walk of the cloister nearest to the church (i.e. the south walk) does not, as is usual, lie against the wall of the nave, but at a distance of several yards, leaving a small court between nave and cloister, as in many of the houses of friars; (3) the dormitory lay over the western range. All the claustral buildings have vanished, save for foundations; the small isolated fragment north-east of the church is part of the west wall of the infirmary hall.

To the north of the church and cloister the two gatehouses still stand. The inner one was converted into a lodging for the prior, and is still a dwelling; the outer and

larger one is roofless. The site has been excavated and planned, but in view of the peculiarities observed a second investigation conducted in the light of more recent knowledge would be of interest.

Description and plans (unusually good for their date), by J. R. Holliday in *Transactions of the Birmingham and Midland Institute*; Archaeological Section, vol. for 1874 (published 1878), pp. 56–105. The writer in the *Victoria County of Warwickshire*, IV (1947), 136–7, appears to accept, without either amplification or explanation, the conclusions put forward by Holliday.

99

BROOKE

AUGUSTINIAN

BROOKE PRIORY, the only foundation of a religious order in Rutland, lies three miles south-west of Oakham. It was a small Augustinian house, a cell of Kenilworth, and was founded shortly before 1153. It never contained more than two or three canons, and at the end only the prior; and at one time and another gave considerable trouble to the mother-house. For most of its existence it can have been little more than the administrative centre of its land.

The photograph shows a terrain particularly rich in archaeological evidence, the interpretation of which lies outside the scope of this book. The site came into the possession of the family of Noel, later raised to the peerage with the viscounty of Campden in Gloucestershire, and their seat is still at Exton Park, Rutland. Brooke House, the mansion built by them, has disappeared save for the gateway and octagonal porter's lodge, shown in the photograph. Some of the masonry of the priory was incorporated in the farmhouse visible to the left at the bottom of the view; this is known to-day as the priory. It is uncertain whether the numerous banks and terraces near the house are medieval (which is unlikely, considering the small numbers at Brooke) or, as local tradition has it, the work of the Parliamentary forces which lay for some time in strength at Burley Hill near Oakham. Beyond the little river Gwash are further banks and trenches, and traces of a dam across the river. Some of these are almost certainly prehistoric. The 'rig and furrow' cultivation of the fields to the right may be medieval, as it clearly extended across the road, and perhaps also across the site of the terraces.

There is a description in the *Victoria County History of Rutland*, II, 37; cf. I, 117.

KMS

217

28

100

KIRBY BELLARS

AUGUSTINIAN

THIS WAS A SMALL and unusually late (1359) foundation of Austin canons replacing a previously existing college of secular priests. It lies near the River Wreak, between Melton Mowbray and Leicester. In the photograph the parish church of St Peter, with its spire, can be seen near the river; the small conventual buildings, probably inherited from the college, lay somewhere between it and the large three-armed depression which may have been fishponds. The ground enclosed by the arms is, however, raised somewhat above the rest of the field and may have been the site of a building.

For a description and sketch-plan of the earthworks, see the *Victoria County History of Leicestershire*, I (1907), 267.

101

ULVERSCROFT

AUGUSTINIAN

THE AUGUSTINIAN PRIORY OF ULVERSCROFT lies within the bounds of Charnwood Forest, some seven miles north-west of Leicester; it was founded soon after the middle of the twelfth century. The site is in a valley, in a 'dearne and solitary place', as a seventeenth-century writer has it. The precinct was in consequence both walled and moated. It was roughly oblong: to the west (i.e. towards the top of the plate) a large fishpond extended from the wall to the stream, the course of which is marked by trees and bushes. Round the other three sides was a moat, still visible on the south and east, where it is bounded by the road, and traceable in the plate to the north.

The church has recently been cleared and partially excavated. It consisted of a twelfth-century nave, rebuilt in the following century, and a presbytery or quire without any architectural division from the nave. The nave had a north aisle, added early in the fifteenth century; this was almost as broad as the nave, but shorter. As often with the canons, there was no south aisle. In the fifteenth century a tower was added within the west end of the nave; this still stands to parapet height. The chapter-house has vanished but the south end of the east range, the warming-house under the dorter, and what is probably the subvault of the rere-dorter remain, as does also the south wall of the frater. Part of the western range, probably used as prior's lodging and guest-hall, remains in use as a barn.

The forest abounded in game in medieval times, and the canons, especially in the later centuries, were noted for their addiction to the chase.

Description with plan in *Journal of the British Archaeological Association*, XIX (1863), 165–83; and *ibid.*, New Series, XXXIX (1934), 222–3. Cf. also the short account by Sir A. W. Clapham in *Archaeological Journal*, XC (1933), 391–2.

102

NOTLEY

AUGUSTINIAN

THE REMAINS OF THE AUGUSTINIAN ABBEY OF NOTLEY in Buckinghamshire lie in the parish of Long Crendon, seven miles south-west of Aylesbury, a little west of the direct line of railway from Paddington to Birmingham, the track of which can be seen in the distance. The house was founded *c.* 1160.

The view is taken from the west and the large building nearest to the camera is substantially medieval, being the western range of the claustral buildings (cellarage and guest-rooms), with the abbot's lodging, a late addition of the early sixteenth century, projecting from it at right angles, the whole rebuilt as a large dwelling-house. The long roofed barn and stables, running east from the south-east corner of the house, stand on the site of the frater and warming-house, parts of which they incorporate. The low range of farm-buildings on the site of the eastern range are entirely post-medieval.

The side of the cloister now open was occupied by the church, of which the main axis lay almost exactly north-east. Of this no traces remain above ground, and the excavations made in 1937 by the Oxford University Archaeological Society showed that the foundations had been very efficiently robbed for road-making material. It was, however, possible to ascertain the chief dimensions, and even the period of the construction of the various parts. The mounds visible in the meadow east of the high garden wall indicate the position of the eastern portion of the church. The church had been built in stages: first the transepts and short presbytery; then the nave with north and south aisles; then a long extension of the presbytery (possibly a Lady Chapel) flanked by aisles or chapels. The total overall length was about 250 ft.

The fields east and west of the site show many traces of mounds and trenches—watercourses, ponds and perhaps the divisions of kitchen gardens. Four depressions near the copse, masked by the shadows of its trees, may have been fishponds. The medieval dovecot can be seen 200 yds. from the buildings in the open to the left of the plate; it contained between 4000 and 5000 nests.

Description and plan in the *Buckinghamshire Inventory* of the Royal Commission on Historical Monuments (1912), I, 244–6. There is a fuller description, with plans embodying the results of the 1937 excavations, by W. A. Pantin in *Oxoniensia*, VI (1941), 22–43.

103

BUTLEY

AUGUSTINIAN

BUTLEY, a priory of Austin canons, lay in a district of heath and woodland within a few miles of the Suffolk coast near Orfordness. It was founded in 1171 by Ranulf Glanvil, the celebrated justiciar of Henry II, and had an uneventful and on the whole undistinguished history. It was surrendered to the king in 1538. Considerable remains of the church and conventual buildings remained above ground for several centuries; they gradually disappeared and early in the nineteenth century the site was covered by extensive farm buildings and cottages, and intersected by a metalled road. Nothing remained visible above ground, though fragments had been incorporated in the barns, and much even of the lowest courses of masonry and of the foundations have been plundered. Some twenty years ago such excavations as were practicable were carried out, and the ground plan of the church was revealed. At a distance of some 300 yds. to the north of the priory stands the substantial and beautiful gatehouse, with its remarkable armorial frieze; it has remained intact owing to its conversion into a small country-house.

In the photograph, taken from the north-east, the site of the nave can be seen on the left margin of the plate, just short of a barn; the bases of some of the piers can be distinguished. The conventual buildings lay to the south and have not been excavated. To the right of the plate is the gatehouse. It was first converted into a modern dwelling-house in 1738, and reconditioned in part in 1800 and again in 1926. The pavilion to the east was erected in 1800. Neither the rectangle before the house, laid out as a bowling-green, nor the circle in the garden behind, have any medieval origin, but the dark water among the trees to the west is that of the canons' fishponds. The stone used in the gatehouse has been pronounced to be probably French, from the valley of the Yonne. In the Middle Ages the tidewater came to within 200 yds. of the priory to the south, where excavations have revealed a wharf and canal, together with the foundations of a sea-wall. It was doubtless to this point that the stone was shipped from overseas.

For a description and plan of Butley see *Butley Priory, Suffolk*, by J. N. L. Myres (London, 1934), a reprint of papers in *Archaeological Journal*, XC (1933), 177–281. The gatehouse and its heraldry were discussed in an article by J. G. Mann in *Country Life*, 25 March 1933.

104

ST OSYTH

AUGUSTINIAN

THE REMAINS OF THE AUGUSTINIAN ABBEY OF ST OSYTH or Chiche lie at the head of a creek running down to the Colne estuary between Colchester and Clacton. Founded originally as a nunnery in early Saxon times, the house lost its (legendary) royal abbess, Osyth, when it was ravaged by the Danes, and became derelict. Refounded in 1121 by Bishop Richard Belmeis I of London, it grew rapidly in fame and wealth, its first prior William de Corbeil becoming archbishop of Canterbury. While a number of priories, such as Bolton and Wenlock, have been consistently misnamed abbeys, St Osyth's is almost alone in having retained in common usage throughout the ages its status of priory, which it lost when it was raised to abbatial rank soon after 1160. The buildings, which came into the possession of Lord Darcy soon after the Dissolution, suffered heavily from Tudor demolitions and ambitious rebuildings, and throughout the following centuries have been added to, changed, and abandoned here and there. The external parts of the fabric still standing represent some eighty years of construction, partly the work of the last abbots and partly that of Lord Darcy. Built as they are in flint and red brick, with limestone dressing, they have a mellow warmth and richness of decoration which is peculiar to Essex and East Suffolk, and recall such masterpieces as the gateways of Butley and Layer Marney, and the church of Long Melford.

In the plate, the great gateway is seen in the foreground from the south-south-west; it has been justly characterized as 'unexcelled' in an age and region of great monastic gateways. It dates from *c.* 1480 and is flanked by contemporary or earlier wings forming the offices of the outer court, which lay within to the north. The church, which was totally slighted by Darcy, and has never been excavated, lay from east to west under the present lawn, the west end lying roughly along the drive, and the line of the south wall running just north of the clipped hedge bordering the formal garden. The cloister lay to the north; the ranges along the east and west walks have disappeared, and the wall on the north side is a post-Dissolution curtain-wall which runs across what was the cloister garth a little short of the north walk. The northern extension of the east or dorter range, converted into a dwelling in the sixteenth century, exists in a ruinous condition; abutting on it to the east is the so-called 'abbot's tower', actually built by Darcy *c.* 1555. It is of coarser design and workmanship than the great gateway, and in this and other respects may be compared to a similar structure at Titchfield (p. 181). The gabled building to the west of the tower is the lobby which gave access to the frater. This last-named building, which lay along the north walk, has vanished. The northern extension of the vanished western range began with the so-called 'Bishop's lodging'; at right angles to this is a wing

intended to be part of the abbot's house; both these were put up by the penultimate abbot, Vyntoner, *c.* 1527, an East Anglian counterpart of Abbot Chard of Forde. The adjoining parts of the house and the clock tower are Darcy's work, and beyond this are modern enlargements. The isolated fragment of masonry in the meadow to the north of the house is a remnant of some work of Darcy's.

The fine parish church, served by the canons, and reconditioned by Abbot Vyntoner, is off the plate to the right near the point where the precinct wall and road run eastwards.

Description and plans in the *North-east Essex Inventory* of the Royal Commission on Historical Monuments (1922), pp. 198–204. Plans and fine photographs in H. A. Tipping, *English Homes*, II, 271–93.

105

MICHELHAM

AUGUSTINIAN

THE AUGUSTINIAN PRIORY OF MICHELHAM lies near the River Cuckmere, eight miles north-east of Eastbourne and about the same distance east of Lewes in Sussex. It was founded in 1229, and always remained very small. The precinct is entirely surrounded by a wide moat bordered by trees, which shows to great advantage from the air, and the entrance was by a bridge commanded by the gatehouse which is still standing. The view, which is taken from the south-west, shows the remains of the conventual buildings near the centre of the site. They were for long used as a farm, and were restored with additions as a dwelling-house in 1925. It will be noted that the sides of the cloister are inclined at about half a right angle to those of the moat. The long, low building is the frater, and adjoining it to the west is the beginning of the western range containing the prior's lodging (on two floors), and an undercroft, probably cellarage, at the south end of the west walk of the cloister. The area of the cloister garth is roughly outlined by the buildings and hedges. Of the church not a trace remains above ground.

Description and plan in *Sussex Archaeological Collections*, LXVII (1926), 1–24, by W. H. Godfrey.

106

SHULBREDE

AUGUSTINIAN

THE AUGUSTINIAN PRIORY OF SHULBREDE or Woolynchmere lies in a sheltered valley among the hills two and a half miles south-west of Haslemere, in West Sussex near the meeting-point of Sussex, Surrey and Hampshire. Its situation, isolated, embowered in trees and approached by a lane which falls steeply and crookedly from the ridge of Linchmere, may be taken as typical of many of the smaller Augustinian houses and helps to explain their frequent indigence and their undistinguished and sometimes unedifying history in the later Middle Ages. The existing house, long used as a farm, was converted into a small country house by Sir Arthur Ponsonby (later Lord Ponsonby of Shulbrede) early in the present century.

The precinct, here seen from the south, is surrounded by a moat, still filled with water for much of its course. The principal survival from the medieval priory is the southern portion of the western range, with high gabled roof, containing what was probably part of the prior's lodging on the first floor over an undercroft. A large room contains interesting tempera paintings of which some, representing birds and animals announcing the Birth of Christ, may be of late medieval workmanship. Running at right angles to the east is a post-Dissolution building embodying fragments of the frater and the cloister wall. The church and the original eastern range have disappeared, though fragments of the former were visible two centuries ago. West of the priory, among the trees near the road, are two fishponds.

Account with plan by Sir A. Ponsonby in *Sussex Archaeological Collections*, XLIX (1906), 31–46.

107

CHRISTCHURCH

AUGUSTINIAN

The Augustinian Priory of Twynham, or, as it came to be called very early, Christchurch, lay on the right (western) bank of the Hampshire Avon just above its confluence with the Stour, five miles east of the town centre of modern Bournemouth. Originally a house of secular canons, which had among its deans in the mid-twelfth century Hilary, later bishop of Chichester, the colleague and opponent of Archbishop Thomas Becket, it was refounded for Austin canons *c.* 1150 and became an important and well-to-do house. As the view, taken from the north, shows, the church has a fine situation south of the ruins of the castle and approached through an avenue of elms, at the end of the tongue of land separating the two rivers. Immediately south of the town their united streams form a broad expanse of water studded with small craft.

The buildings of the priory, which lay to the south of the church, have almost entirely disappeared, but the fabric of the church remains intact, surpassed by few parish churches in its majestic length, its architectural variety, and the wealth of its interior ornament. It contains examples of every variety of style from early Romanesque to latest Perpendicular, the tower having been erected only twenty years before the Dissolution and the stalls betraying Renaissance influence.

It is in effect three edifices: the western portion being the medieval parish church, the quire belonging to the canons, and the eastern Lady Chapel being in origin a proprietary church of the lord of the manor. There was originally a low tower at the crossing.

Among the many notable interior features is the chantry erected by Margaret countess of Salisbury to hold the tombs of herself and Reginald Pole. Instead, she found an obscure grave in the precincts of the Tower, a victim to the resentment of Henry VIII which could not harm its true object, her son. The Salisbury chapel, like the stalls, shows in its stonework a blend of the last phase of English Gothic craftsmanship with motifs imported from Renaissance Italy.

There is no account or plan of the conventual buildings; descriptions of the church are numerous.

108

MOUNT GRACE

CARTHUSIAN

The Charterhouse of Mountgrace lies at the foot of the Cleveland Hills some six miles north-east of Northallerton. It was founded in 1398 by the young Thomas Holland, newly created duke of Surrey, the relative of Richard II who lost his life little more than a year later in rebellion against Henry IV. Beautifully situated on an artificially levelled site beneath a steeply rising oakwood, it is notable as being the only English Charterhouse, with the partial exception of the Charterhouse of London, of which the characteristic plan is still clearly visible.

The majority of the buildings were erected *c.* 1400 and are, architecturally speaking, undistinguished and even mean in appearance, perhaps owing to economies rendered necessary by the death, under a cloud, of the founder. The general arrangement is apparent at first glance. The large precinct, here seen from the west, contained two courts: the larger outer court to the south and the great cloister to the north, with the church and community buildings in the middle. The main entrance, which can be seen immediately to the left of some dark trees, stood between the two parts, almost equal in length, of a long range of buildings composing the guest-house and offices of the priory. The portion to the south, now in ruins, is hidden from view in the photograph by foliage; that to the north was converted in 1654 into a dwelling-house by Thomas Lascelles, and has since received minor additions. This block was originally met by one returning at right angles towards the corner of the great cloister and between it and the church lay the kitchen, the refectory (small and unpretentious as always with the Carthusians) and the prior's cell. The church was as unpretentious as the frater, and between its quire and the cloister, where the shadow of the tower falls in the photograph, lay the chapter-house, with the sacrist's cell contiguous to the east. On each of the three other sides of the great cloister were five cells, each with its small garden; the external wall of these gardens can be seen at the western end of the north side; here too the middle cell of the five can be distinguished, which was restored to its original form and roofed by a previous owner, Sir Lowthian Bell, some fifty years ago. South-east of the church a small three-sided court, with six new cells, was built in 1412 as the result of an influx of funds; some of the foundations can be seen in the view.

Outside the precinct to the west lay the monastic fishpond, and to the east, on the summit of a wooded slope just beyond the margin of the plate, stand the ruins of a chapel which survived as a place of pilgrimage long after the Dissolution.

An architectural description of the house, with a plan, by A. W. Clapham, is in the *Victoria County History of Yorkshire: North Riding*, II (1923), 24–7. A history, with illustrations and a large plan, by W. Brown and W. H. St John Hope, is in *Yorkshire Archaeological Journal*, XVIII (1905), 252–309.

109

BEAUVALE

CARTHUSIAN

THE SITE OF THE CHARTERHOUSE OF BEAUVALE is in a valley below a wooded hill, some eight miles north-west of Nottingham. It was founded by Nicholas de Cantilupe, an intimate of Edward III, in 1343, for a prior and twelve monks; forty years later provision was made for two more. Like its sister houses in the order, it remained true to its ideals to the end, and the last prior, Robert Lawrence, was one of the heroic band who suffered at Tyburn in 1535; John Houghton, the prior of the London Charterhouse, who was executed with him, had previously been prior of Beauvale.

Little remains above ground, but systematic excavation was undertaken in 1908, and the principal outlines were recovered. The monastic buildings lay at the centre of an irregular quadrilateral, bounded by walls and ditches, which is seen in the plate from the north-west angle. Within this, the inner precinct was a walled area of oblong shape enclosing the great and small cloisters, prior's house, church, and the rest, with the outer court beyond to the east. At the south-east corner of the precinct lay the small entrance court, surrounded by offices, with the great gateway and guest-rooms at its south-east angle. This court is roughly coincident with the quadrangle of modern farm buildings, and the southern range, with a long high-pitched roof, is in fact the medieval gatehouse.

The Carthusian great cloister (cf. Mount Grace) consisted of cells surrounding a large open space of grass used as a graveyard. This internal area is marked by the hedged enclosure of the farm-house, and outside this on the north, west, and south sides can be seen traces of the walls of the cells. Each stood, abutting on the cloister, in a small walled garden; there was therefore a continuous internal wall round the walks of the cloister, broken only by the doors of the cells, and an external wall enclosing the gardens. Outside this outer wall flowed a stream (the ditch is still visible) which, issuing from a fishpond in the north-east angle of the site, ran round three sides of the cloister serving the function of a drain. Piped water from another source was laid on to every cell. Along the east walk there was only one cell, that of the prior, which had no garden. This cell is still in existence as part of the tall building with two prominent doorways in its western wall. East of it can be seen fragments of

of the north and south walls of the small rectangular church. The south wall of the church, and the east wall of the main cloister (on which the nearer wall of the modern farm-house stands) enclosed a smaller court, on the eastern side of which stood a low range of buildings, including a small chapter-house next to the church and a gateway which formed the only entrance to the inner enclosure of the monks.

Description and plan in *Transactions of the Thoroton Society*, XII (1908), 69–94.

110

PARKMINSTER

CARTHUSIAN

THE VIEW OF ST HUGH'S CHARTERHOUSE, between Cowfold and Partridge Green in Sussex, six and a half miles south-south-east of Horsham, is included for purposes of comparison with medieval sites. It shows a large monastery built in the French Gothic style of the late nineteenth century and deposited ready-made, so to say, in the English countryside. Constructed for French Carthusians, in danger of expulsion from their native country but in no lack of funds, and designed by French architects, it reflects the wishes of planners hampered by no restrictions of purse or site, and it may therefore be taken as a design *à souhait* for a Charterhouse of to-day, whatever may be thought of the architectural shape in which it was embodied. Work began in 1876 and was carried through to completion in the years immediately following.

The great quadrangle, here seen from the north-west, is a parallelogram with cloisters 377 ft. and 440 ft. in length, the northern and southern walks being the longer. The area enclosed by the walks is three and a half acres, and is said to be the largest cloister-garth in the world. It lies to the west of the church, and round it can be seen the small houses and gardens of the fathers. These, as built, numbered thirty-four, including that of the prior and two others, which lie outside the quadrangle at its south-east angle, and two more adjoining the church at its north-west angle and architecturally indistinguishable in the plate. The temporary construction in the southern cloister marks the spot where two cells were destroyed by enemy action in 1940. As can be seen, no windows open upon the outer world, and the houses are so designed that all face south or east. Unlike those of Mount Grace and Beauvale, they are for the most part separated from the cloister by the width of their small gardens.

The high building running south along the cloister from the church is the chapter-house and library; immediately beyond it to the east can be seen the roof of the fathers' and brothers' refectories—never of great architectural importance in a charterhouse—with kitchens beyond. The building in a corresponding position to the refectory on the north side of the church is the lay-brothers' chapel. The large block at the south-east corner of the complex is the guest-house. Immediately to the east of the church, beyond the smaller quadrangle, is the gatehouse. To the north of this quadrangle lie the 'obediences' or workshops of the lay-brothers and their dormitory.

The monks' graveyard lies before the western tower of the church. A precinct wall encloses the kitchen gardens to the south, and a belt of trees to the north and west shields the place from wind and observation. The freedom of the air, however, constitutes a menace to privacy with which no previous generation of monks has had to reckon.

111

HINTON

CARTHUSIAN

THE CHARTERHOUSE known as the Locus Dei at Hinton, five miles south-south-east of Bath in Somerset, lay little more than ten miles in a direct line from what was for a century the only other house of the order in England—Witham, the home of St Hugh before he became bishop of Lincoln. Hinton was founded by Ela, Countess of Salisbury and widow of William Longespee, after a false start at Hatherop in Gloucestershire, and dedicated in May 1232, on the same day as her other foundation of Lacock (p. 265). Always a fervent house, it was the home of several notable monks, including John Luscote, first prior of the London Charterhouse (1371), Nicholas Hopkins, the confessor and, so it was alleged, the abettor of the Duke of Buckingham (1521), and John Batmanson (1529), another Prior of London. The priory surrendered only after heavy pressure had been exerted by Cromwell, and at least two of the monks were among the community of the Marian revival at Sheen.

The site, long neglected, has recently been carefully examined and partially excavated by the present owner, who has recovered and measured the main features of the plan, besides making long-needed repairs to the existing buildings. The photograph, taken from a little west of south, shows the site of the great cloister in the centre of the plate. The small, lofty building with high-pitched gables is the chapter-house, with library and dovecotes over; it is in the Early English style, and must date from the early decades of the house. The church adjoined this to the north-west; it was small, like all Carthusian churches, and was exactly orientated. Due west of the chapter-house and exactly in line with it stands the frater, lying east and west. The sheds and walls north and south of this are not medieval.

The great cloister, 225 ft. square, followed roughly the line of trees south from the chapter-house, turning west along the line of the southern garden-wall and returning north along the broken line of small trees. The white lines in the pasture west of the cloister mark the excavation of the walls enclosing one of the cells and its garden; a cell on the eastern side has since been more fully cleared. To the north of the complex lay the outer court and gatehouse, part of which is incorporated in the sixteenth-century manor house. The quarters of the lay brothers, as at Witham, were situated about a mile away in Friary Wood, by the River Frome.

A description of the buildings and excavations by the owner and excavator, Major P. C. Fletcher, will appear shortly in the *Proceedings of the Somerset Archaeological Society*. The account given above is largely based on information and plans kindly supplied by Major Fletcher.

112

SEMPRINGHAM

GILBERTINE

The site of Sempringham Priory, lost in the fields of Kesteven between Sleaford and Boston, makes in its own way as striking an appeal to the imagination as that of Fountains or Glastonbury. Here at the hamlet of Sempringham, now wholly vanished, Gilbert, the priest of the place, established *c.* 1131 some devout women of the locality in a house on his patrimony which soon became the mother-house of the Gilbertines, a purely English order consisting primarily of nuns (both choir and lay-sisters) with an institute of regular canons to act as chaplains and directors, and lay-brothers to do the farm work and estate management.

The order spread rapidly, and for more than a century and a half (1150–1300) contained the most populous and fervent nunneries in the country. Sempringham, the largest convent and the residence of the Master and his assistants, was a 'double' house—that is, it consisted of two complete sets of conventual buildings, one for the women and one for the men, separated by the church in which both worshipped on different sides of a medial wall which allowed to each choir a view of the high altar. Here, in 1189, Gilbert died and was buried, and here in 1202, after the papal canonization, his relics were solemnly re-buried by Archbishop Hubert Walter in a shrine which was the venerated centre of the order's life and the goal of pilgrimage from all parts. Utterly destroyed within a few decades of the Dissolution, and soon accompanied to oblivion by the mansion of the new owner, the very site of the great complex of buildings was lost. It came to be supposed that it lay to the north of the parish church, the only building that survived among the fields, and the still stranger error prevailed that the church itself was that of the priory—an error encouraged by the nineteenth-century editors of Dugdale's *Monasticon*, who printed an engraving of the church to accompany the article on Sempringham. Even air-photography, when employed in 1937, was unrevealing, and the true site was only identified by the method of trial and error. After the site by the church had been dismissed, work was begun in the field beyond the Marse Dyke, which is seen crossing the centre of the plate (p. 243). Here in July 1938, 'nothing was visible above ground except the rectangular earthwork' which, as was discovered, masked the foundations of the Elizabethan mansion erected by Edward, Lord Clinton, in 1580–5, probably never occupied, and soon deliberately demolished. Traces of a post-Dissolution house were found between the earthwork and the Marse Dyke, and some medieval work was identified, but it was not recognized that, as the second plate shows, this formed part of the canons' monastery, and this line of investigation was abandoned. In the following season, 1939, trenches were cut east of the earthwork, and here the foundations of the great church were uncovered. The nave lay under and within the

wings of, the mansion, with the quire and the single (northern) transept outside it to the east. This was the second church, replacing the original Romanesque building; it was begun in 1301 and not completed for more than a century. It was designed on the grand scale and was 325 ft. in overall length—longer, that is, than the present cathedrals of Ripon and Bristol and only slightly smaller than Chichester; no doubt the height was great in proportion, with a tower or spire. Surrounded by the cloisters and offices of the two monasteries, the one containing 200 nuns and the other some 40 canons and 60 lay-brethren, together with servants and dependants, the whole great mass of buildings must have dominated the landscape of the plain for miles around. A sudden end was unfortunately put to the excavation by the outbreak of war in September, 1939, before the complete plan had been uncovered. It has not yet been found possible (1951) to resume work on the site, which is once more under cultivation, whereas in 1948–9 it was a rough pasture. When excavations are resumed, the air-photographs now available may serve as guides.

The first view, taken from the north-east in 1948, shows the parish church in the foreground, with the tracks and enclosures of the medieval village to the west, and

possibly also to the north-east and south of the church. The ancient causeway to the south-west, with the modern path alongside, no doubt led to the gateway of the precinct. The site of the Clinton mansion, somewhat disturbed by excavation, is clearly visible (above) as an uncultivated square. The patch of scrub to the west of the site (p. 243) marks the fishpond, and the Marse Dyke ran originally from near the centre of its eastern end directly through the site, passing under the transept of the church, where a carrying arch has been discovered. It was diverted to its present channel in the fourteenth century, perhaps after the disastrous floods of 1349, when the cloister and church were flooded to a depth of six feet and more. The site is very low-lying, and from this point of view must have been most unsuitable for a large monastery.

The second plate, taken from the south-west in the early summer of 1950, when the land was under light cereal crop, is extremely revealing, and shows in outline the claustral complex of both canons and nuns, hitherto unidentified by either camera or spade. The earthworks of the Clinton mansion have unfortunately obliterated the nave of the church but the presbytery is visible to the east with its medial wall dividing the quire of the nuns (which in Mr H. Braun's view lay to the south) from that of the canons (to the north). The break in this wall can be distinguished where the excavators found what they took to be the site of the shrine of St Gilbert. Adjoining the north wall a small square building can be seen, which was not discovered by the spade, and beyond it, still further northwards, what may be a large chapel. North of the transept are traces of a line of buildings, presumably the eastern range of the canons' cloister, and what appears to be the outline of the garth. To the west of this is what appears to be another cloister, and to the west of this again the outlines of several more buildings can be seen as crop-marks. To the south of the church the lines of another complex, that of the nunnery, are distinguishable, with what may be a chapter-house projecting eastwards parallel to the presbytery. There are traces of the four walks of the cloister, and possibly other outlying buildings further westwards. It may be added that the prominent parallel lines in the crop are the tracks of a cultivator.

For a description of the excavations and a plan of the church see the article by Mr H. Braun and Dr Rose Graham in *Journal of the British Archaeological Association*, 3rd series, v (1940), 73–101.

113

WATTON

GILBERTINE

THE LARGE GILBERTINE HOUSE OF WATTON lay in the East Riding of Yorkshire, eight miles due north of Beverley on the Driffield road, on flat land which in the twelfth century was largely marsh. The priory was founded *c.* 1150 for nuns and canons (with lay-sisters and lay-brethren) and soon became the largest house of the order, with a community of 70 men and 150 women religious. In the first years of its existence it was often visited by the founder of the order, St Gilbert of Sempringham, and by St Ailred, abbot of the not-far-distant Rievaulx, who describes the place in connection with a curious episode in its history in the tract on *The nun of Watton.* It continued to be wealthy, and was one of the last houses to surrender in December, 1539; the document was signed by nine canons, and there were then at least forty-odd women religious. The nominal superior, Robert Holgate, later became archbishop of York.

Apart from the existing residence, which is an adaptation of the medieval prior's house, nothing but a few mounds and stones are left above ground, but the whole site, being unoccupied, was carefully excavated in 1893–8 by W. H. St J. Hope, and is of interest as being the only Gilbertine 'double' monastery of which the plan has been as yet (1949) completely revealed.

The precinct of the whole establishment was rectangular in shape and is all included in the photograph which is taken from the south-east. Bounded by the road in the foreground, its eastern limit probably followed the line of hedge on the extreme right to a point half-way along the second pasture, whence the line of wall and ditch can be traced across the field past the fishponds (visible in the view) and across an old dyke; it then turns southward at right angles, and regains the road near the parish church of St Mary (in the extreme left of the photograph). The inner precinct of the nuns, bounded along most of its length in medieval centuries by a watercourse, ran from the road in the foreground along the straight row of trees in the centre of the plate, past the long (post-Dissolution) range of stabling, thence turning westward along the second row of trees from the road.

The complete Gilbertine monastery was a 'double' house, i.e. both nuns and canons had a separate cloister with all the usual rooms and offices, but whereas the canons had only a chapel of modest size the nuns had a large church, of which the quire and presbytery were divided into two members by a longitudinal wall, to accommodate the men and women separately for the chief offices. There does not seem to have been any settled plan for the relative positions of the two cloisters and churches. At Watton they lay not alongside, so to say, but in line, i.e. the north walks of the two cloisters were along the same axis, but the nuns' cloister and church

being larger, extended further to the south than did those of the canons. Each cloister lay (contrary to normal practice) to the north of its own church; the dorter and chapter-house in each case lay along the eastern range.

The existing mansion, in the centre of the site, embodies the medieval prior's lodging, which lay at the south-west angle of the canons' cloister; this latter, with its surrounding buildings, lay in the paddock to the north-east of the house, where mounds and some fragments of masonry can be seen. The nuns' cloister lay in a corresponding position in the meadow beyond the row of trees, where more mounds are visible; their great church stood to the south (i.e. nearer to the road). The two complexes were connected by a narrow gallery to the north and the join was marked by a grated parlour near the north end of the present row of trees. The main entrance was not directly from the road in the foreground, but by a lane from the west running to the block of buildings in the centre of the plate, which stands on the site of the outer court. The stream bisecting the whole precinct and acting as drain flows in a stone tunnel under the site of the canons' monastery, and can be seen emerging from under the south wall of the mansion.

There is a full description and plan by W. H. St J. Hope in *Archaeological Journal*, LVIII (1901), 1–34.

114

MATTERSEY

GILBERTINE

THE GILBERTINE PRIORY OF MATTERSEY, founded *c.* 1185, stood on what was then an island in the River Idle in Nottinghamshire, not far east of the present main line of railway between Bawtry and Retford. It was founded for canons only, never becoming a 'double' house. The place is known to have been badly damaged by a fire in 1279. The site came under the guardianship of the Commissioners of Works in 1912, and was partially excavated shortly after.

The view, taken from the south-west, shows the church furthest from the camera. It is a short, narrow, rectangular, aisleless building, without transepts or any architectural division. On the north, what resembles a northern transept is in fact a fifteenth-century tower. It is the opinion of Sir Charles Peers that the western portion—if not, indeed, the whole church—was abandoned after the great fire. The eastern range of the cloister was originally a single room on the ground floor, but the two northernmost bays were later partitioned off and used as chapels, perhaps after the abandonment of the church. There is no architectural evidence of the existence of a chapter-house. The dorter lay along the eastern range on the first floor, with the rere-dorter running east at right angles to the end of the range; the isolated block of masonry supported the wall beyond the drain. The southern range contained the undercroft of the frater, and the frater itself on the first floor; the square building at its south-west corner was the kitchen. Few traces are left of the western range.

Description and plan by Sir C. R. Peers in *Archaeological Journal*, LXXXVII (1930), 16–20, partly reproduced in the *Guide* of the Ministry of Works.

115

CATTLEY

GILBERTINE

THE GILBERTINE PRIORY OF CATTLEY, founded between 1148 and 1154, lay some thirteen miles south-east of Lincoln on the western fringe of the fen bordering the River Witham, almost opposite Tattershall. The visitor to the site, now an open field set among other wide fields of cereals and roots at a distance from any village and in a sparsely populated district, finds it hard to reconstruct in his imagination the complex of buildings which once housed sixty nuns, thirty-five lay-brothers and a group of chaplains.

The site, seen from the north, has been robbed of every stone above ground and has never been excavated. It is however possible, both on the ground and in the plate, to distinguish, half-way along the diagonal fence and a little to the west, what appears to be the cloister garth with traces of the church to the north. To the west of this, near a straight hedgerow, can be clearly seen stone-robbers' trenches outlining a smaller building. As no excavations have been made it is impossible to say whether Cattley had a canons' house which was architecturally a double of the nuns' quarters.

Although the site, like that of other fenland houses, is on the crown of a slight eminence, the water-table lies very near the surface and there is a baffling maze of dykes. Part of the precinct-moat seems clearly indicated, but it has been filled in for some of its length, and it is not easy to discover the purpose of an irregular system of channels in the south-west angle of the precinct. Only one of these can be noted as a fishpond with any degree of likelihood.

There is no plan or description.

116

WALSINGHAM

FRANCISCAN

WALSINGHAM, a small town six miles from the little port of Wells-next-the-sea on the Norfolk coast midway between Hunstanton and Sheringham, was celebrated in the later Middle Ages for its shrine of Our Lady, which was one of the two or three most popular resorts of pilgrims in the land. The shrine was in the church of the Augustinian canons, but there was also a friary on the outskirts of the place. This, one of the last foundations of the grey friars, was for that very reason more elaborate in its plan than the earlier friaries; situated as it was on a free site in the open fields it is the only house of the English Franciscan province of which the plan can be seen in its totality without difficulty by the visitor on the ground or by an observer from the air.

The ruins stand just outside the town with a screen of trees to the north and east; the view is taken from the north. They are an excellent example of a 'monastic' plan adopted in essentials but modified in several respects in accordance with English Franciscan architectural practice. The precinct was probably bounded by a lane to the west (just off the plate), by a road to the east, and by town properties to the north; the southern wall separating the two fields is not medieval, though the precinct line may have lain there. The church, a building of considerable size, 200 ft. long from end to end, lay on the near side of the smaller of the two light-coloured garden-plots. The west end of the nave began at the north-east corner of the northern gable-end; between nave and quire came, as in so many English Franciscan churches, the tall and narrow steeple, with the passage or 'walking-place' beneath it; to the east of this lay the narrow friars' quire and presbytery, the site of which is hidden by foliage in the plate. There were two cloister-courts, one large, the other small. The great cloister, south of the church, is indicated by the walls which enclose the kitchen garden. The walls of the chapter-house exist and can be seen; it lay at right angles to the centre of the eastern walk, but the building stood free, without the sacristy, parlour and passages that flanked it in monastic houses. To the south lay the undercroft of the small dorter, which probably (another common Franciscan practice) extended over the walk of the cloister, perhaps owing to the cramped sites of so many of the urban friaries. No rere-dorter is visible, but the steep fall of the ground to the east would be suitable to a normal position.

The frater lay, as in the traditional monastic plan, along the south wall, but (again in conformity with normal Franciscan practice) was on the first floor and extended over the walks of the great cloister to the north and of the little cloister to the south. The principal support was therefore the south wall of the cloister, which has disappeared.

Description, with photographs and plan, by A. R. Martin, in *Franciscan Architecture in England* (British Society of Franciscan Studies, XVIII, 1937, 124–37).

117

AYLESFORD

CARMELITE

THE CARMELITE FRIARY OF AYLESFORD lies on the right bank of the River Medway, three miles below Maidstone and some eight miles above Rochester. It was one of the two earliest Carmelite foundations, being founded in 1241–2 by the original exiles from Palestine, on a site given by Richard Grey, Lord of Codnor. Hulne, the other, was probably a few months the junior.

The first hermitage was bounded by the river on the south, and a moat on the other three sides; the area is now covered partly by the square river-side spinney and partly by the open court of the friary, the eastern arm of the moat having been filled up at an early date. In the middle of the fourteenth century a new set of buildings of normal monastic plan was begun north-east of the original site; part of the latter became the walled *curia* of the new friary.

In the photograph, taken from the south-west, the outer gatehouse can be seen covering the approach north of the claustral block. The conventual buildings still in existence and recently in use as a dwelling are the southern range, with the frater at first-floor level on an undercroft, and the western range, containing the prior's lodging; the short block running west from this at its north end contains the inner gatehouse, flanked by other rooms. The plan of the church has been recovered by excavation, traces of which can be seen; it was an aisleless structure, with quire and presbytery slightly narrower than the nave, from which they were divided by a narrow crossing, used as a passage, over which stood a slender tower. These features, and also the space between the north wall of the cloister and the south wall of the church, are typical of the developed church plan of the Franciscan and other friars. The dorter has vanished; a flood-wall of earth covers its foundations, and those of the chapter-house, to a depth of several feet. The *curia* is surrounded by buildings which replace or embody those of the medieval period. The range on the river bank has been identified as the guest-house; it has a doorway opening directly upon the river. There was also a small inlet with a quay at the south end of this block, almost hidden by trees in the plate. The dwelling-house was completely gutted by fire in 1930, but the walls stood, and the whole was carefully restored. Recently (1949) the whole site has come into the possession of Carmelite friars, who are thus once more the occupiers, after an interval of a little over four hundred years. The frater is in use as a temporary chapel.

There is no description or plan in print, but Mr H. F. Braun kindly allowed the use of the plans he had drawn up and of the paper which he delivered before the Society of Antiquaries in December, 1949.

118

HULNE

CARMELITE

THE CARMELITE PRIORY OF HULNE in Northumberland lies two miles north-west of Alnwick on the north bank of the Aln. The Carmelites, originally groups of hermits on the slopes of Mount Carmel, were dislodged from Palestine early in the thirteenth century, and settled in various countries of the Levant and Europe. Among the first of such settlements were the two English priories of Aylesford and Hulne; the latter being founded by a Northumbrian, Richard Fresborne, under the patronage of William de Vesci in 1242. The Carmelites, in origin austere and eremitical, were soon drawn into the stream of the friars and became an urban, academic institute like the Dominicans. One or two of their houses, however, in solitary places, retained to the end their early characteristics, and this gives to Hulne a quite exceptional interest. It was excavated by the then duke of Northumberland in 1888–9.

The priory stands on an eminence above the beautifully wooded valley of the Aln, which lies to the right of the area seen in the plate. Like other religious houses in Border territory, it was protected by strong walls and towers (cf. Lanercost, p. 193 and Ewenny, p. 47); the curtain wall is still tolerably complete, with the friary proper forming a second enclosure almost in the centre of the area, which is seen in the plate from its western side. The main gateway lay in the middle of the south side, between the white-roofed house (the infirmary) and the light-foliaged tree; it opened into what was in effect the great court. Along the wall westwards stood a range of offices—brewhouse, malthouse, and the like.

The cloister garth is clearly seen in the centre of the plate. The church, of which the west wall and part of the south wall are standing, was in plan a parallelogram with no architectural divisions. Alongside the church at its south-eastern extremity lay the sacristy, the east and west gables are visible. Between this and the cloister lay a small court; then came a lobby and then the rectangular chapter-house. Over this range lay the dorter, of which the south gable stands; the block running east at right angles was, in part at least, the rere-dorter. The frater, which lay along the south walk, has entirely disappeared; a buttery ended the range, and the kitchen stood in what is now the open area between the cloister and the infirmary. The western range also has disappeared, if it ever existed; the building with the white roof now standing there is a modern summer-house built by the first duke of Northumberland. The building to the west of this is a tower, built as a refuge for the brethren by the fourth earl of Northumberland in 1488.

There is a very interesting survey of the place made about 1567 by one Richard Clarkson for the seventh earl of Northumberland, when the priory was still tolerably complete, though the church was already full of cherry trees. Clarkson's account has been printed more than once (most accurately by Hope in the article noticed below); it allows the reader who has a plan to reconstruct all the offices and outhouses.

Description and plan by W. H. St John Hope in *Archaeological Journal*, XLVII (1890), 105–29.

119

GODSTOW

BENEDICTINE NUNS

GODSTOW, a nunnery following the Benedictine Rule, was founded *c.* 1131–3 on the western (Berkshire) bank of the Thames, two miles upstream from Oxford. The view is taken from the north-west and, as can be seen, very little remains above ground, though the arcading of the cloister was in existence in the eighteenth century, and the western tower of the church stood till 1810, when it was demolished for building material. The walled enclosure represents in part the medieval precinct, the west and south walls being in great part old. The church appears to have stood outside the present north wall, with the west end lying at the break of the north wall and the east end beyond the eastern wall towards the river—which, it should be remembered, is not the ancient stream but a modern canalized diversion; the original river is visible beyond. Of the claustral buildings nothing remains save that at the south-east corner of the enclosure; this was possibly the chapel of the abbess's lodging. The great gateway stood athwart the road near the parked cars.

There is a short description (without plan) in the *City of Oxford Inventory* of the Royal Commission on Historical Monuments (1939), pp. 155–6.

120

ROMSEY

BENEDICTINE NUNS

THE ABBEY OF NUNS following the Benedictine Rule at Romsey was one of the half-dozen important nunneries in Wessex established in Anglo-Saxon times, the others being Amesbury, Shaftesbury, Wherwell, Wilton and Winchester. Of these all have in large part disappeared save for the church of Romsey, which is virtually complete.

The photograph, taken from an angle slightly east of south, shows the abbey on the western fringe of the town, with a branch of the Test visible at the corner of the plate. Built between 1130–60, and attributed in part at least to the great bishop of Winchester, King Stephen's brother, Henry of Blois, it is one of the most perfect English examples of mature and refined Norman architecture and ornament, and the soft grey of the Isle of Wight stone, set off in the interior by excellent restoration and (in recent years) by an unusually tasteful arrangement of altar decoration and flowers, leaves an unforgettable impression on the visitor.

The abbey buildings, of which nothing remains visible save part of the wall of the frater, lay to the south of the church. Like its sister abbeys, Romsey was, in early years at least, something of a preserve for ladies of the aristocracy; Christine, sister of Edgar Aetheling, was abbess shortly after the Conquest, and her niece, Maud, by leaving the cloister to marry Henry I, was the subject of a canonical *cause célèbre*. Fifty years later Mary, daughter of King Stephen and niece of Henry of Blois, was abbess. The only visible relic of the Saxon nunnery (and that a disputed one) is the well-known stone rood, now in the west (exterior) wall of the south transept, anciently part of the east walk of the cloister.

Romsey, a small town eight miles north-west of Southampton, with a number of old houses and inns, owes its existence to the nuns, though it was never, like Battle, entirely controlled by the abbey.

There is no description or plan of the conventual buildings, which have never been excavated.

121

GRACE DIEU

AUGUSTINIAN NUNS

THE AUGUSTINIAN NUNNERY OF GRACE DIEU, in Belton parish, at the north edge of Charnwood Forest, was founded about 1239 by Rohese de Verdon, lady of the manor. It surrendered to Henry VIII just three hundred years later, when the church was destroyed, and the other buildings were subsequently converted into a Tudor mansion by the Beaumont family, obscuring much of the original arrangement. The mansion in its turn has now decayed, the ruins being used for a time as a quarry by road-menders; the visible remains are in poor condition and likely to deteriorate further if conservation is not put in hand.

The site is at the foot of a north-facing slope, near a brook which bounded the precinct on the north and west. The setting of the ruins was somewhat altered by the construction seventy years ago of a railway which runs to the south of the site on a high embankment. In the photograph, which gives a general view from the west, the roofless building with a gabled east end is the chapter-house of the nunnery. There is a fifteenth-century arch in its west wall, and the building has been greatly altered from its original state, the upper part of the walls having been rebuilt, with a Tudor chimney inserted in the north wall. The walls at right angles to the chapter-house define part of the east walk of the cloister. Parch-marks in the grass reveal a long rectangular building to the north of the chapter-house, and on the same orientation. This building, of which a fragment still stands at the north-east angle, may be identified as the church, possibly with a south aisle occupying part of the space between it and the chapter-house. The ivy-covered wall in the form of a right angle to the east of the church does not seem to be original work. The axes of both church and chapter-house aim considerably north of east. Almost all the remaining structures above ground, including a considerable length of east-west wall in which are a number of sixteenth-century fireplaces, doors and windows, appear to belong to the Beaumont mansion. Extensive use has been made of dressed stones from the buildings of the nunnery.

The springers of the arch at the west end of the chapter-house are now but a little above ground level, while in the north wall of the same building an early door is almost entirely buried, so that if this may be taken as a general guide, the floor-levels of the church and conventual buildings may be as much as six feet below the present surface. Not only the immediate neighbourhood of the ruins, but a considerable area around, shows evident signs of disturbance, and much could be learnt by excavation. A long line of parched grass visible to the north of the church may mark some feature in the grounds of the Tudor mansion. The modern building, known as Grace Dieu Manor, standing a quarter of a mile south of the ruins, is a Gothic house, built in the middle of the nineteenth century.

Literary and historical associations cluster round 'forlorn Grace Dieu'. Gasquet, who came across some account rolls of the early fourteenth century, drew a delightful sketch of the life of the house; the visitation records of the same period have since been printed by Professor A. Hamilton Thompson, and give a more realistic picture. Grace Dieu was, however, one of the nunneries which the local commissioners particularly wished to preserve in 1536, thereby earning no thanks from Thomas Cromwell. Half a century after its suppression the mansion built on the site became the birthplace of the poet and dramatist, Francis Beaumont. The Beaumont family continued to live there and in the neighbourhood, and early in the nineteenth century the ruins became familiar to Wordsworth while staying at Cole Orton. A few decades later, the erratic genius of A. W. Pugin left its mark in the neighbourhood in the house designed for Ambrose Phillips.

There is a short note in *Archaeological Journal*, XC (1934), 392.

122

LACOCK

AUGUSTINIAN NUNS

LACOCK, an abbey of Augustinian canonesses, lay near the village of that name, some four miles south of Chippenham in Wiltshire. The house was a late foundation, due to the piety of the Lady Ela Longespee, countess of Salisbury, who founded the nunnery in 1232 and herself took the veil and became abbess in 1238. A wealthy, observant and aristocratic house, it had seventeen religious, all 'of vertuous lyvyng, all desiring to continue religios', in 1536; it was surrendered in 1539. The whole property was sold in 1540, and the grantee, Sir William Sharington, immediately converted the nunnery into a mansion, destroying most thoroughly what he did not use, but preserving many of the conventual buildings unchanged and undefaced.

The procedure adopted by Sharington and his successors was to leave the ground floor unaltered, and to convert the upper floors (with additions) into commodious living-rooms. Consequently, what is for domestic purposes the ground floor of the house is reached by a flight of steps, and the spectator from without (and from the air) sees only a country house of unusually regular design, while the visitor to the nunnery passes through a succession of medieval conventual buildings, with tiled floors and traceried roofs and windows.

The complex of buildings seen in the plate lies with its longer sides almost exactly north and south; of the two courts only the smaller (the southern) is medieval, the larger being post-Suppression. The outer court of the nunnery, wholly obliterated, lay to the westward of the cloister over and beyond the modern gravel sweep. The church, also wholly destroyed by the original owner, adjoined the cloister to the south, the west end being flush with the west end of the southern walk, while the east end coincided almost exactly with the line of the ha-ha to the east of the Tudor turret. The south wall of the church returned from the ha-ha near the spot where the sundial stands. It was without transepts or aisles, but a large Lady Chapel, flanking the quire to the south, was added in the fourteenth century.

The cloister (still preserved) lay to the north of the church and had only three walks. Part of the northern walk is visible and beyond it the wall and roof of the frater which stood on a subvault. Along the east walk lay the chapter-house (in perfect condition) and warming-house, and above them the (converted) dorter; further to the north the short block running eastwards at right angles housed the rere-dorter. The infirmary block, wholly destroyed, lay beyond the ha-ha to the east of this; the lines faintly visible in the meadow may indicate its foundations. The western range, where no walk of the cloister existed, contained the lodging of the abbess and west of this, as has been said, lay the outer court.

The precinct was bounded to the east by the River Avon, which runs just beyond the foot of the plate to the right, and included most of the area shown in the photograph. From near the village church in medieval times a swift stream ran through the long belt of trees to the river, turning the abbey mill on its way; a duct from this, taken right under the main block, served as the great drain. The village of Lacock, consisting almost entirely of medieval or Tudor houses, and now largely the property of the National Trust, lies to the north-west.

Description with plan and photographs by H. Brakspear in *Archaeologia*, LVII (1900), 125–58.

123

DENNEY

FRANCISCAN NUNS

THE SITE OF DENNEY is of some interest as being that of one of the three abbeys of Franciscan nuns (Minoresses or Poor Clares) existing in medieval England, and the only one of which any conventual buildings remain. Denney, as its name suggests, was originally an island in the fens; the site is now a complex of farm buildings some seven miles north-east of Cambridge between the main road to Ely and the River Cam.

Beginning its religious existence as a cell of Ely, the house subsequently passed first to the Templars, who ejected the monks, then to the Hospitallers, and then to the king, by whom it was granted to Mary de St Pol, the widow of Aymer de Valence and countess of Pembroke, who in turn bestowed it in 1336 upon the Minoresses who had settled at the neighbouring Waterbeach, an unsuitable site, in 1294. The Poor Clares were then, as they still are, an austere and fervent order, and Denney drew recruits from the higher levels of society all over England till the Dissolution. One of the nuns *c.* 1500 was a friend and correspondent of Erasmus, and the last abbess, Elizabeth Throckmorton, retired with some of her nuns to her old home at Coughton Court in Warwickshire, where her tombstone remains.

The Minoresses found a small Norman church built by the monks, consisting of a short presbytery, transepts and nave, probably with a south aisle. They replaced the presbytery with a long and wide quire, and apparently divided the church west of the crossing into rooms, some of which formed the abbess' lodging. In the view, which is taken from the north-west, what remains of the church can be seen to the extreme right of the farm-complex, with a garden enclosed by trees and hedges to the south. The nuns' quire has disappeared, and its site has not hitherto been fully excavated, but the original transepts (the building with a high roof running north and south, remain and west of this is the original nave converted by the nuns and now, with an additional wing at the south-west corner, used as a farm-house.

The only part of the domestic buildings now in existence is the large frater, now used as a barn; it may be recognized by its high-pitched roof on the north side of the farm-yard. The frater stood along the north walk of the cloister, which lay to the north of the nuns' quire. As is clear even in the plate, the distance between the frater and the church seems over-great for a cloister of normal proportions. An old plan of Denney exists, drawn in the eighteenth century by one Essex, and this shows a small court between the church and the south walk of the cloister—a feature not uncommon in houses of Franciscan friars, but not hitherto found elsewhere in a nunnery—and

recent excavation has confirmed the accuracy of the Essex plan. The original cloister of the monks' priory lay north of the nave, and there is evidence that the nuns used as their dorter that of the monks which continued the line of the north transept. This dorter lay in the eastern range of the monks' cloister, but thus became part of the western range of the new cloister of the nuns.

The precinct was surrounded by a series of double ditches or moats; the lines of several of these can be seen in the plate, which shows the site in the first light foliage of spring.

Description and plan by A. R. Martin in *Franciscan Architecture in England* (British Society of Franciscan Studies, XVIII (1937), 256–65), and information supplied by Mr E. A. R. Rahbula from notes prepared for the forthcoming *Cambridgeshire Inventory* of the Royal Commission on Historical Monuments.

34-2

124

STANBROOK

BENEDICTINE NUNS

THIS VIEW is included to show a modern nunnery in being, with its contrasts and resemblances to a medieval house. The Abbey of Our Lady of Consolation was founded by English ladies at Cambrai in 1625. Driven out at the French Revolution, the community settled at Abbot's Salford, near Evesham, from 1807 to 1838, when they purchased Stanbrook Hall, four miles south of Worcester on the right bank of the Severn, a few miles north-east of the Malvern Hills. Here the nuns, who gradually increased in numbers to a large community, added building to building, the younger generations of the Pugin family supplying the designs. The complex as seen in the view from the south is quite irregular in plan; the church consists of a large quire and chancel, with some added chapels. The quadrangle to the south is the graveyard; that to the north has cloisters within the buildings on two sides, and is open to the west. The refectory, chapter-house and library are not architecturally distinguishable, and the dorter has been replaced by 'cells' opening upon corridors. The original Hall, now the residence of the chaplains, is in the foreground, to the west of a wide sweep of gravel; behind it are the domestic and garden offices. The precinct, which in post-Tridentine houses of Benedictine nuns is also an 'enclosure', is surrounded by a high wall, which follows the belt of trees.

125 AND 126

MILFIELD AND YEAVERING

THESE TWO SITES, revealed by crop-markings in oats, were discovered by chance in 1948–49 in the course of reconnaissance of the Till valley, near Wooler in Northumberland. No traces of any structures are now to be seen on the surface, and there seems to be no local tradition that there had ever been buildings at either place. The first site is in the parish of Milfield, half a mile east of the church, on a level gravel terrace, near the river Till, which is visible in the top, left-hand corner of the plate. It is seen from the west in the photograph. The site at Yeavering lies two and a quarter miles to the south-south-west, in a prominent position within the valley of the Glen, a little less than a mile east of Kirknewton church, and close to the site of the traditional Dark Age *villa* of Old Yeavering. It is viewed in the photograph from slightly west of north.

The two places have a number of features in common. At each there is a long range, apparently of timber buildings, reconstructed more than once. The principal building, oriented to the east, is a rectangle in plan, perhaps 30 ft. long, having buttresses outside the longer walls, and extensions at one or both ends. At Milfield, there is a small, detached building a little to the east, on the same axis, and the two structures are surrounded by a roughly rectangular enclosure. The significance of the other marks on the photograph is not apparent. At Yeavering, the main range is composed of overlapping buildings of several different periods, while there are a number of isolated rectangular structures, of which three are visible to the north of the main range, and two more lie outside the limit of the photograph to the right. The two broad, parallel lines to the left of the photograph, probably mark the ditches of a native fort, obliterated by ploughing.

The plan of the principal building with buttresses outside the longer walls implying provision for a structure of some height, the site at Milfield, within a rectangular precinct, the orientation to the east and the position, within a known area of Dark Age occupation, raise the question whether these may be early Christian churches or Dark Age halls. The exact orientation of both sites can hardly be chance, while the small buildings at Yeavering recall the isolated cells at Whitby, though widely scattered. Whether ecclesiastical or domestic, excavation of these two sites would surely yield results of the greatest interest.

The site at Milfield lies in field 59 on the Ordnance Survey plans, 25 in. scale, Northumberland sheet X, 15 and 16: that at Yeavering is in field 25 on sheet XV, 7.

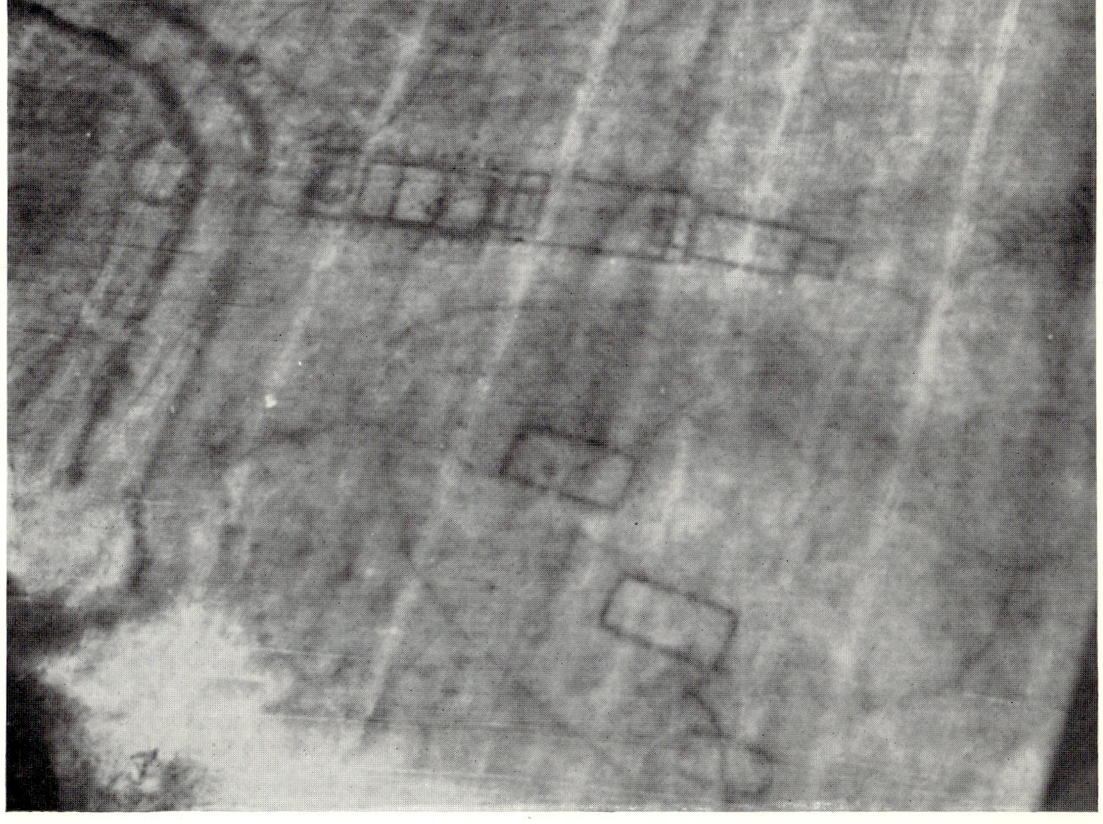

127

WELLS

THE PHOTOGRAPH OF WELLS shows the influence of the monastic plan on cathedral architects, and a number of features common to monastic and other great medieval buildings.

By the beginning of the thirteenth century a cloister was considered an integral part of a great cathedral, even if neither monks nor regular canons used it. That at Wells, begun by Bishop Joceline (1206–42) and completed by Bishop Beckington (1443–65), was a piece of architectural luxury rather than a necessity; it has three sides only, being closed to the north by the nave of the cathedral, and is oblong in shape. Beyond it to the south-west is the bishop's palace, of which the core is medieval, dating from Joceline's day. The chapel and the great banqueting hall which adjoined it were added by Bishop Burnell (1275–92), Edward I's great but worldly Chancellor. The hall is now an incomplete shell. The precinct was splendidly moated, walled and crenellated by Bishop Ralph (1329–63), the water coming from St Andrew's well, which can be seen near the left-hand margin of the plate. The palace is approached by an outer court entered from the main street of the little city through one of Bishop Beckington's magnificent gateways. It will be noted that the polygonal chapter-house, of which the roof is just visible in the left-hand bottom corner of the plate, is separated from the cloister by the whole breadth of the cathedral —another striking departure from traditional planning which may be contrasted with the more normal arrangement at Salisbury.

128

CAMBRIDGE

A VIEW OF CAMBRIDGE is not inappropriate as a tailpiece to a series of monastic sites, for not only were colleges of one sort or another the last and most diluted embodiment of the monastic idea in the Middle Ages, but the colleges of the two universities were the only religious communities of the medieval world to escape the Tudor bonfire and to remain, almost within living memory, the only bodies of celibate clergymen in England with a status recognized by authority. Added to this, two Cambridge colleges occupy parts of the conventual buildings, and two more the site, of a religious house (to say nothing of smaller houses absorbed in the thirteenth and fourteenth centuries), while a fifth has inherited the buildings of a monastic house of studies. Finally, in the hall, raised on an undercroft, and in the cloisters of Nevile's Court at Trinity College, we can trace relationship to, if not descent from, the frater and garth of the abbey.

The view, taken from the south-west on an afternoon of spring, shows part at least of all the medieval colleges save for the oldest of all, Peterhouse, which lies just off the right margin of the plate. In the centre, the group formed by Clare College and the chapel and Gibbs' Building of King's College shows to advantage, with the far-flung courts of Trinity and St John's beyond. Half-way up the left-hand margin a portion can be seen of Magdalene College, once, as Buckingham College, the resort of monks from Ely, Crowland and other fenland houses. In the middle distance the grounds of Jesus College form a spacious *enclave* in the riverside commons; it was established by Bishop Alcock out of the suppressed nunnery of St Radegund. Between Jesus and King's Chapel the trees of the garden of Sidney Sussex mark the site of a Franciscan friary, while on the right-hand margin of the plate, just short of another grove, the roofs can be seen of the old buildings of Emmanuel, which embody part of the Dominican priory. In the foreground the house of the Carmelites stood where is now part of the garden of Queens' College.

CATALOGUE OF AIR PHOTOGRAPHS OF RELIGIOUS HOUSES IN THE UNIVERSITY COLLECTION

This catalogue gives a complete list of all photographs of religious houses in the Cambridge University Collection (at January 1952), whether the sites are illustrated in this book or not. The entries against each name are the photograph numbers: thus, for Worcester there are five photographs numbered respectively, Z91, Z92, EY41, EY42 and EY43.

The photographs are oblique views, taken with an air survey camera, from heights between 800 and 2000 feet. The Collection is under the care of the University Curator in Aerial Photography, and is housed temporarily in the Museum of Classical Archaeology, Little St Mary's Lane, Cambridge.

BENEDICTINE

Abbotsbury AS 7
Arbroath GP 85–9
Bardney BR 94; BS 1–3
Bath AO 61
Battle AU 4–5
Binham CP 66–73
Bradwell FK 12–13
Buckfast AX 72–5
Bury St Edmunds AU 41–2
Canterbury CW 41–6
Cerne AQ 47–8; AY 10–11; FC 62–6
Chester BN 26–7; EK 74–6
Crowland ET 48–52
Deerhurst EY 55–7
Downside CX 64–9
Dunfermline DJ 95–7
Durham W 65–9; BG 86–9; BT 17–20
Ely CC 62–71; CP 8–14; FN 5–6
Ewenny BW 76–7; CZ 49–50
Finchale BT 11–15; DC 65–7
Glastonbury AW 53–5; CK 60–4; FM 3–6
Gloucester AN 82; CH 86–91; EP 88–91
Great Malvern EY 52–3
Hurley GC 56–7
Jarrow BG 75
Leominster FA 80–2
Leonard Stanley FY 41; GX 54–61
Lindisfarne M 55, 57–8; BG 12–14
Lindores GP 82–4
Malmesbury GA 5–6
Milton FC 70–5
Muchelney CK 68–76
Peterborough R 22–3; FP 77–84
Ramsey FP 86–7; FT 19–20
Rumburgh HC 66–8
St Albans AP 28–9
St Benet's, Holme CQ 18–21
St Mary's, Princethorpe FS 12
St Michael's Mount CG 31–4
Sherborne FC 60–1
Snetteshall DA 4–5
Stogursey CG 82
Tavistock FK 71–6
Tewkesbury EB 53–9
Thorney ET 44–7
Tutbury EX 54
Tynemouth BG 69
Whitby BA 35–7; DP 43–6
Winchester CL 48–53; GE 29
Worcester Z 91–2; EY 41–3
York, St Mary's BH 79–81

Alien Priories

Clare-in-the-Castle EP 153–4; HC 13–17
Wilmington BU 83
Wolston ES 8–10

CLUNIAC

Bromholm FE 63–8
Castle Acre AZ 13–15; FX 11–16; 2/A 37–8
Montacute CF 7–8
Much Wenlock AV 59–61
Thetford BU 9–12

TIRONIAN

Caldy GY 33–5
Kelso DM 97–8
St Dogmael's GZ 18–20

AUSTIN CANONS

CARTHUSIAN

GILBERTINE

BONSHOMMES

FRIARS

NUNS

KNIGHTS HOSPITALLERS

KNIGHTS TEMPLARS

HOSPITAL

ANCIENT MONASTERIES

VARIOUS

DISTRIBUTION MAP

The sites are numbered as in the text. For page references see index.

INDEX OF SITES DESCRIBED IN THIS BOOK

(The references are to pages)